China Insights

This book series collects and presents cutting-edge studies on various issues that have emerged during the process of China's social and economic transformation, and promotes a comprehensive understanding of the economic, political, cultural and religious aspects of contemporary China. It brings together academic endeavors by contemporary Chinese researchers in various social science and related fields that record, interpret and analyze social phenomena that are unique to Chinese society, its reforms and rapid transition. This series offers a key English-language resource for researchers and students in China studies and related subjects, as well as for general interest readers looking to better grasp today's China. The book series is a cooperation project between Springer and China Social Science Press of China.

More information about this series at http://www.springer.com/series/13591

He Tian · Yanbin Lv
Editors

The Chinese Path of Rule of Law Construction

中国社会科学出版社
CHINA SOCIAL SCIENCES PRESS

Springer

Editors
He Tian
Institute of Law
Chinese Academy of Social Sciences
Beijing, China

Yanbin Lv
Institute of Law
Chinese Academy of Social Sciences
Beijing, China

Published with financial support of the Innovation Program of the Chinese Academy of Social Sciences.

ISSN 2363-7579 ISSN 2363-7587 (electronic)
China Insights
ISBN 978-981-16-4129-9 ISBN 978-981-16-4130-5 (eBook)
https://doi.org/10.1007/978-981-16-4130-5

Jointly published with China Social Sciences Press
The print edition is not for sale in China Mainland. Customers from China Mainland please order the print book from: China Social Sciences Press.

Translation from the Chinese language edition: 法治建设的中国路径 by He Tian, and Yanbin Lv,

This Springer imprint is published by the registered company Springer Nature Singapore Pte Ltd.
The registered company address is: 152 Beach Road, #21-01/04 Gateway East, Singapore 189721, Singapore

Series Foreword

Since the Opium War, modern China has come under attack and been bullied for its backwardness; this cultural circumstance has given many Chinese people a psychological inferiority complex, as China has lagged behind other countries technologically, institutionally and culturally. Efforts to change the situation in which Western countries were strong but China was weak and to revitalize China needed to start with cultural criticism and culture renovation. Therefore, the Chinese people turned their eyes to the outside world and learned from Japan, Europe, the USA, and even Soviet Russia. We have always been overwhelmed by stress and anxiety and have had a burning desire to reverse the state of being bullied as a result of underdevelopment, poverty and weakness and to catch up with and surpass the Western powers. In pursuing the more than one-hundred-year-old dream of building a powerful country and reviving China, we have focused on understanding and learning from others, but seldom, if ever, have others learned from and understood us. This has not greatly changed in the course of modernization since China's reform and opening up in 1978. The translation and introduction of many Western works in the 1980s and 1990s is a very good example. This is the history of the Chinese people's understanding of the relationship between China and the rest of the world since the beginning of modern times.

At the same time, in pursuing the dream of turning China into a powerful country and rejuvenating it through material (technological) criticism, institutional criticism and cultural criticism, the Chinese people have struggled to find a path that would make the country prosperous and the people strong while preventing the country from being ruined and the race from being destroyed. This path first represents a thought, a banner and a soul. The key issue has been what kind of thought, banner and soul can save the country, making it prosperous and the people strong. For more than one hundred years, the Chinese people have constantly carried out experiments and attempts amidst humiliation, failure and anxiety. They have experienced failure in adopting advanced Western technology and thought on the basis of safeguarding China's feudal system and practicing a constitutional monarchy after the collapse of the Western capitalist political path and a great setback in worldwide socialism in the early 1990s. The Chinese people ultimately embarked on a path towards a successful revolution with national independence and liberation; in particular, they have adopted a path leading to the socialist modernization of China—a road towards socialism with Chinese characteristics—by combining the theoretical logic of scientific socialism with the historical logic of China's social development. After more than 30 years of reform and opening up, China's socialist market economy has rapidly developed; tremendous achievements have been made in economic, political, cultural and social constructions; comprehensive national strength, cultural soft power and international influence have substantially improved; and a great success has been achieved in socialism with Chinese characteristics. Although the latter project has not yet become full-fledged, its systems and institutions have basically taken shape. After more than one hundred years of pursuing dreams, China is rising among the nations of the world with a greater degree of confidence in the path it has chosen, the theory it has adopted and the institutions it has created.

Meanwhile, we should be aware that given the long-standing cognition and cultural psychology of learning from Western countries, we seldom take the initiative in showcasing ourselves—historical China and current China in reality—to the world, though China has emerged as a great world power. Due to a deeply rooted view that "Western countries are strong and China is weak", developed through Western-Chinese cultural exchanges, Western people and nations seldom have a sense of Chinese history or the current developments in China, let alone an understanding of China's developmental path and such in-depth issues as the scientificity and effectiveness of China's theory and institutions or their unique value for and contributions to human civilization. As self-recognition is not displayed, the "China Collapse Theory", "China Threat Theory", "China State Capitalism" and other so-called theories coined by certain people with ulterior motives and differing political views have been widely spread.

During our development, based on "crossing the river by feeling the stones", we have paid attention to learning from Western countries, understanding the world and learning to know ourselves through Western experience and discourse but have neglected self-recognition and efforts to let others know us. When we strive to become part of the world in a more tolerant and friendly way, we are not objectively, truly understood. Therefore, we should describe the path to the success of socialism with Chinese characteristics, tell Chinese stories, disseminate Chinese experiences, use international expressions to show a real China to the world, and help people around the world realize that the Western manner of modernization is not the endpoint of human historical evolution and that socialism with Chinese characteristics is also a valuable treasure of human thought. This is undoubtedly a very important task for an academic cultural researcher with a sense of justice and responsibility.

In this connection, the Chinese Academy of Social Sciences organized its top-notch experts and scholars and several external experts to write the *China Insights* series. This series not only provides an overview of China's path, theories and institutions but also objectively describes China's current development in the areas of political institutions, human rights, the rule of law, the economic system, finance, social governance, social security, population policies, values, religious faith, ethnic policies, rural issues, urbanization, industrialization, ecology, ancient civilization, literature, art, etc., thus depicting China in a way that helps readers visualize these topics.

We hope that this series will help domestic readers more correctly understand the course of the more than 100 years of China's modernization and more rationally look at current difficulties, enhance the urgency for and national confidence in comprehensively intensifying reform, build a consensus on reform and development and gather strength in this regard, as well as deepen foreign readers' understanding of China, thus fostering a better international environment for China's development.

Beijing, China
January 2014

Zhao Jianying

Introduction

From "Advancing the Rule of Law" to "Comprehensively Advancing the Rule of Law"

The law is vital to the governance of a country, and the rule of law is an important support for China's system and capacity for governance. Comprehensively advancing the rule of law is a major choice made by the Communist Party of China (CPC) and the Chinese people after thoroughly summing up the successful experience and harsh lessons in China's socialist construction.

Since the reform and opening up, the CPC and Chinese leaders have repeatedly emphasized the importance of "law" and have actively planned and deployed to promote the rule of law and build a socialist country under the rule of law. In December 1978, Deng Xiaoping stated at the 3rd Plenary Session of the 11th CPC Central Committee that "To ensure people's democracy, we must strengthen our legal system." In September 1982, the 12th CPC National Congress proposed that "We should continue to improve socialist democracy and legal system." In October 1987, the 13th CPC National Congress emphasized that "We must promote economic development and reform and at the same time build a legal system. Building the legal system must run through the whole process of reform." In October 1992, the 14th CPC National Congress further stated that "Without democracy and legal system, there would be no socialism or socialist modernization." In September 1997, the 15th CPC National Congress clearly stated that "We should improve the socialist legal system, advance the rule of law, and build a socialist country ruled by law" and "The rule of law is a fundamental principle by which the Party leads the people in running the country." The rule of law was confirmed for the first time as "the fundamental principle" in the form of the highest political document of the CPC Central Committee. In March 1999, the 2nd Session of the 9th National People's Congress deliberated and adopted the *Amendments to the Constitution*, and "advancing the rule of law and building a socialist country ruled by law" was written into the *Constitution* so that "the rule of law" becomes a constitutional principle and has changed from a proposition of the CPC into the will of the state.

In the 20 years since the 15th CPC National Congress, the rule of law has been continuously advanced in China, and law-based governance has been developing in depth and breadth. In November 2002, the 16th CPC National Congress proposed that "The key to developing socialist democracy is to combine the need to uphold the Party's leadership and to ensure that the people are the masters of the country with the need to rule the country by law." It further identified the essential characteristics and development path of governing the country according to law and took further improvement of the socialist democracy and socialist legal system and comprehensive implementation of the rule of law as important goals for building a moderately prosperous in all respects. In October 2007, the 17th CPC National Congress stated that governing the country according to law is the basic requirement of socialist democratic politics and emphasized the need to "fully implement the fundamental principle of governing the country according to law and accelerate the building of a socialist country under the rule of law." In March 2011, the Standing Committee of the National People's Congress announced at the 4th Session of the 11th National People's Congress that we had brought into being a socialist system of laws with Chinese characteristics as scheduled. In November 2012, the 18th CPC National Congress introduced a series of new concepts, new propositions and new tasks centering on the strategic objective of "advancing the rule of law in all respects and accelerating the building of a socialist country under the rule of law", confirmed that the rule of law is the basic way to run the country, and emphasized the need to give greater scope to the important role the rule of law plays in the country's governance and in social management.

Since the 18th CPC National Congress, the Party Central Committee with Xi Jinping at the core has raised comprehensively advancing the rule of law to an unprecedented level of importance, incorporated it into the blueprint of "The Four-Pronged Comprehensive Strategy", introduced a series of new concepts, new ideas, and new strategies for comprehensively advancing the rule of law, created a new realm of theories and practices of comprehensively advancing the rule of law and ushered in a new era of socialist rule of law with Chinese characteristics. In November 2013, the 3rd Plenary Session of the 8th CPC Central Committee took "building China under the rule of law" as an important task of comprehensively deepening reforms and proposed for the first time that "We must pursue coordinated progress in law-based governance, law-based exercise of state power, and law-based government administration, and promote the integrated development of rule of law for the country, the government, and society." In October 2014, the 4th Plenary Session of the 18th CPC Central Committee focused on the major issues concerning comprehensively advancing the rule of law and adopted the *Resolution of the CPC Central Committee on Major Issues Concerning Comprehensively Advancing the Law-Based Governance of China*, which specifies the overall objectives, blueprint, road maps and construction drawings of our drive to comprehensively advance the rule of law. This is the first plenary session in the history of the Chinese Communist Party that laid out strategic plans for comprehensively advancing the rule of law in China. It is a major milestone in the history of rule of law in China. In October 2017, the 19th CPC National Congress emphasized that "law-based governance is an essential requirement and important guarantee for socialism with Chinese characteristics" and "advancing law-based governance in all fields is a profound revolution in China's governance" and identified "ensuring every dimension of governance is law-based" as a part of the basic policy that underpins our endeavors to uphold and develop socialism with Chinese characteristics in the new era. The 19th CPC National Congress has deepened the understanding of law-based governance in all respects, formulated a timetable for completing the building of a country, government, and society based on the rule of law, established the organizational guarantee for law-based governance in all respects, and formulated the basic policy for law-based governance in all respects as the action program and guidelines for comprehensively advancing the rule of law. This will surely lead China to embark on a new journey of comprehensively advancing the rule of law.

We have completed the transition from "the rule of the legal system" to "the rule of law" and from "the rule of law to "the rule of law in all respects." We should ensure that there are laws to abide by; that laws are observed and strictly enforced; and that lawbreakers are prosecuted. We should make laws in a scientific way, enforce them strictly, administer justice impartially, and ensure that everyone abides by the law. All these factors reflect the CPC's keen understanding of the laws governing the country and its tireless exploration of law-based governance in all respects. The five years since the 18th CPC National Congress have witnessed historic achievements and historic changes in the cause of the Party and the country. China has initiated an unprecedented new stage in the cause of comprehensively advancing the rule of law.

First, the Party's leadership over law-based governance has been continuously strengthened, and law-based governance of the country and the Party has been further promoted. The leadership of the Communist Party of China is the most essential attribute of socialism with Chinese characteristics and the fundamental guarantee for comprehensively advancing the rule of law. Since the 18th CPC National Congress, the CPC has continuously strengthened the overall planning and leadership over a comprehensively advancing rule of law, ensuring that the Party plays its role as the leadership core in exercising overall leadership and coordinating the efforts of all, and exercising Party leadership at every point in the process and over every dimension of law-based governance. The 4th Plenary Session of the 18th CPC Central Committee focused on the major issues concerning comprehensively advancing rule of law. It is the first plenary session of the CPC Central Committee dedicated to the study of the rule of law, the first plenary session of the CPC Central Committee that has made a major decision to comprehensively advance the rule of law, and the first plenary session of the CPC Central Committee that put forward the new goal of building a rule of law China. It identified a new path for the rule of law in China, established a new policy for the rule of law in China, and specified a new method of building a rule of law China. It has great strategic guiding significance for comprehensively promoting the rule of law and building a socialist country under the rule of law. The report to the 19th CPC National Congress called for establishing a central leading group for advancing law-based governance in all areas to exercise unified leadership over the initiative to build rule of law in China. In February 2018, the 3rd Plenary Session of the 19th CPC Central Committee adopted the *Decision of the CPC Central Committee on Deepening the Reform of the Party and State Institutions* and the *Plan for Deepening the Reform of Party and State Institutions*, which proposed establishing the commission for comprehensive law-based governance of the CPC Central Committee to be responsible for top-level design, overall layout, overall coordination, overall promotion, supervision and implementation," and the leadership system for comprehensive law-based governance was unprecedentedly strengthened. Since the 18th CPC National Congress, the CPC Central Committee has focused on the layout of "The Four-Pronged Comprehensive Strategy" and has successively made arrangements for law-based governance of the country and rule-based governance over the Party. The 3rd Plenary Session of the 18th CPC Central Committee proposed that we must deepen the reform of the Party building system by centering on enhancing the Party's capacity to govern in a scientific and democratic way and in accordance with the law. The 4th Plenary Session of the 18th CPC Central Committee took shaping a sound system of intra-Party regulations as an important part of building a system of socialist rule of law with Chinese characteristics and an important content of the overall goal of comprehensive law-based governance. The 5th Plenary Session of the 18th CPC Central Committee pointed out that we must uphold law-based exercise of state power and comprehensively improve the Party's ability to run the country in accordance with the Constitution and the laws and to govern the Party in accordance with the intra-Party's regulations to raise the rule-based governance over the Party to an unprecedented level to ensure "institution building for the Party." The 6th Plenary Session of the 18th CPC Central Committee embarked on a Journey of rigorous governance over the Party, institution building for the Party and rule-based governance over the Party. During the five years from the 18th CPC National Congress to the 19th CPC National Congress, the CCDI had investigated 440 officials at or above the provincial or corps level and other centrally administered officials; disciplinary inspection and supervision departments across the country registered 1.545 million cases of corruption, punishing 1.537 million people; 58,000 people who were suspected of being involved in crimes were transferred to judicial departments.

Second, we should make laws in a scientific way and continuously strengthen the socialist legal system with Chinese characteristics. Since the 18th CPC National Congress, the CPC Central Committee has proposed a series of new concepts, new ideas, and new strategies for ensuring sound lawmaking according to the new situation, new tasks, and new requirements we are facing in comprehensively advancing the rule of law. To comprehensively advance the rule of law, we must first ensure that there are laws to abide by, prioritize lawmaking and make the most of the role of lawmaking in spearheading its efforts; we will harmonize lawmaking with the making of reform decisions so that major reform measures are lawful and these legislative efforts meet the needs of China's reform drive as well as its economic and social development. To improve the mechanism for sound and democratic lawmaking, we should focus on improving the quality of legislation and making the socialist rule of law good law and good governance. The CPC Central Committee proposes that arrangements will be made to allow peoples' congresses that have legislative power to play the dominant role in lawmaking and give play to the leading role of the people's congress and its standing committee in legislative work. Those involved in legislative work must have a strong sense of political integrity. They must possess the ability to respect objective laws, promote democracy, coordinate more effectively with others, and build consensus to provide important guidance for strengthening and improving legislative work in the new historical period. During the five years from the 18th CPC National Congress to the 19th CPC National Congress, China formulated or revised 48 laws, 42 administrative regulations, 2,926 local regulations, and 3162 rules. Meanwhile, it has successively revised 57 laws and 130 administrative regulations through a "package" scheme, initiated the compilation of the Civil Code, and promulgated the *General Provisions of Civil Law*, so the socialist legal system with Chinese characteristics is constantly improved. The Communist Party of China has issued a large number of symbolic, fundamental, and key intra-Party regulations and formulated and revised nearly 80 Central Committee regulations, accounting for more than 40% of the existing intra-Party regulations; thus, the building of the system of intra-Party regulations has made unprecedented major achievements. The efficient implementation system for the rule of law, the strict supervision system for the rule of law, and the powerful guarantee system for the rule of law have yielded remarkable results and played a role of significantly promoting comprehensively advancing the rule of law.

Third, we should adhere to strict law enforcement, and the building of a law-based government has entered a new stage. The 18th CPC National Congress has identified basically building a government under the rule of law as an important goal of building a moderately prosperous society in all respects by 2020. The 3rd Plenary Session of the 18th CPC Central Committee identified promoting law-based government administration and accelerating the building of government under the rule of law as a major task for comprehensively advancing the rule of law. Governments at all levels must operate under the leadership of the Communist Party of China in keeping with what the rule of law requires. China will put in place a system of law-based government administration that balances powers with responsibilities and that is both authoritative and effective and redouble its efforts to build a law-based government that undertakes its duties in a scientific way, is vested with lawful powers and responsibilities, enforces the law stringently, and is transparent, impartial, clean, efficient and credible to identify the direction and tasks for speeding up the building of a law-based government. In December 2015, the CPC Central Committee and the State Council promulgated the *Implementation Outline for Building a Government under the Rule of Law 2015–2020*, which established the overall objective and action plan for building a government under the rue of law by 2020. During the 5 years from the 18th CPC National Congress to the 19th CPC National Congress, the reforms to streamline the government, delegate power, and improve government services were strengthened. The State Council successively canceled and delegated 618 administrative approval items and canceled all non-administrative review items, which greatly stimulated the vitality of the market and society. All provincial-level governments were required to release their list of powers and list of responsibilities, and 31 provincial governments released the list of powers and responsibilities of the three-level government departments of provinces, cities and counties. A government legal counsel system was established to ensure administrative decision-making in a more scientific and democratic way and strengthen the role of rule of law in administrative decision-making. In February 2016, the General Office of the CPC Central Committee and the General Office of the State Council issued the *Opinions on Comprehensively Promoting Transparency in Government Affairs* to implement oversight conducted through the random selection of both inspectors and inspection targets and the prompt release of results and continuously strengthen in-process and subsequent supervision. Administrative law enforcement reforms will be bolstered. Laws will be enforced strictly in a standardized, impartial and humane manner. The evaluation system for the construction of a government under the rule of law is taking shape, and supervision and inspection efforts have been significantly strengthened. Law-based government administration is promoted according to law, and the construction of a government under the rule of law is accelerated at an unprecedented pace.

Fourth, we should uphold judicial impartiality, write a new chapter in judicial reform and raise public confidence in judicatory reform. In February 2013, General Secretary Xi Jinping emphasized during the 4th Group Study Session of the Political Bureau of the 18th CPC Central Committee that we should strive to make people feel fairness and justice in every judicial case. It established new objectives for judicial reform and judicial construction in the new historical period. Since the 18th CPC National Congress, the CPC Central Committee has attached great importance to the reform of the judicial system. The 3rd Plenary Session of the 18th CPC Central Committee proposed 17 judicial reform tasks, and the 4th Plenary Session of the 18th CPC Central Committee introduced 84 reform tasks in the judicial field and made feasible top-level design and strategic arrangement for the reform of the judicial system. The Leading Group for Comprehensively Deepening Reforms of the 18th CPC Central Committee convened 37 meetings, of which more than 20 meetings were dedicated to studying and discussing issues related to judicial reform and adopted more than 40 documents, including regulations, plans and opinions on (or involving) judicial reforms. Among the documents, the *Framework Opinions on Several Issues on Piloting the Reform of the Judicial System* adopted at the 3rd Meeting of the Central Leading Group for Comprehensively Deepening Reforms in June 2014 is a programmatic document for judicial reform in the new era. The reform of the judicial system focused on building a socialist rule of law system with Chinese characteristics, building a socialist country under the rule of law, and safeguarding social fairness and justice. Reform measures were promptly implemented, important progress was made, and the main framework of reform was basically established. Since the 18th CPC National Congress, the reform of China's judicial accountability system has been fully implemented. The reform of the trial-centered criminal procedure system was deepening. Local courts and procuratorates below the provincial level have gradually implemented unified management of personnel, funds, and properties, and the system for the recording, notification and accountability investigation of leading officials for interventions in judicial activities has been established and implemented. The Supreme People's Circuit Court, International Commercial Court, Intellectual Property Court, Internet Court and other specialized courts, and cross-administrative division courts and procuratorates were established. The case filing registration system was implemented, the system of reeducation through labor was abolished, a number of major criminal cases involving unjust, false, or wrongful charges were redressed, the allocation of judicial powers was continuously optimized, law enforcement and judicial standardization construction was further strengthened, and judicial transparency was vigorously promoted. The right to know and to supervise the parties concerned and the public was effectively guaranteed. Judicial quality, efficiency and credibility have been greatly improved, and people's sense of gain for fairness and justice has been significantly enhanced.

Fifth, we must ensure that everyone abides by the law, and new strides have been made in building a society ruled by law. A society under the rule of law is an important foundation and basic prerequisite for building a country and a government under the rule of law. Only when the whole society has universal belief in the rule of law can we provide a solid ideological foundation for comprehensively advancing the rule of law. Only by continuously creating a rule of law environment in which the entire society respects, believes in, observes and applies the law can we provide a broad social foundation for comprehensively advancing the rule of law. Since the 18th CPC National Congress, the CPC has attached great importance to building a society under the rule of law. The 3rd Plenary Session of the 18th CPC Central Committee regarded "promoting the integrated development of rule of law for the country, the government, and society" as an important task of "building China under the rule of law." The 4th Plenary Session of the 18th CPC Central Committee regarded building a society under the rule of law as an important aspect of our efforts to comprehensively advance the rule of law and proposed that "we must raise awareness of the rule of law among the general public and building a society under the rule of law." The 4th Plenary Session of the 18th CPC Central Committee further deepened the development of the rule of law culture, clearly stated that we should vigorously strengthen the development of the socialist rule of law culture, strengthen the supporting role of moral values in the rule of law culture, incorporate education on the rule of law into our initiatives for cultural and ethical progress, and carry out mass cultural activities for promoting the rule of law. In December 2016, the General Office of the CPC Central Committee and the General Office of the State Council jointly issued the *Guiding Opinions on Further Integrating the Core Socialist Values into the Building of Rule of Law*, which specified the concrete requirements for the development of the rule of law culture. Since the 18th CPC National Congress, the CPC and the Chinese government have attached greater importance to strengthening education on the rule of law, further promoting universal understanding of the law. A series of results had been achieved in law popularization during the 6th Five-year Plan Period, and law popularization work started smoothly in the 6th Five-year Plan Period. In November 2014, the 11th Session of the 12th NPC Standing Committee adopted the decision on the establishment of the national Constitution day. In July 2015, the 15th Session of the 12th NPC Standing Committee decided to implement the constitutional oath system to demonstrate the dignity and authority of the Constitution. China attaches greater importance to the mediation and resolution of social conflicts and disputes, and the diversified dispute resolution system is constantly improved. We have improved mechanisms to reward people for good faith when they abide by the law and punish them for bad faith when they break it and significantly strengthened the fostering of social integrity. The 5th Plenary Session of the 18th CPC Central Committee requires that "We should promote the spirit of the socialist rule of law, raise awareness of respecting, learning about, observing, and applying the law in the whole society, especially public servants, and form a good atmosphere for the rule of law in the whole society and the rule of law habits." The system for leading officials to take the lead in respecting, learning about, observing, and applying the law has been constantly improved, and the ability and level of using law-based thinking and approaches has been significantly improved. The authority of socialist rule of law is gradually established, and respecting and observing the law has become the common pursuit and conscious action of all people.

Contents

Chapter 1
Well-Conceived Legislation: Perfecting the Legal System

Yanpeng Liu

1.1 Introduction

Over the six years from 2012 to 2018, China continuously explored the path of advancing lawmaking by effective and democratic means, had the courage to break new ground, and embarked on a path of legislation that suits China's national conditions and has Chinese characteristics. Although a socialist legal system with Chinese characteristics has been formed, China's legislative tasks have continued unabated. In the past seven years, in terms of both quantity and quality, Chinese legislation has achieved tremendous results. From 2012 to 2018, the National People's Congress and its Standing Committee enacted 38 laws and revised or amended 192 laws (see Table A.1 in Appendices for details). The State Council formulated 44 administrative regulations and revised, amended or repealed 280 administrative regulations (see Table A.2 in Appendices for details). The legislative work in the past seven years mainly focused on the following aspects: The first is to adapt to social development and respond to social needs; the second is to ensure reforms in order and the unification of the legal system; the third is to adhere to the people-oriented approach and promote the protection of rights; the fourth is to pay attention to environmental legislation to prevent environmental pollution; the fifth is to ensure the quality of legislation with enactment, revision, repeal of laws and regulations simultaneously the sixth is to expand the main body of legislation and promote local legislation; the seventh is to persist in open-door legislation and practice democratic legislation; the eighth is to rely on evaluation and inspection to promote well-conceived legislation.

Y. Liu (✉)
Institute of Law, CASS, Beijing, China

H. Tian and Y. Lv (eds.), *The Chinese Path of Rule of Law Construction*,
China Insights, https://doi.org/10.1007/978-981-16-4130-5_1

1.2 Legislative Status

1.2.1 *Adapting to Social Development and Responding to Social Needs*

The legal system as the superstructure should adapt to economic and social development; otherwise, it will lose its vitality. During 2012–2018, the NPC Standing Committee revised or amended a total of 192 laws, and the State Council revised, amended or abolished a total of 280 administrative regulations. The revision of laws and regulations mainly aims to adapt to economic and social development, confirm the results of economic and social development, and guide the direction of economic and social development.

First, in terms of economic development, through enacting and revising the laws, the NPC Standing Committee and the State Council have established market rules, purified the market environment, and promoted orderly economic development. In 2013, the NPC Standing Committee revised the *Trademark Law*, and the State Council revised *Regulations for Computer Software Protection*, *Regulations for the Implementation of the Copyright Law*, *Regulations on the Protection of the Right to Network Dissemination of Information* and *Regulations on the Protection of New Varieties of Plants*. The abovementioned revised laws and administrative regulations added provisions on punitive damages, increased the amount of compensation for infringement, ensured the normal operation of the intellectual property market, and strengthened the protection of intellectual property rights. In 2015, the NPC Standing Committee revised the *Advertisement Law*, the *Law on Commercial Banks*, the *Law on Securities Investment Fund* and other laws that are closely related to economic development. On the one hand, these revised laws regulated the chaotic phenomena in the industry. For example, the *Advertisement Law* added the regulation on spokespersons; on the other hand, they removed institutional obstacles and stimulated economic development. For example, the *Law on Commercial Banks* has deleted the provision that the ratio between the balance of loans and the balance of deposits must not exceed 75%, which greatly improved banks' loan supply ability and intensified lending to the real economy, such as small and microenterprises.

Second, in terms of social management, the NPC Standing Committee and the State Council have formulated new laws to maintain social harmony and revised the old laws that failed to meet social needs. The role of laws and administrative regulations in social management is reflected in the following aspects. First, standardize the industrial rules. Through the guidance of laws and regulations, stricter industry admittance qualifications will be implemented, and industry self-discipline can be strengthened. For example, the *Food Safety Law* revised by the NPC Standing Committee in 2015 was dubbed "the most stringent food safety law in history." It establishes a series of strict systems, such as the real-name system for online sales and the first asking responsibility principle for traders and/or producers to further regulate the food industry and lay a solid institutional foundation for ensuring food safety. Second, strengthen social harmony. Laws and regulations have played an indelible role in maintaining social harmony and protecting the interests of socially disadvantaged groups. For example, in 2016, the NPC Standing Committee enacted the *Anti-Domestic Violence Law*, which includes explicit provisions on prevention, handling, personal safety protective order and legal liabilities of domestic violence and gives special protection on special groups such as the handicapped, minors and the elderly. Third, reduce social risks. Facing the complex social reality, the government needs to enact effective laws and regulations as the basis for administrative decision-making and law enforcement to achieve refined management. For example, as of the end of 2015, the total amount of social security funds had reached RMB 1,913.821 billion, and the task of ensuring the safety of the funds became increasingly arduous. In response to this, the State Council promulgated the *Regulations on the National Social Security Fund* in March 2016, which specifies the nature, purpose and sources of the national social security fund from the level of administrative regulations to reduce the risk of social security funds and safeguard the safety of the national social security fund.

Finally, in terms of culture and education, on the one hand, laws and regulations have strengthened supervision in the realms of culture and cultural relics. For example, the NPC Standing Committee formulated the *Public Cultural Service Guarantee Law*, which provides the legal basis for further strengthening the management and guarantee of public cultural services. The NPC Standing Committee revised the *Law on Protection of Cultural Relics* to delegate part of the power originally belonging to the cultural relics administration department of the State Council to the cultural relics departments of the provincial people's governments to strengthen the protection and supervision of cultural relics. On the other hand, laws and regulations will steer technological innovations and promote the reform of the education system. For example, the NPC Standing Committee and the State Council have amended some of the provisions of the laws and regulations such as *Non-state Education Promotion Law*, *Regulations National Awards for Science and Technology*, and *Regulations on Sino-foreign Cooperation in Running Schools*. This has played a positive role in promoting the effective supply of educational resources and encouraging technological progress. In addition, the promulgation of the *Protection of Heroes and Martyrs Law* in 2018 provides legal protection for the protection of heroes and martyrs, inheriting and carrying forward the spirit of heroism and patriotism.

1.2.2 Ensuring Reforms in Order and the Unification of the Legal System

Reform means changes and improvements to an existing law, social system, or institution. It will not only break the existing balance of interests but also affect the laws and regulations behind the system or institution. In the past, when dealing with the relationship between reforms and systems, reforms were often given priority, while systems lagged behind. This will not only affect the authority of laws and regulations but also easily mislead the reforms. Therefore, before a major reform is carried out, the legitimacy and compliance of the reform should be guaranteed first to ensure that the major reform has a legal basis. Since the 18th CPC National Congress, especially since the 3rd and 4th Plenary Sessions of the 18th CPC Central Committee, China has initiated reforms in various fields from top to bottom, which have had great impacts on China's political structure, economic operation, and social operation. These reforms are not only the processes of reshuffling and reallocation of benefits but also the processes of formulating, amending or revising laws and regulations.

First, laws are formulated to implement reform opinions. For some reform plans that have been written into the laws, to ensure the harmony and unity of the legal system, the main contents and spirit of the reform plan must be reflected in other legal texts. For example, in 2015, the principle of law-based taxation was written into the *Implementing Opinions on the Implementation of the Principle of Law-based Taxation*. Later, in the process of amending the *Legislation Law*, the principle of law-based taxation were taken as an important part of tax legislation. In 2016, the NPC Standing Committee deliberated and adopted the *Environmental Protection Tax Law*, which has become a touchstone for the implementation of the principle of law-based taxation.

Second, laws and regulations were formulated for the implementation of reform opinions. In recent years, China has formed a reform model in which reforms are guided by documents and confirmed by legislation and priority is given to pilot projects. First, reform opinions were issued for the reform in a field, pilot projects were carried out first, and relevant administrative regulations were then formulated and revised after summarizing the experience of the pilot projects. For example, with regard to household registration system reform, the State Council first issued the *Opinions on Further Promoting the Reform of the Household Registration System*, then summarized the experience in the residence permit system in various areas, and finally issued the *Interim Regulations on Residence Permits*, which highlights the empowerment function and service functions of residence permits. On the basis of specifying the nature of residence permits and application conditions, on the one hand, it establishes basic public services and conveniences for residence permit holders; on the other hand, it encourages localities to continuously create conditions to provide services in compulsory education, basic public employment and basic public health.

Finally, the laws and regulations were revised in large quantities to advance the reforms. The 3rd Plenary Session of the 18th CPC Central Committee called for further streamlining administration and delegating more powers to lower-level governments and deepening the reform of the administrative examination and approval system. In accordance with the requirements of the CPC Central Committee, the NPC Standing Committee and the State Council further sorted out the laws and regulations related to the reforms and revised them in batches. For example, the National People's Congress has revised the *Tobacco Monopoly Law* and canceled the tobacco monopoly license, revised the *Law on the Prevention and Control of Environmental Pollution by Solid Wastes* to cancel the import license of solid waste, and revised the *Flood Control Law* to cancel the permit for felling protective trees along banks and embankments. The State Council has even revised administrative regulations many times in packages. In 2013, the State Council revised 16 administrative regulations in one package; in 2014, it revised 29 administrative regulations in two packages; and in 2015, it revised 66 administrative regulations in one package. The revision of most administrative regulations involves streamlining administration and delegating more powers to lower-level governments and society and deepening the reform of administrative examination and approval.

1.2.3 Adhering to the People-Oriented Approach and Promoting the Protection of Rights

The constitution affirms the principle of "the state respects and protects human rights", and this principle needs to be reflected in laws and regulations one by one. During the seven years from 2012 to 2018, China abolished the reeducation through the labor system, cared for the elderly and the weak, women and children, protected consumer rights, improved food and drug regulations, paid attention to disadvantaged groups, and strengthened people's livelihood legislation.

First, China has repealed the reeducation through the labor system to respect and protect human rights. In 2013, the NPC Standing Committee abolished the reeducation through the labor system and implemented community-based corrections instead. This marks the withdrawal of reeducation through the labor system established in the 1950s from the stage of history. This is not only an inevitable requirement for advancing the rule of law but also an important manifestation of the country's respect and protection of human rights.

Second, China has revised laws and regulations to give care for disadvantaged groups. Women, children, and the elderly are relatively disadvantaged groups in society. These groups are likely to be neglected by families, society, and schools, so they need special protection. To this end, the NPC Standing Committee revised the *Law on the Protection of Rights and Interests of the Elderly* twice in 2012 and 2015, revised the *Law on the Protection of Minors* in 2012, and promulgated the *Anti-Domestic Violence Law* in 2016. The formulation and revision of the above-mentioned laws enumerate the rights of disadvantaged groups such as the elderly and minors in detail and provide an institutional basis for making improvements in the protection of the interests of disadvantaged groups.

Third, China has protected the rights and interests of consumers and improved food and drug laws and regulations. In 2014, the NPC Standing Committee revised the *Law on the Protection of Consumer Rights and Interests*, added provisions on punitive damages for fraud and on protection of personal information, and stipulated that consumer associations can institute legal proceedings for public interests to maximally protect the legitimate rights and interests of consumers. The *Food Safety Law* revised in 2015 established the whole-process food traceability mechanism, the food recall mechanism, and the real-name system for selling food online, providing reliable legal support for further ensuring food safety.

In 2018, the NPC Standing Committee deliberated a number of medical and health drafts, including the Draft Amendments to the Drug Administration Law, the Draft Basic Medical and Health Promotion Law, and the Draft Vaccine Management Law, in an effort to build a dam of the medical and health system and tighten the system of citizen health cages.

Finally, attention should be paid to disadvantaged groups to strengthen people's livelihood legislation. In 2014, the State Council formulated the *Interim Measures for Social Assistance*, which incorporated guidelines and policies such as emergency relief, disease emergency assistance, and temporary assistance into legal arrangements. This has far-reaching significance for the construction of China's social assistance system. In 2016, the NPC Standing Committee enacted the *Charity Law*, marking that China's charity activities have moved towards the track of the rule of law. At the same time, civil affairs and relevant departments have issued a series of regulations and normative documents, such as the *Measures for the Recognition of Charitable Organizations* and *Notices on Related Issues, such as the Registration of Charitable Organizations,* as a supporting package.

1.2.4 Paying Attention to Environmental Legislation to Prevent Environmental Pollution

The past three decades have witnessed the rapid economic development of China, but this is always accompanied by serious environmental pollution. Environmental pollution not only affects the growth of crops on land but also affects people's daily lives and greatly harms their physical health. In particular, haze in recent years has gradually aroused people's attention to environmental pollution. For this reason, both the central and local governments emphasized that "Clear waters and green mountains are as good as mountains of gold and silver." At the central level, from 2012 to 2018, the National People's Congress and its Standing Committee and the State Council formulated or revised many laws and administrative regulations related to environmental protection. The amendments to these laws and regulations have armed the environmental protection departments to "the teeth", expanded the power of the environmental protection departments, and enhanced local governments' environmental protection obligations. For example, in 2014, the NPC Standing Committee revised the *Environmental Protection Law*, which established the environmental priority concept of "coordination of economic and social development and environmental protection", defined the government's supervision and management responsibilities for environmental protection, changed the previous concept of "attaching importance to economy and ignoring environment", and changed the previous idea of "pollution before treatment". For another example, the *Law on Prevention and Control of Air Pollution* revised in 2015 has strengthened penalties and set no ceiling on fines for enterprises and institutions that caused air pollution. In addition, the NPC Standing Committee revised the *Air Pollution Prevention and Control Law*, the *Solid Waste Pollution Prevention and Control Law*, the *Animal Epidemic Prevention Law,* and other laws. The State Council formulated the *Regulations on the Prevention and Control of Pollution from Large-scale Livestock and Poultry Farming* and revised the *Regulations on the Prevention and Control of Marine Environmental Pollution by Ships*. Through the promulgation and amendment of the abovementioned laws and regulations, China's governance of environmental pollution has gradually moved towards the rule of law.

In addition to the central government's endeavors, local governments have also continued to strengthen their efforts in environmental protection. They not only intensified the environmental impact assessment of newly launched projects but also implemented the one-vote veto system for leaders' evaluation of environmental protection. Moreover, from the perspective of local legislation, local governments attach great importance to environmental protection legislation. They not only issued detailed provisions on the basis of higher-level laws but also made environmental protection a priority legislation item. For example, Leshan City immediately organized human resources to formulate water source protection regulations after being granted legislative power. In addition to legislation and law revision, the National People's Congress also attaches importance to strengthening environmental protection through law enforcement inspections. From 2013 to 2018, the NPC Standing Committee organized enforcement inspections on one or two environmental protection laws every year on average. On the one hand, it supervised the implementation of local laws, and on the other hand, it urged local governments to strengthen efforts in environmental protection.

1.2.5 Ensuring the Quality of Legislation with Enactment, Revision, and Repeal of Laws and Regulations Simultaneously

With the further development of China's social economy, legislative work has shifted from the pursuit of quantity to the pursuit of quality, from creating new laws to revising old laws, and from filling gaps to interpreting laws. In addition, the suspension of the application of relevant laws and regulations in some regions has become an important way to break institutional constraints, promote local reform practices, and provide experience for central legislation.

First, the number of laws and regulations that were revised was greater than the number of laws and regulations that were enacted. In terms of the legislative work of the National People's Congress and its Standing Committee and the State Council, the ratio of laws that have been revised or amended to the laws that have been enacted of the National People's Congress and its Standing Committee and the State Council is between 5:1 and 6:1, and the number of laws that have been revised or amended far exceeds the number of laws that have been enacted. On the one hand, with the formation of the socialist legal system with Chinese characteristics, the space for purely creating new laws is getting smaller and smaller, so the number of laws that were enacted is gradually decreasing; on the other hand, with the emergence of a new normal in economic development, new measures for social management, reform and innovation have emerged, and laws and regulations have been revised more and more frequently. This reflects the actual situation of legislation in China. The formulation of new laws is no longer the main task of legislation, while the improvement of the existing legal system is the priority of legislation. Although the number of new laws enacted has declined, the procedures for enacting new laws have been further improved, and the quality of legislation has been further improved. Research and investigation before legislation, argumentation in the legislative process and post-enactment evaluation are becoming more scientific and reasonable. Taking legislation evaluation as an example, the *Legislation Law* in 2015 has added the contents of extensive solicitation of opinions, scientific argumentation and evaluation; the legislative regulations of local people's congresses basically stipulate that "evaluation must be carried out one year after a law or regulation is enacted or revised."

Second, a package of laws rather than a single law were revised at a time. In the past, laws and regulations were generally revised because they no longer meet the needs of social development or when new conditions emerged that needed to be regulated, so they were often matured and revised one by one. With economic and social development and the deepening of reforms, a package of laws rather than a single law were revised at one time. Any reform measure often entails the revision of dozens of laws or administrative regulations. For example, to promote price reforms, the central government has gradually canceled or delegated to lower-level governments the power to set prices to create a fairer market environment. For this reason, on April 24, 2015, a package of laws was revised, including the *Tobacco Monopoly Law*, the *Railway Law*, the *Drug Administration Law* and other relevant laws. In the past six years, laws were revised more frequently in a packaging manner, mainly involving administrative review and approval reform, delegation of power, and promotion of service-oriented government. The revision of laws has greatly ensured that the reforms are based on law, the results of the reforms are consolidated, and the pace of the reforms is accelerated.

Finally, the suspension of the application of laws supports reform and innovation. To fully unleash the dividends of reform and improve the level of reform and innovation, the central government has authorized some regions to promote the reform of related content. However, reform means innovation, means a breakthrough in the existing system, and means changing the existing relationship of rights and obligations. The effective advancement of many reforms entails not only the wisdom and courage of those in power but also the support of the legal system, but the actual situation is that the update speed of laws lags behind the speed of the reform. In such cases, to ensure the smooth progress of the reforms and maintain the authority of the legal system, it is necessary to suspend the application of laws in some areas. In the past six years, the National People's Congress and its Standing Committee have repeatedly issued decisions to suspend the application of some laws and regulations in some specific areas. For example, in 2013, the 4th Session of the Standing Committee of the 12th National People's Congress adopted the *Draft Decision on Temporarily Adjusting Certain Administrative Approval Procedures as Regulated by Relevant Laws in China (Shanghai) Pilot Free Trade Zone*. After a reform is successful, the legislature will promptly transform the results of the reform into legislative content and ensure that the reform is advanced in depth by formulating or modifying the relevant laws and administrative regulations.

1.2.6 Expanding the Main Body of Legislation and Promoting Local Legislation

Before 2015, only 49 cities had legislative power, including 27 provincial and autonomous regional capitals, four cities in special economic zones and 18 cities selected by the State Council. With social and economic development, urban management is becoming increasingly complicated. Laws or administrative regulations are unable to directly apply to urban environmental sanitation, city appearance, urban planning and construction, cultural relic protection and other issues. In such cases, cities without legislative power have to carry out urban management based on normative documents. Taking Tangshan and Baoding before 2015 as examples, Tangshan was a larger city with legislative power, while Baoding had no legislative power. However, before 2015, Baoding issued local regulations similar to those of Tangshan in the form of government documents. For example, Tangshan City has *Greening Management Regulations of Tangshan City*, Baoding City had *Gardens and Greening Management Measures of Baoding City*; Tangshan City had *Regulations of Tangshan City on Promoting Scientific and Technological Progress of Enterprises*, and Baoding City had *Measures of Baoding City for Science and Technology Awards*; Tangshan City had *Regulations of Tangshan City on Water Supply Management*, Baoding City had *Measures of Baoding City for Management of Heat Supply and Consumption*. For a long period of time, the normative documents promulgated by the government have played a legislative role, but the procedures for promulgating normative documents are simple without going through rigorous argumentation, which affects the building of the rule of law.

The 2015 amendment to the *Legislation Law* in granted legislative powers to all cities with subordinate districts stipulates that "without any basis in laws, administrative regulations, or local regulations, no rules of a local government may set out any requirements that impair the rights or increase the obligations of citizens, legal persons and other organizations." So far, the regulations of a city with subordinate districts should not be in conflict with the higher-level laws, and it also needs to fully consider the rights and obligations of citizens as legal persons. As a result, China's urban governance has gradually embarked on the road of rule of law.

1.2.7 Persisting in Open-Door Legislation and Practicing Democratic Legislation

Legislation is in essence a process to integrate, balance and coordinate different interests. The best way to balance various interests is to give full play to democracy and solicit opinions from all sides. The 4th Plenary Session of the 18th CPC Central Committee pointed out that "we should carry out lawmaking in a well-conceived and democratic way." Open-door legislation is a prerequisite for advancing law-making in a well-conceived and democratic way. The public can provide legislative opinions only on the basis of a full understanding of the contents, such as legislative background, legislative drafts, and legislative descriptions. In the process of enacting laws, the National People's Congress and its Standing Committee solicit opinions from experts and scholars by holding hearings and expert argumentation meetings to ensure that laws are made in a well-conceived way. In the process of enacting laws, the National People's Congress and its Standing Committee solicit public opinions through its official website to ensure that laws are made in a democratic way. According to statistics from the official website of the NPC Standing Committee, from 2012 to 2018, the average number of people participating in soliciting opinions on legislation was approximately 610,000, and a total of 2,400,000 pieces of opinions were received each year (Table 1.1 in details).

Table 1.1 The average number of people participating in soliciting opinions and Number of opinions

Year	Number of Participants for soliciting opinions(ten thousand)	Number of opinions s(ten thousand)
2012	17	120.8
2013	0.6	4.5
2014	2.9	8.8
2015	10.6	21.5
2016	1.9	8.3
2017	5.9	10.7
2018	22	65.9

1.2.8 Relying on Evaluation and Inspection to Promote Well-Conceived Legislation

To improve legislative quality, we should carry out lawmaking in a well-conceived and democratic way and strengthen the evaluation and enforcement inspection of laws and regulations. In terms of legal evaluation, the NPC Standing Committee will conduct pre-evaluation before a law is about to be promulgated. For example, before the draft tourism law was submitted for deliberation and voting, the Legislative Affairs Commission of the NPC Standing Committee invited some NPC deputies, tourists, tourism operators, experts and scholars to attend a forum to carry out a comprehensive evaluation on the feasibility of the contents of the draft law, the timeliness of its promulgation and possible social effects after enforcement. Through the evaluation, on the one hand, loopholes in the law were found in time, avoiding major mistakes, and the scientific rationality of legislation was improved; on the other hand, public opinions could be widely absorbed to ensure that the laws are made in a democratic way.

In addition to legislative evaluation, the effectiveness of law enforcement can also be evaluated through law enforcement inspection. In the past seven years, the NPC Standing Committee has successively carried out law enforcement inspection activities targeted at the enforcement effect of laws in some fields, including economic and social development (11 laws including *Law on Promoting the Transformation of Scientific and Technical Achievements*, *Law on the Protection of Rights and Interests of the Elderly*, etc.), environmental protection (5 laws including *Law on Prevention and Control of Water Pollution*, *Law on Prevention and Control of Air Pollution*, etc.), education (4 laws including *Compulsory Education Law*, *Vocational Education Law*, etc.), administrative management (*Administrative Reconsideration Law*, *Safety Production Law*, etc.) and culture and cultural relic protection (*Law on the Protection of Cultural Relics*). Law enforcement inspection is of great significance. First, law enforcement inspection enables law makers to keep informed of the enforcement effect of laws. The vitality of any system of law lies in its implementation. Only in practice can we discover the problems of a law and difficulties and obstacles to its implementation. For example, after the inspection of the enforcement of the *Law on Road Traffic Safety*, a report on the enforcement of the *Law on Road Traffic Safety* was issued. According to the report, the backward management of some road safety facilities and the high incidence of illegal behaviors of motor vehicle drivers are the main problems in the enforcement of the law, so it suggested taking comprehensive measures to solve the existing serious problems. Second, law enforcement inspection lays the foundation for the revision of a law. In the process of law enforcement inspection, the NPC Standing Committee will visit all parts of the country, fully listen to the opinions of representatives of all stakeholders, and collect various suggestions on legal amendments to provide useful first-hand materials for the subsequent legislative amendments. For example, in 2012, the NPC Standing Committee launched a round of inspections on the enforcement of the *Cultural Relics Protection Law* and collected a large number of suggestions that were finally reflected in the 2014 amendment to the *Cultural Relics Protection Law*.

1.3 Legislative Outlook

1.3.1 Improving Legislative Efficiency and Quality, Deepening the Reform

In the past seven years, the NPC Standing Committee has formulated 5–6 new laws and revised or repealed 20–30 old laws every year. The State Council has formulated 6 administrative regulations and revised 40 administrative regulations every year on average. In terms of legislative workload, China's legislative efficiency is not low, but compared with the various reforms that China is promoting, the speed of legislation still lags behind the speed of the reforms. At present, a major reform is not promoted through enactment or revision of the law but through the transmission of the spirit of the document, showing that the speed of law enactment or revision is far lower than the speed of reform. Regarding the legal issues involved in the reform process, sometimes the NPC Standing Committee will be asked to suspend the application of some laws in some special areas. However, the vast majority of reforms are still wandering in an area between legal and illegal to hit an edge ball of the law. For example, the reform of the judicial post system can neither find the basis in the *Judges Law* or the *Prosecutors Law* nor does it comply with the specific provisions in the *Organic Law of the People's Courts* or the *Organic Law of the People's Procuratorates*, but it has been rolled out across the country. Thus, it can be seen that the measures to promote the building of a country under the rule of law in practice may not completely meet the requirements of rule of law. Legislation often lags behind reform practice, and the quality and efficiency of legislation often cannot meet the requirements of reform. Therefore, in the future legislative process, it is necessary to further improve the quality and efficiency of legislation so that legislation and reform can march on side by side.

1.3.2 Strengthening Legislative Transparency and Expanding Democratic Legislation

Presently, both the central and local governments attach great importance to lawmaking in a democratic way and regard public participation as an important part of legislative work. To ensure public participation, the legislatures shall publish the draft laws so that the public can learn the contents of the drafts and provide comments and suggestions. In practice, although many drafts are published but fewer opinions are fed back to law makers, many drafts are published, but fewer explanations on the drafts are given. The publication of draft laws to solicit feedback opinions, on the one hand, can urge legislatures to sort out comments and opinions to improve the effectiveness of soliciting opinions; on the other hand, it can increase the enthusiasm of the public to participate in legislation. Publication of explanations on the draft laws is because there are many professional and boring contents in the draft laws, and it is impossible for ordinary people to understand these contents in a short time. Therefore, it is necessary to publish explanations of the contents, significance, and principles of the draft laws. In the future legislative process, it is suggested that legislatures pay attention to publishing the feedback opinions of draft laws and explanations of draft laws.

1.3.3 Strengthening the Legislative Plan and Improving the Legislative Plan

The NPC Standing Committee has formulated a five-year plan of legislation as the priority of future legislation work. In addition, it will formulate a legislation plan based on annual legislative tasks. The formulation of legislation plans will help the legislature identify its work priorities and improve work efficiency. From a national perspective, some local legislatures do not pay much attention to the formulation and implementation of legislation plans. Some legislatures have not formulated any legislation plan for many years, while some legislatures have been unable to complete the legislation plans for a long time. This is due to the lack of reasonable argumentation and scientific judgment at the beginning of legislative planning and legislation plan formulation. On the one hand, the legislatures lacked accurate knowledge of the legislative objects and included immature objects in their legislation plans, causing the legislation projects to be delayed again and again. On the other hand, the legislatures lacked self-awareness and did not have a clear picture of their own human and material resources. At the beginning of legislative planning and legislation plan formulation, they did not recognize their own limitations, resulting in insufficient legislative capabilities and hasty legislation time and ultimately resulting in abortion of their legislative plans. Therefore, it is suggested that both the central and local legislatures pay attention to legislative planning and legislation plan formulation and carry out repeated argumentation to improve the scientific rationality of the plans and promote their completion through the division of responsibilities.

Chapter 2
A Government Under the Rule of Law: Power Contained Within a Cage of Regulation

Xiaomei Wang

In contemporary China, it has become a common choice of the whole society to uphold the rule of law and to clearly establish, safeguard and protect the rights of all citizens through a sound legal system in a bid to build a country ruled by law. The rule of law means good laws and governance. This not only means that good laws should be strictly and effectively enforced but also means that the administrative organs responsible for enforcing the laws should abide by the laws and act within the legal framework. Therefore, in the process of promoting the rule of law, the core is to build a government under the rule of law. The term government is often used in both a broad and a narrow sense. In the broad sense, government refers to the organs and institutions that take control of the public power of the state, including legislative organs, administrative organs and judicial organs, while in the narrow sense, it refers to the organs that take control of the administrative power in the state power system. In China, administrative organs refer to the State Council and its functional departments, local governments at various levels, and functional departments of local governments above the county level.

2.1 The Goal of Building a Government Under the Rule of Law in China

Since the 3rd Plenary Session of the 11th Central Committee of the Communist Party of China (CPC), the rule of law has always been the value orientation for all work and all governance functions in China, but building a government under the rule of law was a construction objective established only a few years ago.

Article 5 of the *Constitution* adopted in 1982 stipulates, "All state organs, the armed forces, all political parties and public organizations and all enterprises and

X. Wang (✉)
Institute of Law, CASS, Beijing, China

H. Tian and Y. Lv (eds.), *The Chinese Path of Rule of Law Construction*,
China Insights, https://doi.org/10.1007/978-981-16-4130-5_2

institutions must abide by the Constitution and the law. All acts in violation of the *Constitution* or the law must be investigated. No organization or individual is privileged to be beyond the Constitution or the law." This provision implies the meaning of a government under the rule of law. In 1997, a report to the 15th CPC National Congress proposed that the rule of law is the fundamental principle by which the Party leads the people in governing the country. In 1999, the *Constitution* was amended to explicitly include the provision on the rule by law, that is, "The People's Republic of China governs the country according to law and makes it a socialist country under rule of law." The core of promoting the rule of law is to exercise government administration in accordance with the law, while the core of building a country under the rule of law is to build a government under the rule of law. In 1999, in the same year that the fundamental principle for governing the country according to law was written into the *Constitution*, the State Council promulgated the *Decision of the State Council on Promoting Law-based Administration in an All-round Way*, and in 2004, the State Council promulgated the *Outline for Promoting Law-based Administration in an All-round Way*, which clearly specifies the goals of building a government under the rule of law. To profoundly carry out the fundamental principle of governing the country by law, comprehensively promote law-based administration, and further strengthen the building of a government under the rule of law, the State Council issued the *Opinions of the State Council on Strengthening the Building of a Government under the Rule of Law* in 2010. It proposes to take the building of a government under the rule of law as the goal, take innovations in the systems and mechanisms related to the overall law-based administration as the breakthrough, focus on raising the awareness and abilities of leaders for law-based administration, improve the quality of institutional building, regulate the exercise of administrative powers, guarantee the strict implementation of laws and regulations, comprehensively promote law-based administration, and constantly strengthen the public creditability and executive capability of the government. The *Decision of the State Council on Promoting Law-based Administration in an All-round Way*, the *Outline for Promoting Law-based Administration in an All-round Way*, and the *Opinions of the State Council on Strengthening the Building of a Government under the Rule of Law* have become the three important documents for building a government under the rule of law.

Since 2012, China has moved into a new historical stage in building a government under the rule of law. The 18th CPC National Congress set basically completing the building of a government under the rule of law as one of the important goals of achieving a moderately prosperous society in all respects by 2020. The 3rd Plenary Session of the 18th CPC Central Committee proposed comprehensively deepening reforms as the proposition of the times and emphasized that "We should transform government functions, deepen the reform of the administrative system, exercise government administration in an innovative way, increase public trust in the government and improve its competence, and build a law-based and service-oriented government." It also proposed that "We must pursue coordinated progress in law-based governance, law-based exercise of state power, and law-based government administration, and promote the integrated development of rule of law for the country, the government, and society." The 4th Plenary Session of the 18th CPC Central Committee, with the theme of "promoting the rule of law in an all-round way", proposed that "We must build a rule of law government which has well-conceived functions and statutorily defined powers and responsibilities; which strictly enforces the law and is impartial; and which operates in an open, clean, and efficient way, with strong credibility." The session profoundly revealed the connotation of building a government under rule of law and explicitly defined the criteria for measuring the level of building a government under the rule of law. To further promote administration according to law, accelerate the building of a government under the rule of law, and achieve the goal of basically completing the building of a government under the rule of law on schedule, at the end of 2015, the CPC Central Committee and the State Council promulgated the *Implementation Outline for Building a Government under the Rule of Law 2015–2020*, which established the grand blueprint and action plan for accelerating the building of a government under the rue of law in the next few years. In 2017, the 19th CPC National Congress announced that socialism with Chinese characteristics entered a new era. The report to the 19th CPC National Congress stated that "We will build a rule of law government, promote law-based government administration, and see that law is enforced in a strict, procedure-based, impartial, and non-abusive way," and set the goal of basically building a country, government, and society based on the rule of law by 2035.

A government under the rule of law involves concepts such as the rule of law and democracy, which have rich and profound connotations. A government under the rule of law signifies that the government's power comes from the law, the operation and behavior of the government are regulated and restricted by the law, and the government should bear corresponding legal responsibilities and safeguard the rights and freedoms of citizens. Since 2012, China has made great progress in four aspects of building a government under the rule of law: accelerating the transformation of government functions, improving the mechanisms for law-based decision-making, deepening the reform of the administrative law enforcement system, and comprehensively increasing transparency in government affairs, laying a solid foundation for completing the building of a government based on the rule of law by 2035.

2.2 Accelerating the Transformation of Government Functions

Well-conceived functions and statutorily defined powers and responsibilities are important standards for a government under the rule of law. The basic function of the government is to provide public services. The goal of building a government under the rule of law is to maintain a stable and good social order and provide highly efficient and high-quality management services. However, in the past few decades, the government has placed more emphasis on economic development, and its public service functions have been weakened or even ignored. In the time when top priority was given to economic development, the government placed greater emphasis on attracting investment and pursuing higher rates of GDP growth, leading to the dislocation of the functions of the market, the government and society and excessive government intervention in the economy, squeezing the market's adjustment space and affecting the development and growth of society. When directly devoting itself to the market and engaging in economic activities, the government has deviated from its public service function. To uphold the scientific positioning of government functions, we must properly handle the relationship between the government and the market and between the government and society: the government should not exceed its functions and meddle in affairs that can be regulated by the market and should ensure that the market plays a decisive role in the allocation of resources; the government should not intervene in affairs that can be dealt with by individuals or social self-discipline to arouse the enthusiasm of the public and stimulate the vitality of society. To correctly handle the relationship between the government, the market and society and accelerate the transformation of government functions, China has made endeavors in recent years in such aspects as promoting institutional reforms, deepening reforms in administrative examination and approval, reforming the commercial registration system, implementing the power and responsibility list system, cultivating social forces, etc. The report to the 19th CPC National Congress pointed out that the principal contradiction facing Chinese society has evolved, and what we now face is the contradiction between unbalanced and inadequate development and the people's ever-growing needs for a better life. Facing the principal contradiction, the government should further transform its functions to create a good market environment for economic growth, such as an honest and faithful contractual spirit and a fair competition order, to ultimately meet the demands of the people for democracy, rule of law, fairness and justice, security, and a better environment.

2.2.1 Steadily Promoting Institutional Reforms

The initial motivation for the reform of government institutions in China was that the bloated bureaucracy severely affected the efficiency of government operations and restricted economic development. Therefore, the reform of government institutions initially focused on streamlining administrative structures, including abolishing life tenure in leading posts and bringing younger cadres to leading posts. Since it did not shake the highly centralized planned economic system and we were not keenly aware of the importance of transforming government functions, the reform stopped as a halfhearted attempt and was caught in a vicious circle of repeated streamlining and bloating. In the late 1980s, China began to launch the reform of government institutions targeting transforming government functions and identified the reform direction of establishing greater government departments.

The so-called reform to establish larger government departments is to reorganize and define the functions and boundaries of government departments and merge government departments with similar functions and business areas to enable the government to focus on macromanagement, avoid and reduce its intervention in the microeconomy. The decentralized department setup causes shirking and friction between departments, increases fiscal expenditure, and is conducive to the realization of a service-oriented government. In 2008, the institutional reform plan of the State Council clearly proposed the system of "larger government departments." The reform of the State Council in 2013 set the tone for the reform to establish larger government departments, which should be "advanced steadily." In 2013, the CPC Central Committee and the State Council promulgated the *Opinions on Functional Transformation and Institutional Reform of Local Governments* (ZF No. [2013] 9), proposing to further transform government functions by means of reducing overlapping and decentralization of departmental duties to ensure that various departments effectively perform their economic and social management functions. It focused on integrating the same or similar duties dispersed in different departments of the State Council and smoothing the functional relationship among departments. In this round of reforms, functions such as food and drug supervision, broadcasting, television and publishing management, and maritime law enforcement were integrated; the Ministry of Railways was dismantled, and the State Railway Administration and China Railway Corporation were established to perform the administrative functions and business functions of the former ministry separately. Presently, China has established larger government departments in some fields, such as the Ministry of Communications, but such reforms still need to be advanced further to establish larger departments in the fields of finance, commerce, agriculture, and culture. In addition, the State Council has also decided to integrate the real estate registration functions dispersed in different departments so that these functions are undertaken by one department.

In 2018, the institutional reforms that had entered a new stage were further accelerated and intensified. The purpose of institutional reforms is to establish a Party and state institutional function system that is well conceived, fully built, procedure based, and efficiently functioning and to form a CPC leadership system that ensures that the Party always provides overall leadership and coordinates the efforts of all involved and a law-based administrative governance system with clear functions and responsibilities. Based on the conditions and practical requirements in the new era, in the institutional reform of the State Council in 2018, we have strengthened and improved the role of the government in economic regulation, market oversight, social management, public services, and environmental protection and established the Ministry of Natural Resources, the Ministry of Ecology and Environment, the Ministry of Agriculture and Rural Affairs, the Ministry of Culture and Tourism, and the Ministry of Emergency Management. To strengthen judicial and administrative work and ensure that all our government work is performed in accordance with the law, the institutional reform of the State Council in 2018 integrated the functions of the Ministry of Justice and the Legislative Affairs Office of the State Council and restructured the Ministry of Justice to coordinate administrative legislation, administrative law enforcement, legal affairs management, law popularization and other functions. The institutional reform of the State Council in 2018 also brought about great changes to China's taxation system. The national and local taxation organs at and below the provincial level were integrated and subject to the dual leadership of the State Administration of Taxation and the governments of provinces, autonomous regions or municipalities directly under the Central Government. The greatest characteristic of this round of the State Council's institutional reform is that the reform of the administrative system is advanced in a synergetic manner under the framework of the reform of state institutions and systems, and it has smoothed the relationship among the Party committee, the government, the people's congress, and the CPPCC, so it is a profound transformation to advance the modernization of China's system and capacity for governance.

2.2.2 Deepening the Reform of Administrative Examination and Approval System

Deepening the reform of the administrative examination and approval system is the breakthrough point for the transformation of government functions. The administrative examination and approval system is an important means of the government to implement prior management of social and economic affairs and an important method for prior control, management, intervention and guidance. Reforming the administrative examination and approval system and implementing the *Law on Administrative Permission* is the breakthrough point in the reform of the administrative management system and an important content of transforming government functions, building a service-oriented government and exercising government administration in accordance with the law. The reform of administrative examination and approval involves not only the transformation of government functions and functional positioning and power adjustment of government departments but also the key to smoothing the relationship between the government and enterprises, the market, and society. The 3rd Plenary Session of the 18th CPC Central Committee proposed that "We will further streamline the administration and delegate more power to lower levels, deepen the reform of the system concerning matters subject to government examination and approval, and reduce the central government's administration in micro affairs to the greatest extent. We will cancel all administrative approval procedures for economic activities under the effective regulation of the market mechanism. We will manage matters that require administrative approval according to procedures and with high efficiency. We will transfer large-scale and widely participating social and economic projects to local and community-level management for convenience and efficiency."

The *Implementation Outline for Building a Government under the Rule of Law 2015–2020* proposes to promote work on relatively centralized administrative approval power and support local governments in launching pilot reform projects for relatively centralized administrative approval. We should comprehensively review and regulate intermediary services for administrative approval, implement list management for the retained intermediary services requiring administrative approval and publish the list to the public. We should resolutely rectify "red-top intermediaries," cut off the interest chain between administrative agencies and intermediary service agencies, and promote fair competition in the intermediary service industry.

Reviewing and streamlining examination and approval items is the foundation and the primary content of the reform of administrative examination and approval. To effectively prevent the number of administrative licensing items from increasing while decreasing and the number of items to be explicitly reduced and implicitly increased, the *Circular of the State Council on Strictly Controlling the Establishment of New Administrative Permission*s (GF No. [2013] 39) was delegated by the State Council in September 2013. It stated that we should strictly observe the requirements of the *Law on Administrative Permission* and strictly establish the standards for administrative permission. In addition, the NPC Standing Committee and the State Council have successively revised a number of laws and regulations to respond to the reduction of administrative examination and approval items. To prevent the disguised establishment of administrative licensing items for citizens, legal persons or other organizations in the name of illegal administrative licensing approval, the State Council delegated the *Circular of the State Council on Reviewing Items Requiring Non-administrative License Examination and Approval by the Departments of the State Council* (GF No. [2014] 16) in 2014, requires reviewing all items requiring non-administrative license examination and approval, cancel all items requiring non-administrative license examination and approval by various departments of the State Council for citizens, legal persons or other organizations, and cancel and adjust items requiring non-administrative examination and approval by the local governments, etc. To change management philosophy, simplify the procedures, and establish a sound national vocational qualification system, the State Council has successively issued the *Decision of the State Council on Canceling a Group of Professional Qualification Licensing and Certification Items* (GF No. [2015] 41) and the *Decision of the State Council on Canceling 13 Items Subject to Administrative Examination and Approval by the Departments of the State Council* (GF No. [2016] 10), aiming to cancel the administrative licensing of professional qualifications. According to the 2018 government work report, the administrative examination and approval items of the State Council departments were reduced by 44%, the non administrative license examination and approval was completely ended, the enterprise investment projects approved by the central government level were reduced by 90%, the intermediary service items of administrative examination and approval were reduced by 74%, and the professional qualification licensing and identification were greatly reduced during the five years from 2012 to 2017. On August 5, 2018, the General Office of the State Council issued the *National Plan for Deepening the Reform of "Decentralization, Administration, Services" and Transformation of the Key Tasks of Government Function Video and Telephone Conferences*, which made detailed arrangements for deepening the reform of "Decentralization, Administration and Services". In 2018, China's reform of streamlining administration and delegating powers, combining deregulation with management, and optimizing services, intensified. It has further promoted streamlining administration, reduced taxes and fees, and cancelled a number of administrative licensing matters. As a result, the business environment has improved significantly.

In addition to removing and delegating examination and approval items to lower-level governments, the reform of administrative examination and approval also involves the horizontal centralization of administrative examination and approval power. There are two modes of horizontal centralization of administrative approval power. One is physical centralization, where the departments with examination and approval power are stationed in the government service halls; the other is to centralize the examination and approval power of various departments so that it can be exercised by a special examination and approval bureau. Presently, physical centralization is the primary mode, and the mode involving the exercise of power by a special examination and approval bureau is still under exploration on a pilot basis. Like the vertical decentralization of administrative examination and approval power, the horizontal centralization of exercise of examination and approval power also aims to make it convenient for people to handle matters requiring administrative examination and approval and to effectively supervise the standardized operation of the examination and approval power. The *Implementation Outline for Building a Government under the Rule of Law 2015–2020* proposes that "For reserved administrative licensing and approval items, we will explore directory or coding-based management, and fully carry out one-window handling, in-parallel handling, time-limited handling, normative handling, transparent handling and online handling to improve administrative efficiency and stimulate social vitality." To further facilitate the provision of convenient services, in November 2015, the General Office of the State Council issued the *Circular of the General Office of the State Council on Simplifying and Optimizing the Public Service Procedures to Facilitate the Public to Get Access to Government Services and Start Their Own Business*, aiming to further improve the quality and efficiency of public services and provide the public with fair and accessible services so as to better promote mass innovation entrepreneurship and and stimulate market vitality and social creativity. To implement the documents of the central government, the Hainan provincial government took the lead in formulating the *Administrative Measures for Government Services of Hainan Province* on the basis of the original "Three Centralizations" reform, clearly implementing directory-based management of administrative examination and approval and specifying the functions and powers of government service management agencies and stationed departments. In addition, Hainan Province has further launched online approval work, solidifying each approval process into an online process, and using technical means to reduce the intervention of human factors in the approval process. In 2016, Zhejiang Province promulgated the *Circular of the General Office of the People's Government of Zhejiang Province on Optimizing the administrative Procedures and Promoting Online Examination and Approval* to meet the overall requirements for streamlining administration and scaling back administrative power, lifting participation in major administratior exercising regulations where necessary and providing better services. It aims to provide problem-oriented and innovative services and use "Internet+" thinking and methods, supported by data resource sharing and interconnection, to further simplify and optimize the administrative approval procedures, strengthen inter-departmental business collaboration, vigorously promote online approval, and continuously improve the level of approval services to facilitate the public to get access to government services and start their own business. In September 2016, the *Guiding Opinions on Accelerating the Promotion of the Work for "Internet + Government Services"* was issued by the State Council. It proposes to meet the development needs of "Internet+ government services," further enhance the service capabilities of administrative service halls, accelerate integration with online service platforms, and form a new administrative service model that has online and offline functions complementing each other. In 2018, "Internet+ government services" deepened, various regions explored and promoted a number of distinctive reform measures, and the convenience of enterprises and the people in handling affairs continued to increase.

2.2.3 Reforming the Commercial Registration System

In the process of comprehensively advancing the reform of the administrative examination and approval system, the reform of special examination and approval systems in China started from the commercial registration system that is most closely related to economic development. To further reduce the burden of business operation and release economic vitality, the State Council proposed reforming the registered capital registration system to relax controls over market entry and change the registered capital system from actual paid-in of registered capital to commitment to payment of registered capital. The reform of commercial registration completely overturned the original administrative examination and approval system and mode. The reform involves separation of operation permits from business licenses, registration upon commitment to payment of registered capital, separation of business entities' residences from their business premises, and implementation of a business scope and paid-in capital filing system and "one business license with multiple addresses" and "one address for multiple business licenses." The reform focused on simplifying the procedures for industrial and commercial registration and reducing the registration items and the types of business licenses. One of the highlights of the reform of the commercial registration system is to change some preapproval items for enterprise registration to postapproval items. Before the reform, administrative licensing was a preapproval registration item, and operators could not obtain a business license without going through it. After the reform, the administrative approval for special business items was changed to a post-approval item, thus simplifying the procedures for business registration. In June 2016, the General Office of the State Council promulgated the *Circular of the General Office of the State Council on Accelerating the Reform of the Registration System of "Incorporating Five Certificates into One and One Code for One License"*, and the reform aims to introduce the social insurance registration and statistics registration certificates into the previous "Three Certificates in One" reform (business license, organization code certificate and tax registration certificate), which upgraded the business license to include five certificates. In 2017, China rolled out the reform separating permits and certificates from business licenses nationwide. With the main thrust of this reform being to cut back on the permits and certificates now required once a business license is issued, all that can be cut will be cut, and all that can be merged will be merged. This will further trim a chunk off the time it takes to complete all the procedures required for starting a business. The reform separated permits and certificates from business licenses In 2018, the reform of "separation of licenses and licenses" was implemented nationwide, the start-up time of enterprises was greatly reduced, and the types of industrial production licenses were reduced by more than one-third.

2.2.4 Implementing the System of List of Rights and Responsibilities

The Chinese government has made proactive efforts to put in place a transparent system whereby the powers of local governments and their departments are cataloged to ensure that these powers are exercised according to the law. To clarify the powers of the governments and prevent the governments from setting and withdrawing approval powers in disguised form, the State Council required governments at all levels to formulate the lists of powers and responsibilities and make them available to the public. After reviewing and delegating powers, the approval items retained by governments at all levels have been greatly reduced. In 2015, the General Office of the State Council issued the *Plan for Implementing Trials for Compiling Lists of Powers and Responsibilities of Departments under the State Council*, and the *Guiding Opinions on Implementing the System of List of Powers for Working Departments of Local Government at Various Levels*, clearly requesting that various ministries and commissions of the State Council and local governments at all levels should organize to compile lists of powers and responsibilities. The compilation of lists of powers and responsibilities involves both horizontal and vertical aspects. Horizontally, lists of government powers catalogue the powers and responsibilities between different departments in a view to put identical and similar affairs under the administration of the same department and change the phenomenon of "nine dragons taming the water" in the past; vertically, lists of government powers clarify the division of management functions among the governments at various levels of provinces, cities, counties, and towns to overcome the problem of excessively micro management by the higher-level government, especially the provincial-level government, and to avoid the problem that the township, district and county governments exercise overly macroscopic and improper administration as the executive organs, or shift the powers and responsibilities that should belong to the governments at this level to the governments at the higher level. Therefore, the compilation of lists of government powers and responsibilities plays an important role in clarifying the powers and responsibilities between the government and the market, the government and society, the provincial government and the governments at the city, county and district levels. Behind lists of government powers and responsibilities, there are also requirements for the unification of power and responsibilities, which will have a certain effect on curbing the much-criticized phenomenon of "fighting for interests while shirking responsibilities." At present, various ministries and commissions under the State Council have issued their lists of powers and responsibilities, and 31 provinces (autonomous regions and municipalities) have published lists of powers and responsibilities of the three-level government departments of provinces, cities and counties, so the government power responsibilities are apparent to the eye.

If, so to speak, the system of list of government powers aims to legalize government powers and functions, then the building of the administrative approval and negative list systems aims to define the reasonable boundary between the government and the market. In October 2015, the *Opinions of the State Council on Implementing the Negative List System for Market Access* (GF [2015] No. 55) was promulgated. Pursuant to the Opinions, the market access negative list system would be piloted in local areas and then would be promoted throughout the country from 2018. The establishment of the market access negative list system is conducive to further deepening the reform of the administrative approval system, greatly reducing the scope of government approval items, innovating government supervision modes, facilitating investment and trade, and thus fundamentally promoting the transformation of government functions. The system of lists of government powers the administrative examination and approval system complement each other and has played an important role in building a government under rule of law since the 18th CPC National Congress. In 2018, China further deepened the reforms to streamline the government, delegate power, improve government services, and fully implemented a unified national market access negative list system.

2.2.5 *Laying Emphasis on Cultivating Social Forces*

The function of the government is to provide public management and services, but this kind of public service is at the cost of huge government operating costs, and due to professional restrictions, the public services provided by the government in certain fields and aspects cannot be compared with those provided by professionals on the market. Therefore, in endeavors to transform government functions, streamline administration and delegate powers, we should subdivide public services, and the services that can be provided by the market at lower cost should be separated from government functions and transferred to the market and society. To this end, the *Guiding Opinions of the General Office of the State Council on the Government's Purchasing Services from Social Forces* (GBF No. [2013] 96) proposes that through the role of market mechanisms, some public service items directly provided by the government to the public will be handed over to qualified social forces through some methods and procedures, and the government will pay them according to the quantity and quality of the services. It also stipulates the contents of the services that can be purchased and the promoting mechanism.

In recent years, a noteworthy phenomenon in the field of government public services has been that privatization mainly through public–private partnerships (PPPs) is attracting increasing attention. This kind of privatization mechanism is mostly seen in the fields of municipal transportation, medical care, and elderly care. In 2015, under the strategic deployment of the central government, the PPP model was further promoted in the public service field. On February 3, 2015, ten ministries and commissions under the State Council, including the Ministry of Civil Affairs and the Ministry of Finance, jointly issued the *Implementing Opinions on Encouraging Private Capital to Participate in the Development of Elderly Care Industry* (MF No. [2015] 33), which proposed various measures to encourage social forces to develop elderly care services. On April 21, 2015, six ministries and commissions under the State Council, including the Ministry of Finance and the Ministry of Housing and Urban–Rural Development, jointly issued the N*otice on the Use of Public–private Partnership Model to Promote Public Rental Housing Investment Construction and Operation Management* (CZ No. [2015] 15), encouraging local governments to use the PPP model to promote public rental housing investment construction and operation management and requiring all regions to cooperate on public rental housing projects within 2015. In May 2015, the Ministry of Finance, the National Development and Reform Commission, and the People's Bank of China jointly formulated the *Guiding Opinions on Promoting the Public–private Partnership Model in the Public Service Field* and decided to further adopt the PPP model in public service fields such as energy, transportation, water conservancy, agriculture, science and technology, medical care, health, and old-age insurance to attract society capital to provide people with high-quality and efficient public services. Privatization and public–private cooperation mechanisms have yielded outstanding results in the process of building the government under the rule of law in 2015, and public–private cooperation methods will play an increasingly important role, especially in the areas of administrative benefits such as affordable housing and social security. To enhance the vitality of state-owned enterprises and comprehensively promote the governance of enterprises according to law, the *Guiding Opinions of the CPC Central Committee and the State Council on Deepening State-owned Enterprise Reform* was issued in August 2015. It proposed to develop a mixed-ownership economy, promote mixed-ownership reform of state-owned enterprises, and introduce non-state-owned capital to participate State-owned enterprise reform, in the fields of oil, natural gas, electricity, railways, telecommunications, resource development, public utilities, etc., to introduce non-state-owned capital projects that are in line with industrial policies and are conducive to transformation and upgrading, and carry out various types of government and social capital cooperation pilots, and gradually Promote the cooperation model between government and social capital. In October 2015, the supporting document *Several Opinions of the State Council on Reforming and Improving the State-owned Assets Management System* was released, proposing coordinated promotion of supporting reforms. In the second half of 2018, in accordance with the *Implementation Opinions on Promoting the Pilot Reform of State-owned Capital Investment and Operating Companies* issued by the State Council, the mixed ownership reform pilot work progressed smoothly.

2.3 Improving the Government's Law-Based Decision-Making Mechanism

Decision-making is the starting point for the operation of administrative power and the focal point for the regulation of administrative powers. Administrative decision-making refers to the process of behavioral design and decision-making carried out by administrative leaders to perform administrative functions in the interests of the public based on the principle of fairness and justice. Administrative decision-making is an important way for an administrative agency to determine the main tasks of itself and its subordinate organs in a specific period. Administrative decisions have certain authoritativeness and are binding not only to members of administrative organs but also to enterprises, public institutions, and social organizations and individuals within the jurisdiction of administrative organs at various levels. Administrative decision making is usually authorized only by legislation, and when power is exercised, it must be exercised in accordance with legislation. Unlike specific administrative actions such as administrative punishment and administrative permission, administrative decisions do not directly determine the specific rights and obligations of administrative counterparts, but an established administrative decision is often the basis for a large number of specific administrative actions and affects a wide range of objects. Therefore, how to regulate decision-making procedures and ensure that decisions are made in a well-conceived manner according to law is particularly important. Law-based decision-making is an important task for advancing administration according to law and building a government under the rule of law. Improving the law-based decision-making mechanism is mainly carried out by institutionalizing and proceduralizing the requirements for making major administrative decisions and improving the accountability system.

2.3.1 Institutionalization of Administrative Decision-Making

Pursuant to the *Implementation Outline for Building a Government under the Rule of Law 2015–2020*, "scientific, democratic and law-based administrative decision-making" is one of the measurement standards for a government under the rule of law and is also a key indicator for evaluating the country's capacity and level of governance. To achieve the goal of decision-making in accordance with the law, various localities have been explored to establish relevant systems to regulate administrative decision-making. As of June 2017, 17 provincial governments and the municipal governments of 23 comparatively larger cities in China issued regulations to standardize major administrative decision-making procedures. For example, the *Interim Regulations of the People's Government of Zhongshan City on the Major Administrative Decision-making Procedures* (ZF No. [2013] 2) implements the legality review system for major administrative decisions and the post-evaluation system for the implementation of major administrative decisions and clarifies the scope of major administrative decisions of the municipal government and specific procedures.

The endeavors of institutionalization of administrative decision-making in various localities, fields, and links have gradually converged to produce synergic effects, ensuring that there are clearly defined guidelines for the whole process involving administrative decision-making from agenda setting, initiation, public participation, expert consultation and argumentation, program selection and implementation, and accountability. To address the practical problems in administrative decision-making, such as not fully respecting the objective laws and not fully soliciting public opinions, the State Council decided to issue administrative regulations to uniformly standardize major administrative decision-making procedures. In June 2017, opinions were openly solicited from the public for the *Provisional Regulations on Major Administrative Decision-Making Procedures (Draft for Comments)* to implement and improve the law-based decision-making mechanism, promote scientific, democratic, and legalized administrative decision-making, and improve the quality of decision-making. The *Provisional Regulations on Major Administrative Decision-Making Procedures (Draft for Comments)* further clarified the scope of major administrative decision-making. The so-called major administrative decisions refer to matters made by the government that have a major impact on economic and social development or involve the vital interests of the public, such as preparing important plans for economic and social development, formulating major public policies and measures for public services, market supervision, and social management and environmental protection, formulating major public policies and measures for development, utilization and protection of important natural resources, making decisions on major public construction projects to be implemented in the administrative region, and making decisions on matters that have a major impact on economic and social development and involve vital interests of the public.

2.3.2 Administrative Decision-Making Procedures

To ensure that the government makes correct decisions prudently, major administrative decisions should follow certain steps, including public participation, expert argumentation, risk assessment, legality review, and decisions by collective discussion. The procedures for making major administrative policy decisions aim to identify matters related to overall economic and social development, with wide social coverage, and closely related to the interests of citizens, legal persons and other organizations as major matters that require administrative decision-making by the government, and include them in the major decision-making procedures and in the government's annual catalogue of major matters requiring administrative decision-making.

1. Public Participation

Public participation in major administrative decision-making means that decision makers should adopt a way that facilitates public participation to widely solicit the opinions of the public on matters related to the vital interests of the public or that have a significant impact on their rights and obligations, except those that should be kept secret according to law. Before making a major administrative decision, the government should solicit opinions from the public through various means to ensure that the decision is in line with the interests of the majority. According to the scope and extent of public influence of major administrative decisions, public participation includes publicly soliciting public opinions, holding hearings, holding seminars, soliciting opinions in writing, questionnaire surveys, public opinion polls, field visits, etc.

Local governments should attach great importance to the concept of public participation in decision-making and the building of corresponding systems. Taking decision-making hearings as an example, hearings are generally introduced into the procedures for administrative decision-making in various parts of the country. For example, in 2011, the Guangzhou Municipal Government issued the *Tentative Measures for Holding Hearings before Making Major Administrative Decisions,* and in 2013, the Guangdong Provincial Government issued the *Regulations of Guangdong Province on Hearings for Holding Hearings before Making Major Administrative Decisions*. These documents specify the scope, functions, procedures, and results of hearings so that public opinions can be fully expressed, fully discussed and collected. Public participation in decision-making has changed the government's one-way governance model to a co-governance model, representing the direction of the transformation of government governance, and is an important way for the government to absorb the wisdom of the people, listen to their opinions and build consensus on major decisions.

2. Expert Argumentation

Expert argumentation is to organize experts in relevant fields or entrust special agencies and research institutions to expound and appraise the scientificity, rationality and feasibility of the contemplated decisions on matters that are highly professional and technical. Information on the study and handling of argumentation opinions and relevant reasons should be fed back to the experts and special institutions that provided the argumentation opinions. Expert argumentation can take the form of argumentation meetings, written consultations, and entrusted consultations and argumentations. Professionalism and broad representation should be emphasized in the selection of experts and special institutions to ensure that all parties holding different opinions should have representatives to participate in the argumentation when there is a substantial divergence of opinion on an issue. It is not allowed to select experts or special institutions that have a direct interest in the matters requiring decision-making. The relevant information of experts and special institutions should be disclosed to the public. At present, most provinces, autonomous regions, municipalities directly under the central government, and even many cities and counties have established decision-making consultation and argumentation expert databases. For major administrative decisions with strong expertise, experts in certain fields should be randomly selected from expert databases. Expert argumentation can provide external intellectual support for government decision-making and compensate for the shortage of professional and technical personnel in government departments. In addition, relying on the social reputation of experts and scholars, the authoritativeness of the decisions made by the government will increase, making them more likely to be accepted by the public. Therefore, expert consultation and argumentation can not only overcome the technical risks of administrative decision-making but also weaken the social risks of administrative decision-making.

3. Risk Assessment

The implementation of major administrative policy decisions may adversely affect the ecological environment, social stability, etc., so risk assessment should be carried out. Risk assessment can be conducted through public opinion tracking, sample surveys, field visits, consultation analysis, etc., to comprehensively identify risk sources and points, and qualitative and quantitative analysis methods can be used to scientifically predict and comprehensively judge decision-making risks. During risk assessment, the opinions of relevant departments should be solicited, and a risk assessment report should be formed to identify the risk level and propose risk prevention measures and control plans. At present, all major policies and decisions on major projects related to social development and the interests of the people must be assessed for legitimacy, rationality, feasibility, and controllability. Without risk assessment, no decision should be made. In many places, social organizations and special institutions are introduced to conduct third-party assessments as needed. The results of risk assessment have become an important basis for making major administrative decisions.

4. Legality Review

The *Provisional Regulations on Major Administrative Decision-Making Procedures (Draft for Comments)* clearly states that matters requiring decision-making that have not been reviewed for legality or are deemed illegal after being reviewed shall not be submitted to the decision-making agencies for discussion. Legality review covers three aspects: first, whether the matters requiring decision-making comply with the statutory authority of the decision-making organ; second, whether the decision-making procedures comply with the statutory procedures; third, whether the contents of the decisions comply with the relevant laws, regulations and rules. The decision-making organs' legal bodies shall conduct a legality review and must give full play to the role of government law advisers and lawyers. In 2016, the General Office of the CPC Central Committee and the General Office of the State Council jointly issued the *Notice on Issuing the Opinions on Promoting the Legal Adviser System and the Government Lawyer and Corporate Lawyer System*, requiring the legal advisers of Party and government organs to provide legal opinions on major decisions and major administrative actions.

Nationwide, practices similar to the preposition of legal affairs are carried out in many places, and typical examples include legal advisory groups in townships and subdistricts in Changzhou, the legal affairs forefront project of Luotian County, law, legal inspection in Mengjin County, and the preposition of legal affairs in Yuhang, Hangzhou. These practices aim to bring state administration and social governance into the framework of the rule of law to ensure that public power is exercised justly, the legality for major decision-making is prechecked, and decisions are made according to the law. Qingdao Municipal Government has further improved the legal advisory work mechanism and printed and issued the *Implementation Rules for the Administration of Legal Advisory Panel* and the *Appraisal Measures for the Members of the Legal Advisory Panel* to give full play to the role of legal advisers, strengthen the review of major legal affairs, and effectively prevent decision-making risks.

5. Decision by Collective Discussion

Decision by collective discussion refers to the process in which the draft decision, expert opinions, risk assessment materials, and legality review opinions are discussed at the executive meeting or plenary meeting of the decision-making organ, and a decision is made by the chief administrator on the basis of collective discussion. Decision by collective discussion aims to limit the authority of the chief administrator and curb arbitrary actions. In practice, when making administrative decisions, especially when making major administrative decisions, the government tends to yield leadership preferences, and administrative decisions tend to obsessively reflect the personal will of the leaders. As a result, decisions may lack scientific justification, rationality and rigidity and always become inconsistent with changes in leadership. In regard to decision-making, General Secretary Xi Jinping particularly emphasized that "Before being introduced, policies and measures must be subjected to repeated debate and careful evaluation to ensure that they are practical and effective and can stand the test of time. The stability and continuity of policies should be maintained to prevent too much chopping and changing."

2.3.3 System of Lifelong Responsibility for Decision-Making

Administrative decisions, especially major administrative decisions, are often related to the vital interests of the people and public safety. Once a decision-making organ of the government makes any mistake in decision-making or makes decisions unscientifically, this will seriously impair public interests and cause greater losses to local politics, economy, and society, and ultimately the whole society has to bear the losses from public decision-making. To oversee decision-making organs to make decisions scientifically and prudently, the *Provisional Regulations on Major Administrative Decision-Making Procedures (Draft for Comments)* not only establishes the necessary procedures for making major administrative decisions but also further specifies the legal responsibilities of decision-making organs. Article 38 of the Regulations stipulates that "Where decision-making organs violate these Regulations by making serious errors in decision-making, or going a long time without making a decision where one should be made, causing heavy losses or heinous impacts, the chief administrator, other leaders bearing responsibility and directly responsible personnel, shall be given sanctions in accordance with the law."

In practice, local government work reports on the rule of law in many places point out that it is necessary to establish a follow-up, feedback and accountability mechanism for major decision-making. Administrative decision-making must follow legal procedures. If the government makes decisions without following legal procedures and causing heavy losses, government officials in charge must assume lifelong responsibilities. The mechanism for lifelong responsibility and retroactive investigation into accountability for major decisions was established because some administrative leaders and chief administrators have made arbitrary decisions on vanity projects and image projects to pursue political achievements. Such disorderly decision-making, illegal decision-making, decision-making not in accordance with democratic procedures, and decision-making not in accordance with scientific laws often occur. To build a government under the rule of law, we must start with correcting arbitrary decisions. To achieve accountability investigation, it is necessary to establish a mechanism to evaluate major administrative decisions after their implementation, actively introduce a public evaluation mechanism, take public satisfaction as the basic criterion for evaluating the effectiveness of administrative decisions, strengthen tracking and feedback on the implementation of administrative decisions, and promptly correct problems in our work.

2.4 Deepening the Reform of the Administrative Law Enforcement System

The government should not go beyond its duties to meddle with others' affairs, nor should it allow market players to disrupt the market environment of fair competition. Therefore, the government should lift or exercise regulations where necessary, strengthen administrative law enforcement and fully perform government functions and responsibilities. Administrative law enforcement refers to the actions taken by the administrative subject in accordance with the law that directly or indirectly affect the rights and obligations of administrative counterparts or the actions to supervise and inspect administrative counterparts' exercise of rights and performance of duties.

The vitality of law lies in its enforcement. Administrative law enforcement is a key link in law enforcement and a basic function of the government. Therefore, deepening the reform of the administrative law enforcement system has a direct bearing on whether the government can fully perform its functions in accordance with the law and on modernization of China's system and capacity for governance and sustained and healthy economic and social development. General Secretary Xi Jinping pointed out, "Administrative organs are important subjects in the enforcement of laws and regulations. They must take the lead in strict law enforcement, safeguard public interests and people's rights and interests, and maintain the social order." In recent years, as the notion of rule of law has been gradually rooted in the hearts of the people and the system for developing democracy and the rule of law has been continuously improved, great improvements have been made in law enforcement and law-based government administration, but there are still some problems, including misconduct in law enforcement, violation or distortion of the law, and acts of nonfeasance and misfeasance/inaction and abuse of power in law enforcement. The phenomena of selective, emotional and entrapped law enforcement are serious. There are many reasons for the chaos in law enforcement, including the poor law enforcement system, imperfect law enforcement procedures, and low quality of law enforcement personnel. Moreover, the purpose of law enforcement in some industries deviates from public interests, law enforcement is driven by interests, and law enforcement officials impose fines to create income. The existence of these problems has seriously affected the fairness and authority of the law and seriously impaired the image of the Party and the government. They have become serious problems of widespread concern in all aspects in the field of administrative law enforcement. For this reason, the 4th Plenary Session of the 18th CPC Central Committee proposed to "deepen the reform of the administrative law enforcement system, and rationally allocate law enforcement forces based on the power and functions of different levels of government, and in accordance with the principles of reducing levels, integrating teams, and improving efficiency." As an important part of the reform of China's administrative system, the reform of the administrative law enforcement system includes two levels: vertically straightening out the powers and functions of government at various levels and reducing the levels of law enforcement and horizontally promoting integrated law enforcement and cross-department law enforcement to integrate and reduce the types of law enforcement teams. To deepen the reform of the administrative law enforcement system, we must first straighten out the law enforcement system and promote comprehensive law enforcement; second, we must strictly follow law enforcement procedures and standardize enforcement behavior; third, we must raise the entry threshold for administrative law enforcement personnel and implement the system of working with legal certificates and qualification management. In addition, it is necessary to strengthen the standardization of special administrative law enforcement in key areas.

2.4.1 Promoting the Comprehensive Law Enforcement System

As traditionally a highly fragmented and segmented management system was implemented, departments in different sectors have set up law enforcement teams. The so-called phenomenon that "big lip caps can be found everywhere" not only led to the dispersion of law enforcement forces but also tended to cause repeated inspections and penalties, increasing the burden on enterprises and the public. In response to the phenomenon of fragmented law enforcement, many places have carried out reforms and innovations in law enforcement systems, implemented cross-departmental integrated law enforcement on a trial basis, and exercised centralized law enforcement power. So-called comprehensive law enforcement refers to an administrative law enforcement system in which a law enforcement body comprehensively exercises the statutory power of multiple administrative bodies within a reasonable range of management based on certain legal procedures. Comprehensive law enforcement is conducive to breaking down departmental barriers and solving problems such as duplicate law enforcement or buck-passing law enforcement in the traditional law enforcement system. Presently, the reform of the comprehensive law enforcement system has been carried out in areas such as urban management, cross-departmental comprehensive law enforcement in cultural systems, relatively centralized administrative penalty power in agriculture, transportation and other fields, and a relatively centralized administrative licensing power system based on local administrative service centers.

Straightening out the urban management system and promoting comprehensive law enforcement in urban management are key areas for deepening the reform of the administrative law enforcement system. The report of the 3rd Plenary Session of the 18th CPC Central Committee proposed that we will straighten out the urban management law enforcement system and improve the level of law enforcement and service quality. In December 2015, the CPC Central Committee and the State Council issued the *Guiding Opinions on Deepening the Reform of the Urban Law Enforcement System and Improving Urban Management*, which pointed out the direction for urban management and urban law enforcement in the new era, improved administrative law enforcement management at the city and county levels, promoted comprehensive law enforcement in areas such as food and drug safety, industrial and commercial quality supervision, public health, production safety, cultural tourism, resources and environment, agriculture, forestry and water conservancy, transportation, urban and rural construction, and commerce, and supported areas where conditions permit the implementation of cross-departmental comprehensive law enforcement. The opinions also proposed that by the end of 2017, we would realize the centralized exercise of the power of administrative punishment in the field of urban and rural housing construction. Since 2016, governments in various localities have formulated guiding opinions on promoting comprehensive administrative law enforcement in cities and counties based on the opinions mentioned above. For example, in 2017, Hainan Provincial People's Government issued the *Guiding Opinions on Deepening the Reform of the Administrative Law Enforcement System and Promoting Comprehensive Administrative Law Enforcement in Cities and Counties* (QF No. [2017] 19), which proposed that by the end of 2017, cities and counties should establish a comprehensive administrative law enforcement system that meets the requirement of "multiple plans integration" and the regulatory requirements in urban management and other key areas, and build a scientific and sound comprehensive supporting mechanism to realize the goal that the responsibilities and functions of comprehensive administrative law enforcement organs and government functional departments are clearly defined, and the administrative law enforcement system is intensive, efficient, coordinated in operation, and standardized and orderly. To reform the market supervision system and implement unified market supervision, China instituted the State Administration for Market Regulation in the institutional reform of the State Council to further promote comprehensive law enforcement in market supervision in 2018.

2.4.2 *Strict Administrative Law Enforcement Procedures*

The report to the 3rd Plenary Session of the 18th CPC Central Committee proposes that we will improve the procedures of administrative law enforcement, specify areas of discretion, strengthen supervision over administrative law enforcement, and comprehensively implement the responsibility system as well as government funding for administrative law enforcement to promote strict, standardized, fair and civilized law enforcement. Many local governments have issued the *Implementing Opinions on Improving and Strengthening Administrative Law Enforcement* to carry out special inspection of administrative law enforcement and review of administrative law enforcement case files to further standardize administrative law enforcement and improve the level of administrative law enforcement. The governments of many provinces have formulated the *Measures for Regulating Administrative Punishment and Discretion Power* to implement dynamic management of discretionary standards for administrative punishments, review and revise the discretionary standards and publish them to the public in accordance with the law to ensure that the intensity of punishment is commensurate with the severity of violation and the degree of damage. We should improve the financial guarantee mechanism for funding for administrative law enforcement, increase financial support to law enforcement organs, and strictly implement the system of "separation of revenue and expenditure." To promote strict, standardized, fair and civilized law enforcement by administrative organs, the government has further improved the law enforcement procedures and established three systems, including the administrative law enforcement publication system, the recording system of law enforcement in the whole process and the legal review system of major law enforcement decisions, focusing on regulating administrative licensing, administrative punishment, administrative compulsion, administrative inspection, administrative expropriation and requisition, and other enforcement actions. The recording system of law enforcement in the whole process was established to ensure that the traces in the whole process of administrative law enforcement were recorded and that all links were well documented. The legal review system of major law enforcement decisions was established to ensure that major law enforcement decisions are made after being reviewed by the organs in charge of legislative affairs. An administrative law enforcement publication system was established to ensure that the subjects of administrative law enforcement, basis, procedures, results and other information were disclosed in a timely manner to the public on government websites to accept supervision. Many local governments have upgraded their administrative law enforcement information publication systems and made significant results in building online big data platforms for administrative law enforcement. By integrating administrative punishment data on the online platforms of cities and districts (cities), they realized one-stop disclosure and inquiry of information on administrative punishment discretion and punishment results within their jurisdiction.

2.4.3 Strengthening the Construction of Administrative Law Enforcement Teams

Administrative law enforcement is directly targeted at enterprises and individuals. The overall quality of law enforcement teams, especially front-line administrative law enforcement officers, has a direct bearing on the interests of the masses and the image of the government. In a sense, administrative law enforcement officers are "the visible government," and the ability of law enforcement officers to enforce the law represents the level of the rule of law in a country.

To improve the ability to enforce the law and establish a good image of the government, governments at all levels have set strict requirements on building contingent law enforcement personnel. First, raise the threshold for admittance of law enforcement officers. The post holding certificate and qualification management system is generally implemented for administrative law enforcement officers. Those who have not passed the law enforcement qualification examination shall not be granted law enforcement qualifications or engage in law enforcement activities. Presently, all localities strictly implement the management system of working with certificates and qualifications for administrative law enforcement officers, carry out special rectification of administrative law enforcement officers and examination of administrative law enforcement certificates in their jurisdictions, and decertify law enforcement officers who are not in law enforcement positions or who do not meet the requirements for holding certificates. Starting in 2018, civil servants in administrative organs who were engaged in review of administrative punishment decisions, administrative reconsideration, administrative ruling, and legal adviser for the first time needed to participate in the national unified legal professional qualification examination. Although it is currently unrealistic to require all administrative law enforcement officers to participate in the unified legal professional qualification examination, it is a trend to include administrative law enforcement officers on the contingent of specialist personnel for the enforcement of rule of law. Second, law enforcement education and professional training should be strengthened for on-the-job officers, the institutionalization and normalization of education and training should be promoted, and the ability of law enforcement officers to resolve serious contradictions and complex problems should be improved. Training courses are held in various regions, including training courses for administrative law enforcement hearing hosts, legal knowledge update training courses for administrative law enforcement officers, and public legal knowledge training courses for newly added administrative law enforcement officers. Third, the administrative law enforcement performance appraisal system should be implemented to strengthen administrative law enforcement accountability. All localities are fully implementing the administrative law enforcement responsibility system, strictly determining the law enforcement accountability mechanism for law enforcement officers of different departments, agencies and positions, strengthening law enforcement supervision, disclosing the basis and results of law enforcement to the public, eliminating interference in law enforcement activities, preventing and overcoming local and departmental protectionism, and punishing law enforcement corruption. Finally, guaranteeing administrative law enforcement forces and funding is the basic condition for strict, fair and civilized law enforcement, as well as a fundamental solution to eliminate the current chaos in law enforcement. More law enforcement forces are allocated to the judicial organs at the basic level, and the staff is scientifically allocated to supplement the front-line law enforcement forces in cities, counties and at the grassroots level to meet the law enforcement needs in key areas. The system of government funding for administrative law enforcement is fully implemented to ensure that law enforcement personnel are paid in full. The management system of separation of penalty decisions from collection of penalty payments and "separation of revenue and expenditure" is strictly implemented. It is strictly forbidden to directly link or link to disguise revenue from fees, fines and confiscations with departmental interests.

2.4.4 *Regulating Public Security Administrative Law Enforcement*

The standardization of public security law enforcement is related not only to social stability, fairness and justice but also to the personal and property rights of the people. Every move will arouse high attention from society. Public security is the law enforcement team that has sacrificed the most in peacetime. They have made great contributions to national security and social stability. However, some public security officers have also been criticized for being brutal in law enforcement. Therefore, it is imperative to promote the standardization of public security law enforcement. In September 2016, the General Office of the CPC Central Committee and the General Office of the State Council issued the *Opinions on Deepening the Standardization of Public Security Law Enforcement*, and the General Office of the State Council issued the *Opinions on Regulating the Management of Auxiliary Police in Public Security Organs* and *Opinions on Deepening the Standardization of Public Security Law Enforcement*. These documents have clarified the focus of public security law enforcement work in the future, guided the direction of public security law enforcement team building, and laid the foundation for deepening the construction of a government under the rule of law in the future. To implement the requirements of the *Regulations on the Use of Information System for Law Enforcement and Case Handling of Public Security Organs* formulated by the Ministry of Public Security, local public security organs have unified local law enforcement case handling systems, fully implemented online case handling, and strengthened standardized management and overall process control of law enforcement case handling.

2.5 Comprehensively Promoting Transparency in Government Affairs

In the modern context of rule of law, law-based government administration and building a government under the rule of law not only require the government to obtain and exercise power in accordance with the law but also require the process of exercising administrative power to be transparent. In 2007, the State Council promulgated the *Regulations on the Disclosure of Government Information*, which established China's government information disclosure system in the form of administrative regulations for the first time. Since then, great progress has been made in government information disclosure at both the national and local levels. The notion that government agencies are obliged to disclose government information and protect the public's right to know has gradually gained popularity, and government information disclosure has gradually become the government's routine work. Disclosing government information and promoting transparency in government affairs are the cornerstones of building a government under the rule of law and an important guarantee for building a service-oriented government. The report to the 18th CPC National Congress proposed that we should make the exercise of power more open and standardized and increase the transparency of party, government and judicial operations and official operations in other fields to ensure that power is exercised in a transparent manner. The 3rd Plenary Session of the 18th CPC Central Committee put forward that "We will introduce a list of the powers of local governments and their working departments at all levels, and publicize the power-exercise process in accordance with the law. We will improve information disclosure in Party, government and other fields, so as to promote transparency in decision-making, management, services and results." The report to the 4th Plenary Session of the 18th CPC Central Committee further pointed out that: "we should adhere to the principle that information is to be withheld only in exceptional circumstances, and promote transparency in decision-making, management, services and results;" "Local governments and their working departments at all levels must make public their functions, responsibilities, powers, administrative procedures and means of accepting public supervision based on the list of powers and responsibilities." In February 2016, the General Office of the CPC Central Committee and the General Office of the State Council promulgated the Opinions on Comprehensively Promoting Transparency in Government Affairs, which defined disclosure of administrative affairs as an institutional arrangement in which administrative organs should make public the whole process, including decision making, execution, management, services and results; strengthening in-depth interpretation of major policies, response to people's concerns, platform construction, and sharing of administrative information to protect the public's right to know, to participate, to express and to supervise; and increase public trust in the government, and improve its competence. In November 2016, the General Office of the State Council promulgated the *Implementing Rules for Opinions on Comprehensively Promoting Transparency in Government Affairs*. It is planned to select 100 counties (cities, districts) across the country as pilot units to promote nationwide standardization of transparency in primary-level government affairs.

In recent years, the work to promote transparency in government affairs was combined with the Internet and entered a new stage of "Internet+ government affairs." In the Internet age, the scope of work to promote transparency in government affairs has been unprecedentedly expanded in China, with more diversified forms, and it is combined with services to gradually shape a sunny, transparent, and people-friendly image of the government.

2.5.1 Breakthroughs in Some Key Areas

The 4th Plenary Session of the 18th CPC Central Committee proposed that "we will promote the disclosure of government information in the areas such as fiscal budgeting, public resource allocation, approval and implementation of major construction projects, and construction of social welfare undertakings." The *Opinions on Comprehensively Promoting Transparency in Government Affairs* also reiterated the work to promote disclosure of government information in these areas. This will be elaborated in terms of budget transparency and government procurement transparency.

A comprehensive, well-regulated, open and transparent budget system is the foundation and important symbol of the modernization of China's system and capacity for governance and a major reform measure to strengthen budget constraints, regulate government behaviors, implement effective supervision, and ensure that power is exercised in an institutional cage. Budget transparency is an important starting point and driving force for establishing and implementing a comprehensive, well-regulated, open and transparent budget system. In recent years, substantial breakthroughs have been made in promoting budget transparency in China, which is mainly manifested as follows: (1) The legal framework for budget transparency has basically been established. The *Budget Law* revised in 2014 added the provisions on budget transparency and put in place a legal framework for budget transparency with Chinese characteristics guided by the *Budget Law*, the *Regulations on Disclosure of Government Information*, the *Decisions of the State Council on Deepening the Reform of the Budget Management System* and the *Opinions of the General Office of the CPC Central Committee and the General Office of the State Council on Further Promoting Budget Transparency*, covering government budgets, departmental budgets and transfer payment budgets. (2) A budget disclosure system has taken shape in which financial departments disclose government budgets and transfer payment budgets, and various departments disclose departmental budgets. (3) The budget disclosure method is constantly improved, forming a multiplatform and multichannel open pattern of cooperation between government websites and news websites and commercial websites, making it faster and more convenient to disclose and obtain budget information.

Transparency is an essential requirement of the government procurement system, an effective guarantee for building a government under the rule of law and regulating the use of financial funds, and a necessary requirement for regulating government procurement activities and enhancing public awareness and recognition of government procurement. The *Government Procurement Law* and its implementing regulations clearly identify openness and transparency as one of the basic principles of the government procurement system. *The 2015 Implementing Regulations of the Government Procurement Law* clearly requires that "The information on government procurement projects shall be published on the media designated by the financial department of the people's government at or above the provincial level. If the budget of the procurement project reaches the standard set by the financial department of the State Council, the information on the government procurement project shall be published on the media designated by the financial department of the State Council." The Ministry of Finance has also issued documents to detail requirements and standards for transparency. The *Administrative Measures for Government Procurement Information Announcements* stipulate that, the following government procurement information must be announced unless it relates to the state secrets, commercial secrets of the suppliers, or unless it is the government procurement information that shall be kept confidential under the relevant laws and administrative regulations: (1) Relevant laws, regulations, bylaws and other regulatory documents governing the government procurement; (2) The central procurement lists, government procurement quotas and bid quotas as announced by the province-level people's governments or above; (3) The name list of the agencies for the bid business of government procurement; (4) The bidding and tendering information, including the announcements of public bid, announcements of invitation for preliminary examination of qualifications of bidders, announcements of successful bidders, transaction results and corrected items; (5) The contact forms of the finance departments to accept government procurement complaints and the decisions to tackle complaints; (6) The evaluation results concluded by the finance departments over the central procurement institutions; (7) The name list of procurement agencies and suppliers with records of bad conduct; (8) Other government procurement information that shall be announced in accordance with the laws, regulations and bylaws. The Ministry of Finance emphasized in the *Notice on Distributing the Priorities of Government Procurement Work in 2015* that it will focus on improving the transparency of government procurement and reiterated the requirement for disclosure of government procurement information in the *Notice on Promoting the Disclosure of Government Procurement Information*. In 2017, the Ministry of Finance issued the *Notice on Matters Regarding Further Promoting the Disclosure of Government Procurement Information* (CK No. [2017] 86), proposing that since September 2017, transaction records will be published; a unified publishing platform will be established, and local subnetworks will be established by relying on the China Government Procurement Network to fully disclose government procurement information. In 2018, the rapid development of e-commerce, 23 regions in the country through self-built e-stores or relying on other e-commerce platforms, achieved part of the goods and services of e-commerce, greatly improving the transparency of procurement.

2.5.2 Three-Dimensional and Diverse Development Trend of the Platform

In the context of the era of "Internet+ government affairs", the government has continuously created new ways to promote transparency in administrative affairs and strengthened the building of Internet-based government information and data service platforms. At present, mobile terminals have gradually become the main way for the public to obtain information. Various departments of the State Council and local governments at various levels have keenly grasped this trend, actively expanded the channels for promoting transparency in government affairs, and explored new media applications. Weibo, WeChat and NewsAPP have become the normal modes of government information disclosure. The development of government information disclosure platforms follows the path from offline to online, from PC to mobile, and from "square speaker" to "circle communication." In addition to the traditional ways of publishing on portal websites, many local governments and their departments disclose information on administrative affairs simultaneously through Weibo, WeChat, and NewsAPP, making it more convenient for people to obtain and download government information.

2.5.3 Change from One-Way to Interactive Mode

In recent years, China has attached great importance to information disclosure and has taken the disclosure of administrative affairs as a means to promote reforms, streamline administration, delegate powers, transform government governance modes, and build a new type of political-citizen relationship. China emphasizes that disclosure of administrative affairs is an important mechanism to serve the people and accept their supervision, and in-depth interpretation of major policies should be increased to respond in a timely manner to people's concerns and has set stricter requirements for information disclosure. Traditionally, the disclosure of administrative affairs is unidirectional. The government discloses information to the public in a one-way manner to guarantee the public's right to know. As their awareness of participation becomes stronger, the public is not only satisfied with being informed but also requires the government to keep promptly informed of and respond to hot issues of concern to the public.

In September 2016, the State Council issued the *Guiding Opinions on Accelerating the Work of "Internet + Government Services,"* which identified a task list and road map for promoting "Internet + government services." In addition to providing richer information and data to the public, "Internet + government affairs" also makes it possible to provide online booking, application submission, prereview and other related services, greatly improving the efficiency of government services and making it easier for enterprises and the public to do business. However, no breakthroughs have been made in sharing data resources among various government departments and interconnecting business systems. Various data centers cannot be interconnected, and repeated construction has resulted in a waste of resources. In response, the General Office of the State Council has issued the *Interim Measures for the Administration of Sharing of Government Information Resources*, which provides basic ideas for promoting information sharing among government departments, and it states that we should adhere to the principle that information is to be withheld only in exceptional circumstances. For unconditional sharing of information, the departments intending to use it can directly obtain it on the sharing platform; for conditional sharing of information, an application is required, and the department providing information should respond within ten working days; for non-sharing information, the departments intending to use it should consult with the department providing information. Local governments have made use of the government service network to effectively expand the scope of online services, making it convenient for people to inquire, handle, and put forward opinions and suggestions through the Internet and strengthening governments' online convenience, efficiency, and transparent administrative service provision function through the Internet. Disclosure of government affairs is no longer a vase-like image undertaking but an undertaking that can truly benefit the people.

2.6 Prospects for the Development of the Rule of Law Government

Since the goal of building a government under the rule of law was fixed, especially since 2012, China has made unprecedented achievements in promoting law-based government administration. By deepening the reform of administrative examination and approval, improving mechanisms for law-based decision-making, enforcing laws in a strict, fair and civilized way according to due procedures, and enhancing government transparency, we have laid a solid foundation for building an open and transparent government under the rule of law and a service-oriented government with statutory remits that ensure sound decision-making and resolute law enforcement. However, the abovementioned achievements have been made in building a government under the rule of law, and many administrators lack a correct understanding of the source and nature of administrative power under the influence of traditional officialdom culture. Their understanding of the rule of law is only superficial, and they still need to inwardly respect rights and laws. To build a government under the rule of law, we should also strengthen the top-level design in certain areas, truly implement the top-level design in some places to reduce the "rule of law on paper" and "oral rule of law", and do more practical work to advance the rule of law.

Taking the reform of administrative examination and approval as an example, we should avoid and reduce interference by the inertial thinking of presupervision and take a pragmatic attitude in canceling and delegating administrative approval items. We should not focus on small things while ignoring what is important and only cancel and delegate insignificant administrative approval items. We should not prettify the reform effects by playing a digital game. Those approval items that shouldn't exist but can bring actual benefits should be really canceled. Only by eradicating the superstition for power and cutting off the interest transmission chain can we achieve substantive progress in administrative approval reform and finally achieve the goal of transforming government functions and defining the boundaries between the government, the market and society. Behind the reform of the examination and approval system is the game of interests between the government and the market and between the central government and the local governments. Presently, the reform of administrative examination and approval should not be monopolized by the government. The public, experts, enterprises and other social entities should be attracted to participate in the reform, and strict legal procedures should be established to regulate the reform process. The retention, modification and abolition of approval items require scientific cost–benefit analysis.

In the process of building a government under the rule of law, there inevitably exist the problems of going through a mere formalism. For example, in the process of promoting law-based decision-making, there is the phenomenon of going through a mere formality in administrative decision-making procedures. Pursuant to relevant provisions, when making decisions on major issues, the government must go through procedures including expert argumentation, but in practice, expert argumentation is often reduced to mere formality. Expert argumentation is mandatory but has not been conducted, and reasonable and viable opinions and suggestions raised by experts are not accepted. In the future, in the process of building a government under the rule of law, it is necessary to prevent and overcome formalism, continuously improve the concept of the rule of law, strengthen awareness of rules, and improve institutional design.

In the process of building a government under the rule of law, there are still controversies over centralized exercise of approval power, comprehensive law enforcement, and ex ante, interim and ex post supervision. To further promote the building of a government under the rule of law, it is necessary to strengthen the study of related theoretical issues. In the future, to build a government under the rule of law, we should not only encourage local governments to carry out innovations in the rule of law but also carry out theoretical argumentation and analysis of the internal structure of administrative power to formulate the top-level design plan for power allocation. The reform direction of vertically flat management and horizontally establishing larger government departments is fixed. As far as the internal structure of administrative power is concerned, the examination and approval power of various departments will be centralized in the hands of the examination and approval bureau, while the enforcement power will be centralized in the hands of the comprehensive law enforcement bureau, which is an inevitable trend. This is because the segmented exercise of power can effectively avoid the phenomena that "administration is replaced by examination" and "administration is replaced by punishment," improve administrative efficiency and solve the contradiction of "heavy workload but shortage of staff."

In addition, to build a government under the rule of law, we need to eradicate the superstitious belief in the almighty government. We must admit that the government has limited power, its management matters are limited, and its management ability is limited. Modern supervision modes mostly emphasize ex ante, interim and ex post supervision. Such supervision modes seem to have no loopholes in all links but are costly and overestimate the government's supervision ability. In fact, the most effective supervision mode should aim to lower the admittance threshold but set up a strict ex post supervision mechanism and phase out illegal market entities with the help of an increasingly sound social credit system to ultimately achieve the effect of purifying the market. Such public law mechanisms for ex post supervision should also be combined with private law mechanisms for infringement compensation and product quality insurance to improve the government's capacity and level for social governance. Without doubt, in the era of information transparency and sharing, government governance is not unidirectional but should interact with society to achieve the goal of social co-governance.

Finally, we must introduce a scientific evaluation mechanism to judge the results of building a government under the rule of law. Administrative appraisal alone can hardly play a stimulating and promoting role, so it is necessary to introduce a neutral and objective third-party evaluation mechanism and establish a scientific and reasonable evaluation index system.

Chapter 3
Judicial Reform: Safeguarding Fairness and Justice

Changming Hu

The judicial system is a major component of the political system, while judicial impartiality is a significant guarantee of social justice. Since the founding of the People's Republic of China, especially since the reform and opening up, China has, based on its national conditions, explored establishing and continuously improving the socialist judicial system with Chinese characteristics and maintaining social justice on the basis of inheriting the outstanding achievements of traditional Chinese legal culture and drawing lessons from human civilization, making great contributions to the rule of law civilization of mankind. The report to the 19th CPC National Congress stated that "Advancing law-based governance in all fields is a profound revolution in China's governance. We must promote the rule of law and work to ensure sound lawmaking, strict law enforcement, impartial administration of justice, and the observance of law by everyone."

3.1 Overview of China's Judiciary System

China's judiciary system is a rigorous people's judiciary system and has a very important position and role in the entire state system.

The judiciary system in general refers to the nature, mission, organizational setup, principles and procedures of judicial organs and other judicial organizations. This system comprises subsystems for investigation, prosecution, trial procedures, jails, judicial administration, arbitration, lawyers, public notaries and state compensation.

C. Hu (✉)
Institute of Law, CASS, Beijing, China

H. Tian and Y. Lv (eds.), *The Chinese Path of Rule of Law Construction*,
China Insights, https://doi.org/10.1007/978-981-16-4130-5_3

3.1.1 Trial System

Pursuant to the *Constitution* and the *Organic Law of the People's Courts*, the People's Courts of the People's Republic of China are the judicial organs of the state. The people's courts shall exercise judicial power independently in accordance with the provisions of the law and shall not be subject to interference by any administrative organ, public organization or individual. All cases handled by the people's courts, except for those involving special circumstances as specified by law, shall be heard in public.

The court system consists of the Supreme People's Court, local people's courts at various levels, and special courts such as military courts. Among them, the Supreme People's Court is the highest judicial organ. The Supreme People's Court supervises the administration of justice by the local people's courts at different levels and by the special people's courts; people's courts at higher levels supervise the administration of justice by those at lower levels. The local people's courts are divided into basic-level people's courts, intermediate people's courts and higher people's courts. Special courts include military courts, railway transport courts (intermediate and primary levels), and maritime courts (equivalent to intermediate people's courts), etc.

China's courts are created by the legislature at the same level—the people's congress, and are responsible to the legislature. The Supreme People's Court is responsible for the National People's Congress and its Standing Committee. Local people's courts at different levels are responsible to the organs of state power that created them.

Adjudication organizations within the court include collegiate benches, sole-judge benches and adjudication committees. The collegiate bench is the basic judicial organization for Chinese people's courts to try cases. It is responsible for trial of ordinary criminal, civil and administrative cases of first instance, trial of cases of second instance, retrial of remanded cases and trial of a case for retrial. A collegial bench consists of three or more judges alone or both judges and assessors. The numbers of members of a collegial bench shall be odd. When deliberating a case, a collegial bench shall observe the principle of minority obeying majority. The deliberations shall be recorded in writing, and the transcript shall be signed by the members of the collegial bench. The dissenting opinions in the deliberations shall be truthfully recorded in the transcript.

The system of sole-judge proceedings is a system in which cases are tried and adjudicated by a single judge alone. The system of sole-judge proceedings is mainly applicable to civil and administrative cases of first instance to which summary procedure applies that are tried by basic-level people's courts and detached tribunals; cases to which a special procedure applies (except for cases concerning qualifications of voters and major difficult cases); non-litigation procedures (except for invalidating judgment procedure in procedure of public summons for exhortation) as well as criminal cases that may be sentenced to less than three years in prison.

The adjudication committee is a unique form of adjudication organization in China. It is the highest adjudication organization in which the people's court decides on the handling of cases. It is the decision-making body for the adjudication business that guides and supervises the trial work of the entire court. Its tasks are to summarize trial work experience and discuss major or difficult cases and other issues related to trial work. The adjudicating committee practices democratic centralism. When discussing cases, the adjudicating committee implements an avoidance system in accordance with the law.

3.1.2 Procuratorial System

Pursuant to the *Constitution* and the *Organic Law of the People's Procuratorates*, the people's procuratorates of the People's Republic of China are state organs for legal supervision. People's procuratorates shall, in accordance with the law, exercise procuratorial power independently and are not subject to interference by administrative organs, public organizations or individuals. China's procuratorates exercise the power of public prosecution, power of arrest approval, power of arrest, and power of protest and have the power to investigate specific crimes involving corruption, negligence of duty, and violations of people's elections. The reform of the supervision system has adjusted the investigation power of the people's procuratorate. The investigation power of job-related crimes has been transferred to the State Supervision Commission, and the people's procuratorate retains the right to investigate cases of illegal detention, extorting confessions by torture, illegal search and other violations of civil rights and damages to judicial justice. China has always regarded procuratorates as judicial organs independent of the government and side by side with courts.

The people's procuratorates are established in correspondacne to the levels of the people's courts. The People's Republic of China establishes the Supreme People's Procuratorate and the local people's procuratorates at different levels, military procuratorates and other special people's procuratorates. The procuratorates are under the dual leadership of the people's congress at the same level and the higher-level procuratorates. The Supreme People's Procuratorate directs the work of the local people's procuratorates at different levels and of the special people's procuratorates; people's procuratorates at higher levels direct the work of those at lower levels. The Supreme People's Procuratorate is responsible for the National People's Congress and its Standing Committee. Local people's procuratorates at different levels are responsible to the organs of state power at the corresponding levels, which created them and to the people's procuratorates at the higher level.

3.1.3 Judicial Administration System

The judicial administration system refers to the nature, mission, working principles and norms of judicial administration. It also refers to judicial administrative organs, judicial administrative procedures and judicial administrative laws and regulations.

In China, judicial administrative organs are an integral part of governments at various levels. The Ministry of Justice of the People's Republic of China is a functional department under the State Council. The judicial administrative organs of local governments at various levels are called judicial departments or judicial bureaus. They are not judicial organs that exercise judicial power, so they have no authority to handle specific cases. Specifically, in a broad sense, judicial administration mainly covers functions such as law popularization, governance according to law, penalty enforcement, community correction, community-level people's mediation, reeducation through labor at prisons, judicial authentication management, judicial notarization, and legal aid, except for the part of judicial administrative tasks that are performed by the public security organs, national security organs, procuratorial organs, judicial organs, etc., as internal system management.

3.2 Process and Goals of Judicial Reform

China's judicial system is generally consistent with its basic national conditions at the primary stage of socialism, its state system of people's democratic dictatorship, and its government system of the National People's Congress. Meanwhile, since the reform and opening up, China's economy and society have developed rapidly, public awareness of the rule of law has risen markedly, the judicial environment has changed profoundly, new circumstances and problems appear in judicial work, and the existing judicial system and working mechanism urgently need to be reformed, improved and developed.

In recent years, China has been promoting the reform of the judicial system and its work mechanism vigorously, steadily and pragmatically. This round of judicial reform is not the first judicial reform in contemporary China, and it will never be the last. Since the 1990s, China has undergone several judicial reforms. This round of judicial reforms started in 2012.

The latest round of judicial reform began at the 18th CPC National Congress. The report to the 18th CPC National Congress in 2012 stated that "We should continue to deepen reform of the judicial structure" and regarded the reform of the judicial system an important part of comprehensively deepening the reforms. In addition, unlike previous judicial reforms that were led by the Committee of Political and Legal Affairs of the CPC Central Committee, this round of judicial reform was designed and uniformly arranged by the top leadership of the central government.

Since then, the *Decision of the CPC Central Committee on Several Major Issues Concerning Comprehensively Deepening the Reform* adopted by the 3rd Plenary Session of the 18th CPC Central Committee clearly states that "We will deepen reform of the judicial system and accelerate the building of a just, efficient and authoritative socialist judicial system." The plenary session identified four basic tasks of the reform: unify the management of staffs, funds and properties of courts and procuratorates below the provincial level, improve the classified management system of legal personnel, guarantee the job security of judges, procurators and the police, and improve the accountability system of handling cases by the presiding judge and the collegiate bench, by which the judges hand down verdicts and the collegiate bench is responsible for carrying them out.

The 4th Plenary Session of the 18th CPC Central Committee was dedicated to the study of the major issues concerning comprehensively advancing the rule of law, deliberated and adopted the *Decision of the CPC Central Committee on Several Major Issues Concerning Comprehensively Advancing the Rule of Law*, making special arrangements for comprehensively advancing the rule of law to build legal institutions under socialism with Chinese characteristics and a socialist country under the rule of law. This is the first time that the Party's central plenary was dedicated to the study of the basic strategy of governing the country according to law. This was extremely rare in the Party's history. This also shows that judicial reform has been included in the main policy agenda of the ruling party to an unprecedented extent and has become an indispensable part of the ruling goal of building "a country under the rule of law."

On February 28, 2014, the relevant documents deliberated and adopted at the second meeting of the Central Leading Group for Comprehensively Deepening Reforms clearly identified the goals and principles of deepening the reform of the judicial system, determined the road map and timetable, and provided policy guidance for key and difficult issues. On June 6th of the same year, the third meeting of the Central Leading Group for Comprehensively Deepening Reforms deliberated and adopted the *Framework Opinions on Several Issues Concerning the Pilot Reform of the Judicial System*, marking the official start of the reform of the judicial system in China.

Later, the judicial reform was piloted in local areas. In 2016, with the launch of judicial reform in the third group of pilot provinces, judicial reform was fully implemented in all provinces and cities across the country.

The latest round of judicial reform in China was launched under the following backgrounds.

First, the report to the 18th CPC National Congress regarded "comprehensively advancing the rule of law" as an important deployment for promoting the reform of the political system. The report to the 18th CPC National Congress clearly proposed advancing the rule of law in an all-round way and further deepening the reform of the judicial system as one of the important measures to "advance the rule of law in an all-round way." The report also states that "we should uphold and improve the socialist judiciary system with Chinese characteristics and ensure that judicial and procuratorial bodies independently and impartially exercise their respective powers pursuant to law;" "Everyone is equal before the law. .... No organization or individual has the power to overstep the Constitution or the law; and no one in a position of power is allowed in any way to override the law with his own orders, place his authority above the law, violate the law for personal gain, or abuse the law." The 18th CPC National Congress opened the door to this round of judicial reform and regarded it a part of the reform of the political system, showing the particular attention of the CPC Central Committee to this round of judicial reform.

Second, judicial reform is regarded as an important part of endeavors to advance the rule of law and the notion of the rule of law. As early as 1997, the report to the 15th CPC National Congress proposed that "the rule of law is the fundamental principle by which the Party leads the people in governing the country." However, before then, the policy for advancing the rule of law put more emphasis on legislation, law enforcement and law-abiding. That is, "we must ensure that there are laws to abide by; that laws are observed and strictly enforced; and that lawbreakers are prosecuted." It did not highlight the status and significance of judicial impartiality in the legal system. The 18th CPC National Congress confirmed the new policy for governing the country by law and clearly identified judicial impartiality as an important goal of advancing the rule of law. That is, "ensuring our legislation is sound, law enforcement is strict, judicial impartiality is upheld, and the law is observed by everyone," which highlights the importance of judicial impartiality in building a socialist country ruled by law.

Finally, the people have strong expectations and demands for judicial impartiality. As the lifeline of the rule of law, fairness and justice is an important value of judicature and the goal and purpose of this round of judicial reform. Judicial impartiality has an important guiding role in social justice, and judicial injustice has a fatal effect on social justice. General Secretary Xi Jinping emphasized during the 4th Group Study Session of the Political Bureau of the 18th CPC Central Committee that "we should try to make the masses feel fairness and justice in every judicial case, and all judicial organs should firmly center on this objective to improve works and focus on solving deep-seated issues influencing juridical justice and constraining judicial capacity." The people hate judicial corruption and have the strongest expectation for judicial impartiality, which has become one of the fundamental driving forces of this round of judicial reform.

3.3 Measures and Effects of Judicial Reform

This round of reform aims to reflect judicial regularity and satisfy the needs of the people and has made major innovations in the following aspects.

3.3.1 Exercising Adjudicative and Procuratorial Powers Independently and Impartially in Accordance with the Law

The independent exercise of adjudicative power by the people's courts and the independent exercise of procuratorial power by the people's procuratorates are the prerequisite and basis for impartial exercise of judicial power, which is also clearly established by the *Constitution of the People's Republic of China*. However, in judicial practice, the exercise of judicial power is interfered with by some external factors, which have a negative impact on judicial impartiality. The fundamental objective of this round of judicial reform is to ensure that the people's courts and people's procuratorates exercise adjudicative power and procuratorial power fairly and independently. This has far-reaching significance.

1. Establishing a System for Recording, Reporting, and Investigating the Responsibility of Leading Officials Interfering with Judicial Activities or Meddling with the Handling of Certain Cases

The Communique of the 4th Plenary Session of the 18th CPC Central Committee stated, "Party and government organs and leading officials at all levels need to support the courts and procuratorates to exercise their functions and powers independently and impartially in accordance with the law. We must establish a system for recording, reporting, and investigating the responsibility of leading officials interfering with judicial activities or meddling with the handling of certain cases. No party or government body or leading official may let a judicial organ commit a breach of their statutory duty or impede judicial fairness, and no judicial body may execute a demand to interfere in judicial activities from a party or government body or leading official. Party or administrative disciplinary action will be imposed where there is interference in a judicial case. If it results in a case involving unjust, false, or wrongful charges, or other severe outcomes, criminal responsibility will be investigated according to the law." A serious warning was given to leading officials who interfere in judicial activities or meddle with in the handling of specific cases.

In February 2015, the 10th Meeting of the Central Leading Group for Comprehensively Deepening Reforms adopted the *Regulations on Recording, Reporting, and Investigating the Responsibility of Leading Officials Interfering with Judicial Activities or Meddling With the Handling of Specific Cases*. In March, the General Office of the CPC Central Committee and the State Council The General Office issued the Regulations, and the Committee of Political and Legal Affairs of the CPC Central Committee issued the *Regulations on the Recording and Accountability Investigation of Staff Members of Judicial Organs for Their Intervention in Case Handling*. These documents stipulate that no leading official should require judicial organs to handle cases in violation of statutory duties or legal procedures; no staff member of a judicial organ should intervene in or meddle with cases being handled by other personnel in violation of the relevant regulations.

The Supreme People's Court, the Supreme People's Procuratorate, local courts, and local procuratorates have successively promulgated the implementation measures or rules for the above documents. This is conducive to providing institutional guarantees for judicial organs to exercise their powers independently and impartially in accordance with the law.

This round of judicial reform, aiming to guarantee the independent exercise of judicial power, has distinctive characteristics. First, the reform targets "leading officials." Leading officials here include not only leading officials within the courts but also leaders of party organs, legislatures, and administrative organs, including cadres, both leading officials and party and government organs themselves. It aims to impose restriction power to strengthen independent exercise of judicial power. Second, in addition to communiques, standardized and detailed regulations and systems have been introduced to require all localities to regularly report information on violation of the above regulations and typical cases of judicial intervention by leading officials to ensure that the reform is implemented institutionally.

2. Establishing a Sound Mechanism for Protecting Judicial Personnel to Lawfully Perform Statutory Duties

Judicial personnel should be fully and effectively protected while performing their statutory duties in accordance with the law. Only in this way will they dare to take on their responsibilities without seeking personal gains, remain loyal to the law and judicial impartiality, and safeguard social fairness and justice as the last line of defense. Therefore, the communiques of the 3rd and 4th Plenary Sessions of the 18th CPC Central Committee stated that "we will guarantee the job security of judges, procurators and the people's police;" "We must establish and improve the protection mechanisms for judicial personnel performing their statutory duties. Judges and prosecutors must not be transferred, dismissed, demoted, removed or otherwise sanctioned without statutory grounds and without undergoing statutory procedures;" and "We must improve the job security guarantee systems, and establish specialist job ranks and salary structures for judges, prosecutors and the people's police."

On April 18, 2016, the Central Leading Group for Comprehensively Deepening Reforms deliberated and adopted the *Provisions on Protection of Judicial Personnel in Lawful Performance of Their Legal Duties* (hereinafter referred to as "the Provisions"). On July 28, the Central Office and the State Council issued the above provisions. It is China's first programmatic document to comprehensively strengthen the protection of judges and prosecutors in performing their duties in accordance with the law. This document, which has a total of 27 articles, has refined the mechanism for protection of various rights of judicial personnel and expands the scope of judicial job protection. First, we should extend the space of security guarantees for the performance of duties to outside courtrooms and beyond working hours. It stresses that those who make false reports or false accusations or intentionally and maliciously make false allegations against judges or those who insult or libel judges or disclose personal information of judges by making use of information networks should be held accountable in accordance with the law. With regard to threats and violent acts against judges, public security organs have the obligation to dispatch police officers to the scene promptly and deal with the case decisively. Second, it establishes the principle that the performance of statutory duties by a judge should not be investigated for liability of misjudged cases without review by the disciplinary committees for judges and prosecutors. No judge should, without statutory causes or without statutory procedures, be transferred, removed or dismissed from his office, or given such punishment as demotion or discharge from his office." Third, it was the first time that the document of the central government clearly stated that "no unit or individual should request judges or prosecutors to engage in matters beyond the scope of statutory duties. People's courts and people's procuratorates have the right to refuse the request of any organization or individual to arrange judges or prosecutors to engage in matters beyond the scope of statutory duties." In this way, we can prevent some localities from apportioning tasks such as investment attraction, land acquisition and demolition, environmental sanitation, and conduct evaluation etc., affecting judges and prosecutors to perform their duties in accordance with the law. Fourth, in terms of standardized evaluation and assessment, the *provisions* clearly require appraisal of the quality of judges and prosecutors in handling cases, and evaluation of their work performance should be carried out based on the principle of objectiveness and fairness and compliance with judicial laws.

On February 7, 2017, the Supreme People's Court issued the *Implementing Measures for the Provisions on the Protection of Judicial Personnel in the Lawful Performance of Their Duties*. The *Opinions on Deepening Procuratorial Reform (Work Plan 2013–2017)* (revised in 2015) issued by the Supreme People's Procuratorate on its official website proposes to "establish and improve a mechanism for protection of judicial personnel in performing their statutory duties." The spirit of the abovementioned *Provisions* was implemented through these implementation methods and work plans.

The above reform measures show that the 3rd and 4th plenary sessions of the 18th CPC Central Committee regarded the protection of judicial personnel in lawful performance of their duties in accordance with the law as a key reform task. First, the Central Office of the CPC Central Committee and the Central Office of State Council jointly issued the document to strengthen the protection of judicial personnel. This reflects that the central government attaches great importance to this reform. Second, the *Provisions* set the requirements for the protection of judicial personnel in the performance of their professional work in all stages, including job security guarantees, protection of their identity, and exemption from liability. Third, *the Provisions* set explicit requirements protection of legitimate rights and interests of judicial personnel. For example, no unit or individual shall request the judge or prosecutor to do anything beyond the scope of his statutory duties; the post of a judge or prosecutor may not be changed on such grounds as ranking of quantity of cases handled, bottom elimination; the performance of statutory duties by a judge or prosecutor shall only be investigated for liability of misjudged cases after a hearing by the disciplinary committee for judges and prosecutors; judges and prosecutors who work for extra hours beyond the legal workdays should take corresponding deferred rest; if no deferred rest can be taken, this should be taken into consideration when distributing performance bonuses.

3. Unifying the Management of Staff, Funds and Properties of Courts and Procuratorates

Judicial administrative affairs administration power is the routine power of the central government, not the routine power of local governments. The ultimate goal of judicial reform is to return all judicial administrative management powers to the state and manage them in a unified manner. However, it is still difficult to return all judicial administrative powers to the state in one step. Presently, it is a transitional measure to unify the management of staff, funds and properties of courts and procuratorates below the provincial level. Therefore, the 3rd Plenary Session of the 18th Central CPC Committee proposed reforming the judicial management system to promote the unified management of staff, funds and properties of courts and procuratorates below the provincial level. The 4th Plenary Session of the 18th Central CPC Committee further proposed reforming the system of management of staff, funds and properties of judicial organs and explored ways to establish a judicial jurisdiction system that is appropriately separated from the administrative divisions.

In 2015, the pilot program for unified management of personnel, funds and properties of local courts below the provincial level was implemented in some provinces to reform the previous mechanism by which local judicial personnel were subject to nomination, management, appointment and removal by the government at the city and county level and judicial funding was guaranteed by the government at the city and county level. In Shanghai, judges and prosecutors are nominated in a unified manner and appointed and removed by level on a trial basis, and selection (disciplinary) committees for judges and prosecutors composed of personnel from various departments and experts have been established. In terms of the management of properties, the properties of judicial organs at the district and county levels are placed under the unified management of the municipal financial authority. According to the pilot plan of Guangdong, in terms of personnel management, the personnel of courts and procuratorates should be placed under unified management at the provincial level. Specifically, presidents of courts and chief prosecutors of procuratorates at the city and county levels should be subject to the management of the Party committee (organization department of Party committee) at the provincial level, and judges and prosecutors should be selected in a unified manner by the Party committee at the provincial level according to the legal procedures. Judges and prosecutors should be selected, appointed and removed according to legal procedures by the provincial-level government in a unified manner. The establishment and staffing of courts and procuratorates should be placed under the unified management of the provincial department for establishment and staffing. In addition, the personnel serving as presidents of courts and chief prosecutors of procuratorates should not only have political integrity to serve as leading officials but also have necessary legal professional knowledge and legal professional experience. In terms of the management of properties, courts and procuratorates at the city and country levels, as the first-level budget units of the finance department of provincial-level government, should directly prepare budgets and submit them to provincial-level finance departments, and budget funds should directly be allocated through the centralized treasury payment system. The pilot program of Hubei stipulates that the selection (disciplinary) committees for judges and prosecutors should be set up at the provincial level, and the proportion of representatives from all walks of life should be no less than 50%.[1]

Through unified management of personnel, funds and properties of judicial organs below the provincial level, local judicial organs at the city and county level can eliminate their personnel and financial dependence on the local governments at the county and city level, thus ensuring courts and procuratorates to independently exercise adjudicative and procuratorial powers in accordance with the law. The original intention of this reform was to reduce improper external interference. As the reform progressed, external interference was greatly reduced, and the judicial environment was improved significantly. However, China's economic and social development is uneven, and the level of judicial protection varies greatly from place to place. There remain a number of difficulties to be overcome in this aspect. Therefore, the central government pointed out that when all provinces, autonomous regions, and municipalities promote the unified management of personnel, funds and properties of local courts and procuratorates below the provincial level, they need to proceed from reality and take measures suited to local conditions and should not insist on absolute consistency. If the conditions permit, unified management will be implemented at the provincial level or the prefecture and city level; otherwise, its implementation can be suspended.[2]

4. Reforming the Selection and Appointment System for Judges and Prosecutors

To build a socialist country under the rule of law, we need to build a strong contingent of personnel to enforce the rule of law with high efficiency, honesty and outstanding professional capabilities. To promote the regularization, specialization, and professionalization of professionals for the enforcement of rule of law and improve their professional quality and competence, the 3rd Plenary Session of the 18th CPC Central Committee proposed that "we should improve the system for unified recruitment, orderly exchange and level-by-level promotion of judges, procurators and the police." The Communique of the 4th Plenary Session of the 18th CPC Central Committee attached great importance to building a strong contingent of personnel for enforcing the rule of law. It proposed that we will improve

[1]Chen Weidong and Zheng Bo, "Judicial Reform: Issues and Prospects," published in *The Blue Book on the Rule of Law: Report on Development of the Rule of Law in China No. 13 (2015)* edited by Li Lin and Tian He, Social Sciences Academic Press (China), 2015.

[2]Qi Jianjian, "New Progress in Judicial Reform in 2016," published in *The Blue Book on the Rule of Law: Report on Development of the Rule of Law China No. 15 (2017)* edited by Li Lin and Tian He, Social Sciences Academic Press (China), 2017.

the system for admission to legal professions and the unified qualification exam for legal professionals. We will establish a system to recruit legislative workers, judges and prosecutors from among eligible lawyers and legal scholars and experts, open up channels for eligible transferred military officers to enter the contingent of professionals devoted to the rule of law, build a more standardized and convenient mechanism for recruiting university graduates majoring in law, and strengthen the building of a contingent of professionals for enforcing the rule of law in border and ethnic minority areas. We will establish a system for level-by-level selection of judges and procurators. Initially appointed judges and prosecutors are recruited uniformly by higher people's courts and provincial-level people's procuratorates and are appointed to grassroots courts and procuratorates without exception. Judges and prosecutors for higher-level people's courts and people's procuratorates are generally selected from excellent judges and prosecutors among the people's courts and people's procuratorates of one level lower.

The 22nd meeting of the Central Leading Group for Comprehensively Deepening Reforms held in March 2016 deliberated and adopted the *Opinions on Establishing a System for the Level-by-level Selection of Judges and Prosecutors* and *Opinions on the Open Selection of Legislative Workers, Judges, and Prosecutors from Lawyers and Legal Experts*. On June 26, the Central Office of the CPC Central Committee issued the *Measures for Open Selection of Legislative Workers, Judges, and Prosecutors from Lawyers and Legal Experts.* Pursuant to these policies, establishing systems for the level-to-level promotion of judges and prosecutors and for the open selection of legislative workers, judges and prosecutors from lawyers and legal experts is an important move to strengthen the regularization, professionalization and professionalization of contingent professionals to enforce the rule of law. We must follow the law of justice, adhere to the correct orientation of personnel selection and appointment, establish an open, fair and just promotion and open selection mechanism, standardize the conditions, standards, and procedures for promotion and open selection, and truly cultivate and appoint outstanding talents with strong political integrity, high professional competence, and good professional ethics. The opinions also set the requirements for steady and orderly advancement of the system, paying attention to institutional convergence, and ensuring the stability of the contingents.

Based on the above opinions and regulations, judicial organs have also started the selection and appointment of judges and prosecutors on a trial basis. In 2015, the Supreme People's Court and the Supreme People's Procuratorate openly selected 8 judges and 10 prosecutors from the courts and the procuratorates at lower levels, respectively. In 2015, Shanghai openly selected judges and prosecutors from society for the first time and successfully selected and appointed a senior judge of third rank and a senior prosecutor of third rank. In January 2017, the Guangdong Provincial Higher People's Court and the Guangdong Provincial People's Procuratorate issued a public announcement to openly select 6 senior judges of fourth rank and first rank and 5 procuratorates of fourth rank and first rank from practicing lawyers, experts and scholars from universities, scientific research institutions, and party and government organs in Guangdong.

The formulation and implementation of the above systems will help broaden the channels for the selection and appointment of judges and prosecutors, optimize the structure of the contingents of judges and prosecutors, and help establish a mutual communication and trust mechanism among legislative workers, judges, prosecutors, lawyers, and legal scholars, promoting the formation of a legal community.

5. Promoting the Quota System and Improving the Classified Management of Judicial Personnel

Establishing a classified management system for judicial personnel in line with their professional characteristics is the basic guarantee for deepening the reform of the judicial system. For a long time, the management mode of judicial personnel in China has been similar to that of civil servants, and so far, we have not yet built a sound contingent of judicial professionals.[3] To this end, the 3rd Plenary Session and 4th Plenary Session of the 18th CPC Central Committee proposed establishing a judicial personnel management system that conforms to professional characteristics and improving the classified management system for judicial personnel. The 3rd meeting of the Central Leading Group for Comprehensively Deepening Reforms adopted the *Framework Opinions on Several Issues Concerning the Pilot Reform of the Judicial System* and the *Work Plan of Shanghai for Judicial Pilot Reform*, setting the requirements for classified management of judicial personnel. Judicial personnel include judges, prosecutors, ancillary judicial personnel, judicial administrative staff, etc. In July 2011, the Organization Department of the CPC Central Committee, the Supreme People's Court and the Supreme People's Procuratorate jointly issued the *Interim Provisions on the Establishment of the Ranks of Judges* and the *Interim Provisions on the Establishment of the Ranks of Prosecutors*, setting up separate ranks of judges and prosecutors to dilute their administrative hues. Based on the different attributes of judicial power and administrative power and the professional characteristics of judges and prosecutors, the management mode of judges and prosecutors should be distinguished from that of civil servants. From the perspective of building the contingency of judicial professionals, we should establish a quota system for judges and prosecutors to raise their judicial capabilities.[4]

As of March 2018, Chinese courts selected 120,138 judges within the quota from 21, 1990 judges, of which the Supreme People's Court selected 367 judges within its quota. We have actively carried out the reform of the ranks of judge assistants and clerks, enrich the trial support force, and ensure that more than 85%

[3]Chen Weidong and Zheng Bo, "Judicial Reform: Issues and Prospects," published in *The Blue Book on the Rule of Law: Report on Development of the Rule of Law in China No. 13 (2015)* edited by Li Lin and Tian He, Social Sciences Academic Press (China), 2015.

[4]Chen Weidong and Zheng Bo, "Judicial Reform: Issues and Prospects," published in *The Blue Book on the Rule of Law: Report on Development of the Rule of Law in China No. 13 (2015)* edited by Li Lin and Tian He, Social Sciences Academic Press (China), 2015.

of the personnel are handling cases in the front line.[5] The quota system for prosecutors has been fully rolled out 87,000 prosecutors within the quota were selected from the original 160,000 prosecutors for handling cases in the front line, and dynamic management of quota is implemented.[6]

The quota system for judges and prosecutors is conducive to reconstructing the internal resource allocation mode of judicial organs in accordance with judicial laws and conducive to highlighting the status and role of judges and prosecutors in judicature. However, the proportion of judges and prosecutors should be controlled below 39% of the judicial and public security staffing quota set by the central government.[7] After the implementation of the quota system, some judges and prosecutors can no longer retain their identity as judges and prosecutors but are listed as judicial assistants or administrative staff. Therefore, this round of judicial reform still faces many challenges, and the quota system tops the list of concerns in the most recent round of judicial reform in China.

Therefore, the following measures are proposed to address the challenges posed by the quota system.

First, the proportion and base number of quotas should be determined flexibly to alleviate the problem of heavy caseloads and lack of staff. The central government introduced the policy to improve the quota system reform and appropriately increase the quotas for the courts and procuratorates at the primary level. First, the personnel previously employed within public institution staffing quotas and through the personnel engagement system who have grown into mainstay staff can be considered the base for determining the quotas. These personnel were originally recruited to alleviate the shortage of judicial personnel because the increase in the judicial and public security staffing quotas was far lower than the increase in cases and solve the problem of a shortage of hands for handling cases. Second, the level of economic and social development varies greatly in different areas in China. When determining the staffing quotas, a "one size fits all" approach is not suitable. Approximately 80% of cases in China were handled at the judicial organs at the primary level. Courts and procuratorates at the primary level that face serious shortages of judges and procurators may include personnel within public institution staffing quotas in the base to determine their quotas to retain the mainstay staff for front-line case handling. Third, if these areas still face severe shortages of judges and procurators, they may consider increasing the quotas to approximately 40%.

---

[5]Zhou Qiang, *Report on the Work of the Supreme People's Court—At the 1st Meeting of the 13th National People's Congress on March 9, 2018.*

[6]Cao Jianming, *The Work Report of the Supreme People's Procuratorate—At the 1st Meeting of the 13th National People's Congress on March 9, 2018.*

[7]Refer to "Comprehensive and Orderly Advancement of the Judicial Reform and Its Remarkable Results," 1st edition of the *Legal Daily*, December 4, 2015. It pointed out that "after the reform, the number of judges and prosecutors in various places should be controlled within 39% of the special establishment of the central government's political and legal system, with room reserved for it"; also see "The Supreme People's Court: No Breakthrough Was Made in The Quota Ratio of Judges in the Judicial Reform," *Southern Metropolis Daily*, July 4, 2015.

The specific proportion and base number can be determined by the leading groups for judicial system reform of the provinces, autonomous regions, and municipalities directly under the central government. For example, Guangdong implemented overall planning and fixed quotas based on caseloads, and judicial organs at the primary level and in areas with more workloads were prioritized with higher quotas. The number of court cases in the five core cities of the Pearl River Delta accounted for nearly 70% of the province, there were many new, difficult and complex cases, and the quotas of judicial organs in these areas accounted for 65.56% of the province.

Second, the presidents and chief judges of the people's courts at various levels within the quota of judges are required to hear a certain number of cases. In the implementation of the judge quota system, the leadership of the court (such as the president, the director) still maintains their identities of judges, but their energy is mainly focused on management, so the number of their cases is small. Therefore, it is requested in the reform that after the presidents and chief judges of the people's courts at various levels are incorporated into the quota of judges upon selection, they shall handle a certain number of cases. Pursuant to the *Opinions of the Supreme People's Court on Strengthening the Work of Case-Handling by Presidents and Chief Judges of the People's Courts at Various Levels (for Trial Implementation)* issued by the Supreme People's Court on April 18, 2017, the presidents and chief judges of the people's courts at various levels shall handle cases according to the judicial work they take charge of and in light of their professional background and personal expertise. Trial priority should be given to major, difficult, complicated, and new-type cases and cases of universal guiding significance in the application of law. The quantity of cases handled by chief judges of the basic-level and intermediate people's courts on a yearly basis shall reach 50–70% of the average quantity of cases handled by judges of the same departments. The quantity of cases handled by the presidents of basic-level people's courts shall reach 5–10% of the average quantity of cases handled by judges of the same people's courts, and the quantity of cases handled by other leaders of the same people's courts that are within the quota of judges shall reach 30–40% of the average quantity of cases handled by judges of the same people's courts. The quantity of cases handled by the presidents of intermediate people's courts shall reach 5% of the average quantity of cases handled by judges of the same intermediate people's courts, and the quantity of cases handled by other leaders of the intermediate people's courts that are within the quota of judges shall reach 20–30% of the average quantity of cases handled by judges of the same intermediate people's courts. All localities are required to actively explore the correct orientation that leading officials can not only do a good job in administrative management but also handle more cases and handle cases impartially and effectively, establish an adept image of leading officials, and raise public confidence in the judicial system.

Third, the scientific rationality of the ratio of judicial professionals to cases was enhanced. In September 2016, the *Several Opinions of the Supreme People's Court on Further Promoting the Efficient Distribution of Complex and Simple Cases and Optimizing the Allocation of Judicial Resources* proposed improving the rationality of the ratio of judicial professionals to cases and making dynamic adjustments of the judicial force of different courts and judicial departments based on accurately calculating the number of judges or prosecutors, caseload and workload. The proportion of judges, judge assistants, and clerks should be determined based on factors such as the court level and case complexity, and their respective functional positioning and interrelationships should be defined to maximize the advantages of the trial contingent.

3.3.2 Optimizing the Allocation of Judicial Powers

Optimizing the allocation of judicial powers is an important move to improve the efficiency of judicial justice and the focus of previous judicial reforms. The 18th CPC National Congress proposed optimizing the allocation of judicial powers, including the promotion of a pilot reform that separates judicial and enforcement powers. The Supreme People's Court should establish circuit courts and explore to establish cross-administrative people's courts and people's procuratorates and the system for procuratorial organs to file public interest lawsuits. After the reform of the public interest litigation system and other content, the allocation of judicial powers will be more in line with judicial laws.

1. Establishing the Circuit Court

The *Decision of the CPC Central Committee on Several Major Issues Concerning Comprehensively Advancing the Rule of Law* adopted at the 4th Plenary Session of the 18th CPC Central Committee determined that the Supreme People's Court should establish circuit courts to hear major administrative, civil and commercial cases across administrative regions. Its purpose is to ensure the uniform and correct implementation of the state laws and adjust the hierarchical jurisdiction system for major civil and commercial affairs and administrative cases across administrative divisions to achieve orderly convergence with the jurisdiction scope of the Supreme People's Court.

In January 2015, in accordance with the *Provisions of the Supreme People's Court on Several Issues Concerning the Trial of Cases by Circuit Courts*, the 1st and 2nd circuit courts of the Supreme People's Court were established in Shenzhen and Shenyang. In November 2016, the 29th meeting of the Central Leading Group for Comprehensively Deepening Reforms deliberated and adopted the *Requesting for Instructions of the Supreme People's Court on Establishing Additional Circuit Courts*, and 4 additional circuit courts were established in Chongqing, Xi'an, Nanjing, and Zhengzhou. To date, the circuit courts of the Supreme People's Courts have covered six regions of Northeast China, Central China, South China, Northwest China, Southwest China, and East China.

Circuit courts are standing judicial organs and branch offices of the Supreme People's Court. The judgments, rulings, and decisions that are rendered or made by the circuit courts are the judgments, rulings, and decisions of the Supreme People's Court. It legally tries major administrative and civil and commercial cases across administrative divisions and handles complaints, petitions, and other cases in accordance with the law. Circuit courts are established to shift the trial work priority to lower levels, resolve disputes on the spot, and make it convenient for the parties to bring actions and the courts to hear major cases involving interprovincial administrative divisions or involving provincial interests. They have great reform and innovation significance in exercise of adjudication power, classified personnel management, and establishment of internal institutions, uniform application of the law, and conclusion of litigation-related complaints by letters and visits.[8] The work report of the Supreme People's Court in 2018 stated that in 2017, the circuit courts concluded 12,000 cases, accounting for 47% of the total number of cases handled by the Supreme People's Court. The trial work of the Supreme People's Court is shifted to lower levels, so the circuit courts are called by the people "the Supreme People's Court near your door." By exerting their advantages of being close to the people and being able to settle disputes on the spot, the circuit courts and received and handled 46,000 letters and visits, and the total number of visits to the headquarters of the Supreme People's Court dropped by 33.2%.[9]

2. Establishing the people's Courts and people's Procuratorates Across Administrative Boundaries

There are currently 3520 local courts and more than 3600 local procuratorates at various levels in China. Most of them are set up corresponding to administrative divisions for convenience in jurisdiction and litigation. However, because personnel, funds and properties are subject to local control, judicial power is likely to be subject to interference from local party and government departments. The communique of the 4th Plenary Session of the 18th CPC Central Committee called for exploring to establish the people's courts and people's procuratorates across administrative boundaries to handle cross-regional cases. The 7th meeting of the Central Leading Group for Comprehensively Deepening Reforms deliberated and adopted the *Pilot Plan for the Establishment of Cross-Administrative District People's Courts and People's Procuratorates*. By establishing cross-administrative district courts, cross-regional civil and commercial, administrative and environmental resource cases can be tried in a centralized manner, thus eliminating the influence of local government on jurisdictions.

Since then, courts and procuratorates have explored establishing cross-administrative district courts and procuratorates in accordance with the requirements of the Central Leading Group for Comprehensively Deepening Reforms and put in place a pattern of litigation in which ordinary types of cases are

---

[8]See He Xiaorong, He Fan and Ma Yuanjie, "Interpretation and Application of Provisions of the Supreme People's Court on Several Issues concerning the Trial of Cases by the Circuit Courts," *People's Court Daily*, January 29, 2015, 5th edition.

[9]Zhou Qiang, *Report on the Work of the Supreme People's Court—At the 1st Meeting of the 13th National People's Congress on March 9, 2018.*

handled in courts and procuratorates within administrative districts, while special types of cases are handled in cross-administrative region district courts and procuratorates to improve the system of judicial jurisdiction. The railway transport courts were transformed into cross-administrative region courts. They mainly hear cross-administrative district cases, major administrative cases, cases that are easily affected by local factors, such as environmental resource protection, corporate bankruptcy, food and drug safety, public prosecution cases initiated by cross-administrative district people's procuratorates, and criminal and civil cases accepted by the original railway transport courts. In 2014, the 4th Intermediate People's Court of Beijing, the 4th Branch of the Beijing Municipal People's Procuratorate, the 3rd Intermediate People's Court of Shanghai, and the 3rd Branch of the Shanghai People's Procuratorate were formally established and began to exercise jurisdiction over and hear cross-regional cases.

In addition, China has further explored establishing specialized courts. For example, in 2014, specialised intellectual property courts were established in Beijing, Shanghai and Guangzhou to focus on hearing technology-related cases, explore and improve the technical investigator system with Chinese characteristics in line with China's national conditions, and raise the scientific rationality, neutrality and objectivity of technical fact identification to ensure the justice and efficiency of trial of technology-related cases.

3. Separating Adjudication from Enforcement and Enhancing Civil Enforcement

Judicial enforcement is the last key link to ensure the execution of judicial inducements and the protection of the rights and interests of the parties concerned. It is also a key link to realize social fairness and justice and raise public confidence in the judicial system. For a long time, "difficulties in the execution of court rulings" for the courts have been criticized by the people, greatly impairing judicial authority. Therefore, the report to the 18th CPC National Congress proposed improving the judicial system and promoting the implementation of the pilot system reform that separates judicial power from enforcement power. The 4th Plenary Session of the CPC 18th Central Committee further proposed deepening the reform of the enforcement system and promoting the implementation of the pilot system reform that separates judicial power from enforcement power. China has established a sound mechanism for the compulsory execution of civil judgment documents and a legal system of credit supervision, warning and punishment over those who fail to perform judicial inducements and has adopted specific enforcement reform measures such as strengthening efforts in reforming judicial auction methods and implementing online judicial auctions.

In June 2016, the 25th meeting of the Central Leading Group for Comprehensively Deepening Reforms reviewed and adopted the *Opinions on Accelerating and Advancing the Establishment of Credit Supervision, Warning and Punishment Mechanisms for Judgement Defaulters*. Pursuant to the *Opinions*, we should establish and improve cross-departmental collaborative supervision and joint punishment mechanisms, raise the capacity of enforcement inquiry and control, improve the system for blacklisting dishonest judgment debtors, improve the system of Party and government departments' supporting the execution work of the people's courts, extend penalty restrictions against people who default on their court orders, clearly define the contents of restricted items, and strengthen information disclosure and sharing to prompt judgment debtors to voluntarily fulfill the obligation specified in the effective legal documents.

In response to this, the Supreme People's Court announced that it would basically overcome difficulties in the execution of court rulings in two to three years. With the continuous improvement of the enforcement system, Chinese courts have achieved remarkable results in their enforcement work. First, a work pattern was formed to comprehensively overcome difficulties in the execution of court rulings. In March 2016, the courts throughout the country formulated work outlines and implementation plans and worked out timetables and roadmaps to achieve the goal of "basically overcoming difficulties in the execution of court rulings in two to three years." Local party and government organs at various levels attached great importance to execution work and generally incorporated overcoming difficulties in the execution of court rulings into the key tasks for advancing the rule of law, effectively forming a joint force for overcoming difficulties in the execution of court rulings.

Second, judicial organs have effectively tackled the difficulties of determining the persons and assets involved and converting assets into cash. More than 10 departments, including the Supreme People's Court, the Ministry of Public Security and the China Banking Regulatory Commission, have jointly established a network execution inquiry and control system to investigate and control judgment debtors and their properties through information-based, networking, and automated means.

Third, the execution and management system and mechanism were continuously improved. In Zhejiang, Guangdong, Guangxi and other regions, pilot programs were carried out to promote the reform that separates judicial power from enforcement power. An execution command center has been established to promote information management throughout the entire process of execution of cases. The execution command systems of courts at four levels have basically been established, and the execution management model has undergone tremendous changes. Thirty-three guiding documents were formulated, including 15 judicial interpretations and "ten prohibitions" on regulating enforcement behaviors. Procuratorates across the country have supervised the handling of cases with strong feedback from the masses and effectively solved problems such as passive enforcement and selective enforcement.

Fourth, a joint credit punishment mechanism was vigorously implemented. The deployments of the Central Leading Group for Comprehensively Deepening Reforms were earnestly implemented, the credit supervision, warning and punishment mechanisms for judgement defaulters were improved, and the list of dishonest judgment debtors was established. More than 60 departments, including the National Development and Reform Commission of the United Nations, have built a credit punishment network, forming a credit punishment system with the combined forces of many departments, many industries and many means. Innovation in the working mechanisms were made. The courts in Jiangxi have established the Dishonest Judgment Debtors Exposure Platform through joint efforts of the courts, the mass media, banks, and courts in Hebei, Shanxi, Inner Mongolia, Qinghai and other regions have carried out special actions to effectively enforce and conclude a large number of cases. During the five years from 2013 to 2018, courts at all levels nationwide had publicly disclosed the information of dishonest judgment debtors for 9.961 million person-times, restricted the purchase of air tickets for 10.148 million person-times, restricted the purchase of bullet train and high-speed train tickets for 3.912 million person-times, and 2.215 million people voluntarily fulfilled their obligations under credit punishment. Punishments against non-execution behaviors were intensified and sentenced 9,824 offenders for refusal to execute judgments and convictions. A credit punishment pattern of "dishonesty once leads to restriction everywhere" was initially formed, which effectively promoted the establishment of a social credit system.[10]

4. Promoting the Practice of Public Interest Litigation

Exploring to establish the system of public interest litigation initiated by procuratorial organs is one of the contents of judicial reform determined by the 18th CPC National Congress. In May 2015, the 12th meeting of the Central Leading Group for Deepening Reforms adopted the *Reform Pilots on People's Procuratorates Initiating Public Interest Litigation*, which pointed out that we should focus on instituting public interest litigation cases in the fields of ecological environment and resource protection, protection of state-owned assets, transfer of state-owned land use rights, and food and drug safety, and a two-year pilot program was launched in 13 provinces.

In July 2015, the Supreme People's Procuratorate began a two-year pilot program allowing prosecutors in 13 provincial divisions to institute public interest litigation in administrative and civil cases. Persuant to the *Measures for the Implementation of the Pilot Program of Instituting Public Interest Litigation by the People's Procuratorates* issued by the Supreme People's Procuratorate on December 16th of the same year, where the people's procuratorate finds during performing its duties that the defendant commits such acts harming the social and public interests as polluting the environment, damaging the ecology, and infringing upon the lawful rights and interests of numerous consumers in the field of food and drug safety, the people's procuratorate may, in the absence of rightful subject or under the circumstance where the rightful subject does not institute any lawsuit, institute a civil public interest litigation in the people's court. Where the people's procuratorate finds that the administrative organ responsible for supervision and management illegally exercised its functions and powers or failed to perform its duties in the fields of ecological environment and resource protection, protection of state-owned assets, transfer of state-owned land use rights, and food and drug

[10]Zhou Qiang, *Report on the Work of the Supreme People's Court—At the 1st Session of the 13th National People's Congress on March 9, 2018*.

safety, which harm national and social public interests, and a citizen, a legal person or any other organization has not and is unable to initiate litigation because there is direct interest between them, the people's procuratorate may institute a civil public interest litigation in the people's court. It also clearly specifies the conditions, scope of application and procedures for the people's procuratorate to initiate public interest litigation, and the participants in public interest litigation, case jurisdiction, allocation for burden of proof, and pilot areas. During the pilot period, people's procuratorates at various levels handled 9,053 public interest litigation cases, covering all the authorized fields such as ecological environment and resource protection, protection of state-owned assets, transfer of state-owned land use rights, and food and drug safety.

The Supreme People's Court explored establishing a case jurisdiction system that matches the system of instituting public interest litigation by the people's procuratorates. In January 2015, the Supreme People's Court issued the *Interpretation of the Supreme People's Court on Several Issues Concerning the Application of Law for the Trial of Environmental Civil Public Interest Litigation Cases*, stipulating that qualified social organizations may initiate environmental civil public interest litigation and play the role of the court. In March 2016, the Supreme People's Court issued the *Measures for the Implementation of the Pilot Program of Trial by People's Courts of Public Interest Litigation Cases Instituted by People's Procuratorates*, which were piloted in 13 provinces, municipalities and autonomous regions, including Beijing, Shandong, Fujian, Guangdong, Yunnan, and Guizhou. Where the people's procuratorate holds that the defendant commits such acts harming the social and public interests as polluting the environment, damaging the ecology, and infringing upon the lawful rights and interests of numerous consumers in the field of food and drug safety, the people's procuratorate may, in the absence of rightful subject or under the circumstance where the rightful subject does not institute any lawsuit, institute a civil public interest litigation in the people's court. In May 2016, the Supreme People's Court issued the *Interpretation on Several Issues Concerning the Application of Law in the Trial of Civil Public Interest Actions regarding Consumption*, stipulating that where the China Consumers' Association ("CCA") and consumers' associations set up in provinces, autonomous regions, and municipalities directly under the Central Government may institute civil public interest actions regarding consumption against business operators that infringe upon the lawful rights and interests of many unspecific consumers or have acts of endangering the personal and property safety of consumers and impairing the public interests. This interpretation shall apply to civil public interest actions regarding consumption instituted by authorities and social organizations as prescribed in the law or authorized by the National People's Congress and the Standing Committee thereof.

In June 2017, the NPC Standing Committee revised the *Civil Procedure Law* and the *Administrative Procedure Law* to formally establish a system for procuratorial organs to initiate public interest litigation. In March 2018, the Supreme People's Court and the Supreme People's Procuratorate jointly issued the *Interpretation on Several Issues concerning the Application of Law for Cases regarding Procuratorial Public Interest Litigation*, improving the procuratorial public interest litigation system. Since July 2017, procuratorial organs have handled 10,925 public interest litigation cases. This reform has gone through the five stages of top-level design, legal authorization, pilot implementation, legislative guarantees, and full roll-out in the past two years and has embarked on a path of public interest judicial protection with Chinese characteristics.[11]

5. Promoting Institutional Reform Within the Judiciary

The reform of internal institutions focuses on judicial professionalization, mainly covering the following aspects.

First, establishing liquidation and bankruptcy tribunals. In June 2016, the Supreme People's Court issued the *Working Plan for Establishing Liquidation and Bankruptcy Tribunals in Intermediate People's Courts*, requiring that an intermediate people's court in each of the four municipalities directly under the Central Government and the intermediate people's courts in the provincial capital cities and sub-provincial cities of 11 provinces, including Hebei, establish their liquidation and bankruptcy tribunals. Whether other intermediate people's courts establish liquidation and bankruptcy tribunals can be determined by the provincial higher people's courts in conjunction with the provincial-level departments for establishment and staffing based on factors such as the level of economic and social development, the number of cases, the power of trial, and the number of bankruptcy administrators. This aims to effectively implement the decisions and arrangements of the CPC Central Committee for promoting the supply-side structural reform and the spirits of a series of important instructions given by General Secretary Xi Jinping on the supply-side structural reform, accelerate the trial of the cases on the compulsory corporate liquidation and enterprise bankruptcy, improve the level of professionalization of trials, improve trial quality and efficiency, and create conditions for the implementation of the market-oriented bankruptcy procedure.

Second, the "three-in-one" trial of cases involving intellectual property rights should be promoted. The *Opinions of the Supreme People's Court on Promoting the "Three-in-one" Trial of Civil, Administrative and Criminal Cases Involving Intellectual Property Rights in Courts Nationwide* issued in July 2016 requires that intellectual property tribunals hear civil, administrative and criminal cases involving intellectual property rights in a unified manner. This is an important move to implement the tasks of the judicial reform determined at the 4th Plenary Session of the 18th CPC Central Committee, the national intellectual property strategy and the innovation-driven development strategy. Its purpose is to build a working mechanism and an adjudication system that conforms to the judicial characteristics and laws of intellectual property rights and to improve the overall effectiveness of intellectual property judicial protection. Promoting the "*three-in-*one" work helps to enhance the joint forces of judicial and administrative authorities and achieve

[11]Cao Jianming, *The Work Report of the Supreme People's Procuratorate—At the 1st Meeting of the 13th National People's Congress on March 9, 2018*.

comprehensive remedy and judicial impartiality; helps to unify judicial standards, improve trial quality and enhance the judicial protection system of intellectual property rights; helps to rationally distribute trial forces, optimize allocation of trial resources, and improve the effectiveness and efficiency of the judicial protection of intellectual property rights; and helps to develop specialized trial teams of intellectual property rights and improve the quality of trial teams of intellectual property rights.

Third, the flattening reform of internal institutions. The central government requires actively promoting the reform of the internal institutions of courts and prosecutors. The provincial and municipal courts and procuratorates that meet the conditions should carry out pilot reforms of internal institutions. The reform must adhere to the combination of flat management and professional construction and the overall consideration of internal institution reform and case-handling organization construction. Institutions should no longer be set up for judicial personnel to strive for administrative ranks. The original organization should also be reduced so that the backbone of the business will return to the front line of handling cases to prevent the section chief from approving cases. At the same time, the original staffing, number of leadership positions and salaries will not be reduced, which will help relieve worries about the reform of internal institutions.

6. Deepening the Reform of the Diversified Dispute Resolution Mechanism

The Supreme People's Court promoted the "Meishan Experience" in Sichuan, the "Weifang Experience" in Shandong, and the "Maanshan Experience" in Anhui, strengthened the linking of litigation and mediation, gave full play to the mediation role of the people, and guided the parties to choose mediation, arbitration and other methods to resolve conflicts. The Supreme People's Court and the Ministry of Justice jointly launched a trial program for lawyer mediation and improved the lawyer mediation system. Adhering to the principle of lawfulness and voluntariness, in the past five years, courts at various levels have handled 13.961 million cases through mediation.

The *Opinions of the Supreme People's Court on Further Deepening the Reform of the Diversified Dispute Resolution Mechanism of the People's Courts* promulgated in June 2016 put forward the following requirements. (1) Improving resource integration, strengthening the construction of the platforms for coordinated litigation and mediation, one-stop dispute resolution and online case-handling information, and a system for linking various dispute resolution mechanisms for reconciliation, mediation, arbitration, notarization, administrative adjudication, administrative reconsideration and litigation. (2) Promoting the construction of the systems for specially invited mediation organizations or mediators, full-time court mediators, lawyer mediation, criminal reconciliation and administrative reconciliation, and exploring to establish mechanisms for neutral evaluation of civil and commercial disputes, recording of non-controversial facts, and recognition of non-objection mediation solutions. In June 2016, the *Provisions of the Supreme People's Court on Specially Invited Mediation by the People's Courts* was issued.

Specially invited mediation organizations or specially invited mediators should conduct mediation in accordance with the law as appointed by the people's court before a case is filed or as authorized by the people's court after a case is filed. (3) Improving procedural arrangements, including establishing a dispute settlement notification procedure, encouraging the parties to reach reconciliation through mediation first, exploring to establish the pre-mediation procedure, improving the appointed mediation and entrusted mediation procedures, improving the mechanism for separating complicated cases from simple ones, promoting the appropriate separation between mediation and adjudication, improving the judicial confirmation procedure, and strengthening the connection between the mediation and supervision procedures. (4) Improving the management mechanism and establishing a reward and punishment mechanism. (5) Promoting the legislative process. Promoting the introduction of relevant local regulations and local government rules in accordance with the local conditions of their respective jurisdictions. (6) Promoting the globalization of the diversified dispute resolution mechanism. We shall further strengthen exchanges and cooperation with judicial organs, arbitration institutions and mediation organizations of other countries and regions and enhance the competitiveness and credibility of China's dispute resolution mechanism. We shall give full play to the advantages of all types of dispute resolution approaches to continuously meet the diverse needs of Chinese and foreign parties concerned with dispute resolution and provide judicial services and guarantees for the implementation of major strategies of the state, such as the Belt and Road.

The *Several Opinions of the Supreme People's Court on Further Promoting the Efficient Distribution of Complex and Simple Cases and Optimizing the Allocation of Judicial Resources* issued in September 2016 requires improving the diversified dispute resolution mechanism. We shall promote all kinds of governance bodies, such as comprehensive governance organizations, administrative organs, people's mediation organizations, commercial mediation organizations, industrial mediation organizations, arbitration institutions and notary institutions, to play the role of preventing and resolving contradictions and disputes, improve the construction of platforms of docking litigation and conciliation, and strengthen organic connections between litigation and non-litigation dispute settlement to promote the division before litigation of disputes. We shall improve the reconciliation and mediation in the criminal procedure, promote administrative mediation and reconciliation and actively support the administrative organs to adjudicate the civil disputes closely related to administrative activities according to the law.

7. Promoting the Efficient Distribution of Complex and Simple Litigation cases

Pursuant to the *Several Opinions of the Supreme People's Court on Further Promoting the Efficient Distribution of Complex and Simple Cases and Optimizing the Allocation of Judicial Resources* issued in September 2016, trial resources shall be scientifically allocated and efficiently applied, simple cases shall be tried in a legal and speedy manner, and the trial of complex cases shall be strictly standardized, so as to realize the speedy trial of simple cases and the elaborate trial of complex cases; the local people's courts at various levels shall, in accordance with the legal provisions, scientifically develop the standards for distinguishing simple cases from complex ones and the rules for distributing them and by taking the method of "giving first place to random distribution of cases and giving second place to designated distribution of cases," ensure that simple cases are tried in a timely manner by the people's courts or speedy trial teams. In principle, serial, mass, or related cases should be tried by the same trial organization. (1) The parties concerned shall be actively guided in agreeing on the application of the summary procedure, small claims procedure, supervision procedure, etc. in the trial of a civil case. (2) Creating a fast-track sentencing mechanism for criminal cases and strengthening the connection and cooperation of investigation, prosecution and trial procedures. We should popularize the establishment of fast-track sentencing offices at detention houses, law enforcement and case handling organizations and other places and promote case information sharing and paperless circulation of files. (3) Simplifying the trial procedure of administrative cases. For administrative cases that have been filed but are not in line with the conditions of prosecution, if it is considered that no trial is required after reading, investigating and inquiring about the parties, a determination to dismiss a prosecution may be made. For a case with clear facts, clear rights and obligations relationships, and minor disputes, we shall explore establishing a mechanism of administrative speedy trial. (4) Exploring the way to implement test case. For serial or group civil and administrative cases, we shall select individual or few cases to implement test cases first and handle other similar cases according to the results of judgments and rulings to efficiently solve batch cases through demonstration handling of individual cases. (5) Carrying out the trial of the case in a concentrated time. For civil cases that are heard for summary procedures and minor criminal cases that are heard for quick trial procedures or summary procedures, we will implement centralized filling, deportation, scheduling, sessions and judgment, and a number of cases will be heard continuously by the same judicial organization in the same period. (6) Developing and utilizing scientific and technological justice, such as promoting electronic payment orders, remote video court sessions, intelligent voice recognition of hearing records, promoting the construction of the smart court and the computerization of the lawsuit archives, and speeding up the transfer of the files between the upper and lower courts in the way of electronic archive. In addition, it also requires promoting the sentence in the court; implementing the division of complexity and simplicity for judgement document; improving cohesive mechanism of case of second instance; popularizing professional trial; promoting the centralized management for auxiliary affairs of trial; improving diversified dispute settlement mechanism; giving full play to the role of lawyers in litigation; guiding the parties to file a lawsuit honestly and rationally.

3.3.3 Regulating the Operation of Judicial Power

"Constant experience shows us that every man invested with power is apt to abuse it and to carry his authority as far as it will go." Judicial power, as one of the powers of modern countries, is obviously no exception. Therefore, to ensure that judicial power is not abused, we should ensure that people feel fairness and justice in every judicial case, and judicial power must also be supervised and regulated. To this end, the report to the 18th CPC National Congress proposed strengthening supervision over judicial activities. The 3rd Plenary Session of the 18th CPC Central Committee further proposed that we will optimize the distribution of judicial functions and powers, improve the system of judicial power division, coordination, checks and balances, and strengthen and standardize legal and social supervision over judicial activities.

1. Improving the Judicial Accountability System

To uphold fair and just judiciary, the report to the 18th CPC National Congress clearly proposed establishing an accountability system for lifelong quality case handling and a system for retroactive investigation into accountability for misjudged cases. Specifically, we will improve the accountability systems of presiding judges, collegial benches, head procurators and lead investigators for the cases they handle to ensure that those who have handled a case assume full responsibility for it and the judges hand down verdicts and the collegiate bench is responsible for carrying them out. These are similar expressions in the Communiques of the 3rd and 4th Plenary Sessions of the 18th CPC Central Committee.

In August 2015, the 15th meeting of the Central Leading Group for Comprehensively Deepening Reforms adopted *Several Opinions of the Supreme People's Court on Improving the Judicial Accountability System of the People's Courts* and *Several Opinions on Improving the Judicial Accountability System of the People's Procuratorates*. Pursuant to these opinions, the exercise of judicial power in a scientific manner is a prerequisite for improving the judicial accountability system. We should establish a system for protecting judicial personnel in lawfully performing their duties, hold judicial professionals accountable for the quality of case they handle for the rest of their life, establish mechanisms and procedures for the identification and investigation of judicial responsibility, and identify 7 illegal trial circumstances into which the responsibility should be investigated and 8 circumstances in which the performance of statutory duties by a judge should not be investigated for liability of misjudged cases and 19 circumstances where prosecutors should be held accountable. In July 2016, the 26th meeting of the Central Leading Group for Comprehensively Deepening Reforms adopted the *Opinions on the Establishment of a Disciplinary Punishment System for Judges and Procurators (for Trial Implementation)*, which stated that the establishment of a disciplinary punishment system is of great significance to implement the judicial accountability system, urge judges and prosecutors to exercise their powers in accordance with the law and maintain social fairness and justice.

Further improving the judicial accountability system is one of the four basic tasks of this round of judicial reform. It is considered the rudder for steering this judicial reform, or the "nose of an ox", as described in some policy documents. The main part of the judicial accountability system is to clearly define the powers and responsibilities of judicial personnel, rationally establish the rules for accountability investigation that conform to judicial laws, and effectively protect judicial personnel in lawfully performing their duties.[12] Improving the judicial accountability system is conducive to establishing and improving a mechanism for exercise of adjudicative power that conforms to judicial laws and establishing a mechanism for fair and efficient exercise of procuratorial power.

The core of improving the judicial accountability system lies in two aspects: "the judges hand down verdicts and the collegiate bench is responsible for carrying them out." "The judges hand down verdicts" is to establish a mechanism for exercise of adjudicative power with clear definition of power and responsibilities, unification of power and responsibilities and supervision in an orderly manner. Previously, the Chinese court system was such a hierarchical organization that the lower-level judges must obey the superiors. For example, the superiors have the power to review the judgment drafted by the lower-level judges and decide whether to approve the judgment. "The collegiate bench is responsible for carrying the verdicts out." In accordance with the principle of unification of powers and responsibilities, we should clarify the responsibilities and exemption conditions of chief umpire judge, prosecutor, and collegial panel and its members, realize the effective connection of evaluation mechanism, accountability mechanism, disciplinary mechanism, withdrawal mechanism and guarantee mechanism, clarify that the premise for judicial personnel to assume responsibilities must be deliberate violation of law or gross negligence, strengthen judicial personnel's duty performance and identity protection under circumstances where they should not be held accountable, and severely punish those who are at fault, and resolutely hold them accountable.

2. Advancing the Trial-Centered Reform of Procedures

The 18th CPC National Congress proposed advancing the trial-centered reform of procedures to ensure that the facts and evidence of cases under investigation, examination and prosecution can stand the test of law. We should fully implement evidentiary judgment rules; collect, fix, preserve, investigate, and use evidence strictly according to the law; improve systems for witnesses and experts appearing in court; ensure that courtroom hearings play a decisive role in ascertaining the facts, identifying the evidence, protecting the right of action; and adjudicating impartially.

In June 2016, the 25th meeting of the Central Leading Group for Comprehensively Deepening Reform deliberated and adopted the *Opinions on Advancing the Trial-centered Reform of the Criminal Procedure System*. In July,

[12]Wang Minyuan, "Overcoming the Difficulties in the Implementation of the Judicial Accountability System," *People's Court Daily*, September 26, 2015, 2nd edition.

the *Opinions* was jointly issued by the Supreme People's Court, the Supreme People's Procuratorate, the Ministry of Public Security, the Ministry of State Security, the Ministry of Justice and the Ministry of Justice. It reiterates that the people's courts, the people's procuratorates and the public security authorities shall, in handling criminal cases, divide their functions, take responsibilities for their own work, coordinate their efforts, and restrict each other. It points out that 16 systems remain to be improved, 7 systems to be established and 6 systems to be established and improved. Pursuant to the Opinions, we should establish and improve guidelines on the collection of evidence; explore and establish a system to make video and audio records of such significant cases as homicide cases in the process of examination, search, identification, etc.; improve the rules for the transfer, examination, court investigation and use of technical investigation evidence and out-of-court verification procedures; and explore and establish a system for verifying the legality of interrogation before conclusion of investigation of a significant case. Evidence has been collected by illegal means of extorting confessions through torture, violence, etc. shall be excluded in accordance with the law and shall not be used as a basis for requesting approval of arrest and transferring a case for examination before prosecution. The Opinions stated that we should give to play the important role of trials, especially court trials, in ascertaining facts, determining evidence, protecting litigation rights, and making fair judgments based on China's national conditions and judicial reality. The opinions also require focusing on solving serious problems affecting the impartiality of criminal judicature, implementing evidence judgments in all links of criminal litigation, excluding evidence collected by illegal means, implementing the system for witnesses and appraisers to appear in court to testify, improving legal aid, advancing the separation of complicated and simple cases, and establishing a criminal procedure system that conforms to consistent judicial laws.

The reform of the trial-centered procedure system helps to realize cross examination of lawsuit evidence in court, ascertainment of case facts in court, presentation of opinions on accusation and defense in court and formation of juridical reasons in court, to make activities of investigation and examination before prosecution always get in line with trial procedures and to realize the substantive fairness of the judgment of the case through the fairness of the court trial procedures, prevent cases in which people were unjustly, falsely or wrongly charged or sentenced, and promote judicial justice.

3. Strengthening the Legal System of Procuratorial Supervision

The supervisory power of the procuratorial organ is an important part of improving the mechanism for judicial power division, coordination, checks and balances and an important move proposed by the 18th CPC National Congress to strengthen judicial supervision. In accordance with the spirit of the 4th Plenary Session of the 18th CPC Central Committee, we will improve the legal system for procuratorial organs to exercise their supervisory power, strengthen legal supervision over criminal, civil and administrative procedures, and focus on the supervision of prosecutorial organs' investigation of criminal offence occurring during law enforcement activities including case registry, arrests, detention or freezing of assets, filing complaints, etc. Specifically, we will strengthen internal supervision, investigation supervision, execution supervision, and administrative litigation supervision.

First, internal supervision should be strengthened over case handling. Pursuant to the *Provisions of the People's Procuratorates on the Work of Case Process Monitoring (for Trial Implementation)* implemented in July 2016, the objects to be supervised by the people's procuratorates are the procedural issues of cases being accepted or handled by the procuratorates. People's procuratorates should conduct real-time dynamic supervision, prompting, prevention and control of whether case-handling procedures are lawful, standard, timely and complete in cases that are currently being accepted or handled. It involves case acceptance, compulsory measures, property in dispute, legal documents, time limits for case handling, rights protection, information disclosure, online case handling, etc. When a substantive problem is found, it should be made known to the case-handling department and reported to the chief prosecutor for supervision. In addition, after the conclusion of the case process, a quality assessment can be organized to conduct in-depth analysis of substantive and procedural contents to confirm whether there is any problem. This is conducive to strengthening the supervision and management of people's procuratorates over case handling, further regulating case handling behaviors, and promoting fair and efficient judicature.

Second, investigation supervision should be strengthened. Strengthening investigation supervision strengthens people's supervisors' supervision and refines the conditions for arrest. First, we demonstrate people's supervisors' supervision over self-investigation cases. In July 2016, the Supreme People's Procuratorate disclosed four typical cases where people's supervisors supervised the procuratorial organs' direct acceptance of the investigation work, including the circumstance where a case should be filed for investigation by a public security organ but the latter has not done; the circumstance where the criminal suspect is suspected of bribery and the case was to be withdrawn; and the circumstance where the criminal suspect was not satisfied with the decision of arrest; the circumstance where Mr. Chen was suspected of corporate bribery and the case was not prosecuted. In some of these cases, the people's supervisors were selected by the bureau of justice through the System for Random Selection of People's Supervisors to participate in the supervision and evaluation. There was also one of two reconsideration cases nationwide since the reconsideration procedure was specified by the *Plan for Deepening the Reform of the System of People's Supervisors*. These cases have gone through complete supervision procedures by the people's supervisors, which are endeavors to explore supervisory reconsideration procedures. People's supervisors' supervision in these cases has achieved good legal and social effects. Second, to refine the social harmfulness conditions for arrest. The *Provisions of the Supreme People's Procuratorate and the Ministry of Public Security on Several Issues concerning Social Harmfulness Conditions for Arrest (for Trial Implementation)* implemented in October 2016 stipulate that the public security organs should be responsible for proof of social harmfulness for arrest. Where the evidence proving a criminal fact fails to prove that the criminal suspect has social harmfulness, the procuratorate may request the public security organ to supplement relevant evidence. If the public security organ fails to supplement and transfer evidence, the procuratorate should make a decision of not to approve the arrest. It defines specific social harmfulness circumstances, including 7 circumstances where the suspect may commit a new crime; 4 circumstances where there is an actual danger to national security, public security, or social order; 4 circumstances where the criminal suspect may destroy or forge evidence, interfere with the testimony of witness, or make a false confession in collusion; 4 circumstances where the criminal suspect may retaliate against a victim, informant, or accuser; and 5 circumstances where the criminal suspect attempts to commit suicide or escape, etc. This helps reduce pretrial detention.

Third, supervision should be strengthened over criminal execution. Supervision over criminal execution is strengthened from two aspects: supervision over the execution of involuntary medical treatment and supervision over the execution of property-oriented penalties. First, supervision should be strengthened over the execution of involuntary medical treatment. In June 2016, the *Measures for the Procuratorial Supervision of Execution of Involuntary Medical Treatment by People's Procuratorates (for Trial Implementation)* was promulgated, requiring the people's procuratorate to supervise whether the delivery execution activities of people's courts and public security authorities are legal; supervise whether the receipt and treatment, medical treatment, supervision and other activities of involuntary medical treatment institutions are legal; supervise whether the temporary protective restraint measures adopted by the public security organs on the mental patients involved in the compulsory medical treatment institution are legal; investigate duty-related crimes occurring in the execution of involuntary medical treatment, and prevent duty-related crimes; accept the accusations, reports and appeals filed by the personnel subject to involuntary medical treatment and their legal representatives and close relatives. This is conducive to safeguarding the legal rights of persons subject to involuntary treatment and ensuring that compulsory treatment enforcement activities are carried out in accordance with the law. Second, to strengthen supervision over execution of property-oriented penalties. In August 2016, the *Notice on the Nationwide Procuratorial Organs' Special Prosecution Activities for Execution of Property-oriented Penalties* decided to carry out special prosecution activities for execution of property-oriented penalties throughout the country from August to December 2016, and the targets were the cases involving execution of property-related penalties determined by the people's courts from January 1, 2013 to June 30, 2016, focusing on the five types of crimes in which execution of property-related penalties have not yet completed, mainly including duty-related crimes, financial crimes, gang-related crimes, crimes of undermining protection of environmental resources, and crimes endangering food and drug safety. With regard to fine penalties, penalties of confiscation of property, confiscation of illegal income, order to return compensation, and confiscation of personal property used for crimes, it is necessary to check and identify the basic number of cases and improve the execution of property-oriented penalties. For cases that should be transferred for execution in accordance with law but not transferred, the procuratorial organ should be coordinated with the criminal trial department to transfer the cases for execution in a timely manner. For cases that have entered the execution procedure but the execution has not yet completed, the procuratorial organ should strengthen efforts to conclude the execution as soon as possible.

Fourth, supervision should be strengthened over administrative litigation. In April 2016, the *Rules for Supervision over Administrative Proceedings by the People's Procuratorates (for Trial Implementation)* was promulgated, specifying 4 circumstances where a party may file a request for supervision with a people's procuratorate; 8 circumstances where a party files a request for supervision with a people's procuratorate, the people's procuratorate shall not accept the request; 3 circumstances where a people's procuratorate shall, according to its functions and powers, supervise an administrative case. It also gives procuratorial proposals for 12 kinds of illegal acts of judges in trial procedures and 16 kinds of illegal enforcement activities. It summarizes 17 specific circumstances in which the main evidence for ascertaining the facts is insufficient, there is definite error in the application of the law and legal proceedings are violated, which are likely to affect fair judgment. This is conducive to supervising the people's courts' trial and execution in accordance with the law, prompting administrative agencies to exercise their powers in accordance with the law, and maintaining judicial justice and authority. In May 2016, the Supreme People's Procuratorate disclosed 10 typical cases of administrative litigation supervision to guide and strengthen the supervision over administrative litigation.

4. Improving the people's Assessor System

The people's assessor system is one of the judicial systems with Chinese characteristics, which helps to broaden the channels for people's orderly participation in trials and improve judicial democracy and transparency. The 4th Plenary Session of the 18th CPC Central Committee proposed improving the people's assessor system, safeguarding citizens' right to participate in case trials, expanding the scope of participation in case trials, improving random selection methods, and increasing public confidence in the people's assessor system. The assessor system will gradually introduce people's assessors who will no longer hear the issue of the application of the law and only participate in the issue of fact finding.

In response to the long-standing phenomenon for people's assessors of "presenting without hearing" and "hearing without discussing," the latest round of judicial reform proposed ensuring public participation in judicial activities such as judicial mediation, judicial hearings, and petitions involving litigation, safeguarding citizens' right to participate in case trials, expanding the scope of participation in case trials, and raising public confidence in the people's assessor system. In April 2015, the 11th meeting of the Central Leading Group for Comprehensively Deepening Reforms adopted the *Pilot Program for the Reform of the People's Assessor System*, pointing out that the people's assessor system is an important part of socialist democratic politics, and proposed to conduct pilot reform of important links of the assessor system. In May, the Supreme People's Court and the Ministry of Justice jointly issued the *Implementation Measures for the Pilot Reform of the People's Assessor System*, stipulating that in principle assessors should participate in hearing of cases in which criminals may be sentenced to more than ten years of fixed-term imprisonment and major cases involving demolition, environmental protection, and food and drug safety. The *Measures* raises the age qualification for assessors to 28 and relaxes the requirement for educational background to a high school education or above. It requires that the number of people's assessors in the basis-level courts be no less than three or five times the number of judges in the court; the selection and appointment of people's assessors should be carried out once every five years; the assessors should independently express their opinions and vote on the issues of fact ascertaining, but no longer participate in the voting on the issues of the application of the law for the case.

The *Interim Report of the Supreme People's Court on the Pilot Reform of the People's Assessor System* published in October 2016 pointed out that the pilot work has achieved phased results, showing "four changes." First, the assessor selection mode has changed from recommendation of assessors by organizations to random selection of assessors. Second, the power of assessors to participate in trials has changed from full participation to only participating in finding factual issues. Pilot courts in Beijing, Hebei, Henan and other places have formulated operating rules for separating factual issues from legal issues. Third, the mode of assessors' participation has changed from a three-member collegiate panel mode to a large-scale collegiate panel mechanism with more than five members. Fourth, in the trial of cases, assessors' attention has changed from focusing on the number of cases to focusing on quality. The average age of the assessors was 45 years old, and the total number of assessors was 4.3 times the number of judges.

1. Constructing sunshine judicature to promote justice through openness

Sunlight is said to be the best of disinfectants. The 4th Plenary Session of the 18th CPC Central Committee proposed that "create a mechanism that keeps the judiciary in the sunshine, making it open, dynamic, transparent, and convenient for the public to access." We will ensure openness of adjudicative, procuratorial police and prison affairs, promptly publish law enforcement and judicial basis, procedures, processes, results, and effective legal documents according to the law, put an end to put an end to backroom dealings, strengthen the explanation and interpretation of legal documents, and establish an online integrated open inquiry system for effective legal documents.

In recent years, the Chinese judiciary has continuously broadened channels for judicial openness, created platforms for information disclosure, and upgraded the relevant systems to continuously improve the level and quality of judicial transparency.

In terms of trial openness, the Supreme People's Court has issued a number of normative documents on promoting judicial openness and standardizing judicial openness, such as "opinions of the Supreme People's Court on Further Deepening Judicial Openness", which promotes judicial openness to strengthen the restriction on the operation of power, and guarantees the people's right to know, participate, express and supervise, As well as carry forward the socialist core values, promote the height of strengthening the national awareness of the rule of law. Since the 18th CPC National Congress, the Supreme People's Court has successively established four major judicial open platforms for judgment documents, trial procedures, execution information, and public hearings. China Judgments Online has become the world's largest judgment document website. As of December 31, 2018, the website has published more than 61 million effective judgment documents of courts at all levels across the country, with more than 21.2 billion visits. The search function is gradually improving. Visitors come from more than 210 countries and regions around the world. The documents published by China Judgments Online not only involve five categories of criminal, civil, administrative, enforcement and compensation cases but also publish judicial documents in Mongolian, Tibetan, Uyghur, Korean and Kazakh, with a wide range of types and languages. China Court Trial Online has opened trial live broadcasts, trial previews, live reviews, trial recordings, major cases, hotspot rankings, court navigation, data disclosure and other columns to meet the needs of the parties and the public for watching court trial videos at different levels. As of December 20, 2018, live broadcasts and videos of more than 2.2 million cases have been published through the website, and a total of more than 13.5 billion visits have been made to websites across the country. Disclosure of execution-related information to the parties helps to realize the parties' right to know, and also helps to expose the execution work to the public, reduce black-box operations and power rent-seeking, and at the same time strengthen the deterrence of execution. Since the launch of zxgk.court.gov.cn, at present, the site can query national court enforcement case information, information on persons subject to enforcement, information on consumption restrictions, final case information, enforcement legal documents, announcements, enforcement guidelines and other information. In addition, untrustworthy persons subject to enforcement, consumer restrictions, and enforcement disclosure are broadcast on the homepage, which has enhanced the deterrence of enforcement disclosure. As of December 31, 2018, the website has published a total of more than 35.98 million enforcement cases, more than 51.89 million pieces of information on persons subject to enforcement, and more than 9.92 million pieces of information on untrustworthy persons subject to enforcement. The China Judicial Process Information Online is a unified platform of judicial openness that the Supreme People's Court has been striving to build in recent years. At present, the network has achieved full coverage of courts at all levels across the country. Through this network, parties can contact Supreme Court judges, sign documents, and inquire about the progress of cases in courts across the country. In addition, the public can inquire about the institutional settings, disclosure guidelines, judge lists, court openings, roster information, litigation guidelines and other information of most courts across the country through this website and put forward opinions and suggestions, which has become another highlight and business card of judicial disclosure.

In terms of the openness of procuratorial affairs, the Supreme People's Procuratorate has built a nationwide system of case information disclosure to strengthen the openness of procuratorial affairs with case information disclosure as the core.[13] In February 2015, the *Opinions of the Supreme People's Procuratorate on Comprehensively Promoting Public Procuratorial Affairs* was officially promulgated. This opinion puts forward the overall requirements for advancing the disclosure of procuratorial affairs: "It is necessary to focus on strengthening the disclosure of information in the case-handling process, further expand the scope of disclosure of procuratorial affairs, enrich the forms of disclosure of procuratorial affairs, improve the mechanism of procuratorial affairs disclosure, and strengthen the protection of procuratorial affairs disclosure. Improve the effectiveness of procuratorial affairs disclosure, focus on promoting the transformation of procuratorial affairs disclosure work from general affairs disclosure focusing on publicity to case information disclosure, from static disclosure of judicial basis and results to dynamic disclosure of case handling process, and from one-way announcement to two-way disclosure The interactive and open transformation will better protect the people's right to know, participate, express, and supervise the procuratorial work, and continuously improve the affinity, credibility, and satisfaction of the procuratorial organs".[14] The opinion also further clarified the contents, ways and methods of procuratorial affairs publicity, and formulated the requirements for strengthening the construction of procuratorial affairs publicity mechanism and work implementation.

In addition, the *Provisions of the Supreme People's Procuratorate on Implementing the System of Interpreting Laws with Cases by Public Prosecutors (for Trial Implementation)* clearly stipulates that prosecutors shall interpret laws and explain reasoning to litigation participants without delay under circumstances whereby they are required to do so in the course of handling cases; explain the law to the parties and litigation participants, and at the same time deal with cases that may trigger petitions or mass incidents.

6. Promoting Information Construction and Building Smart Justice

The report of the 18th CPC National Congress pointed out that to improve the scientific level of social management, it is necessary to strengthen the construction of social management laws, institutional mechanisms, capabilities, talent teams, and informationization. The 19th CPC National Congress implemented and developed the discourse on informatization of the 18th CPC National Congress and mentioned the importance of informatization in many tasks and in different fields. The

[13]Wang Zhiguo, and Dai Jia, "Procuratorates Legally Protecting Lawyers' Practicing Rights," *Procuratorial Daily*, August 19, 2015, 1st edition.

[14]*Opinions of the Supreme People's Procuratorate on Comprehensively Promoting Public Procuratorial Affairs.*

construction of judicial informatization is a powerful means to ensure openness, transparency, fairness and efficiency of the judiciary, an important way to promote justice for the people, and an important guarantee for the people to feel fairness and justice in every judicial case. In 2016, the construction of the "smart court" was incorporated into the national informatization development strategy and plan, and significant results were achieved in the active response and pioneering and innovative practice of courts at all levels. The full coverage of the court's private network has laid a solid foundation for all-business online processing. Disclosure and litigation service platform construction accelerated the promotion of full-process trial execution elements to be disclosed in accordance with the law, and the provision of intelligent services to judges, litigation participants, the public and government departments achieved initial results. Informatization has made the work of people's courts more convenient and intelligent. Trends and characteristics such as integration, high execution efficiency, openness and normalization, scientific management, and precision decision-making. With the joint efforts of courts at all levels across the country, the main framework of Chinese Court Information 3.0 has been established, the basic pattern of full-service online processing of smart courts has been formed, and the entire process is basically realized in accordance with the law. The direction of all-round intelligent services has been clarified and has shown broad prospects. Advanced information technology has promoted an overall change in the court's trial enforcement methods and has effectively promoted the modernization of the trial system and trial capabilities. After the CPC 18th National Congress, the Supreme People's Procuratorate issued the *Opinions on Deepening the Construction of Smart Procuratorate*, which clarified the development plan for smart prosecution before the end of 2020 and 2025. *National Procuratorate Smart Prosecution Action Guidelines (2018–2020)* propose a roadmap for comprehensively building a new era of smart prosecution ecology by the end of 2020. In recent years, the Ministry of Justice of the PRC has researched and deployed network security and informatization work, such as the construction of a "digital rule of law, smart justice", requiring integration as the theme, maximizing the integration of resources, optimizing resource allocation through information technology, and innovating government services and legal service models. It will let people feel happier and more secure in sharing the achievements of scientific and technological information development.

3.3.4 Judicial Protection of Human Rights

Respecting and safeguarding human rights is one of the basic values in judicature. Strengthening the judicial protection of human rights and tightening supervision over judicial activities were included in the report to the 18th CPC National Congress. The 3rd Plenary Session and the 4th Plenary Session of the 18th CPC Central Committee regarded the improvement of the judicial human rights protection system as an important aspect of judicial reform, and the reform was carried out in the following aspects.

1. Repealing the System of Reeducation Through Labor

The system of reeducation through labor is an administrative punishment measure to deprive citizens of personal freedom for a long time without going through judicial procedures. With the continuous development and progress of democracy, rule of law and human rights in China, the system of reeducation through labor has been increasingly criticized.[15] The *Decision of the CPC Central Committee on Several Major Issues Concerning Comprehensively Deepening the Reform* adopted at the 3rd Plenary Session of the 18th CPC Central Committee clearly stated that the system of reeducation through labor should be repealed. On December 28, 2013, the 6th Session of the Standing Committee of the 12th National People's Congress adopted the *Decision on Repealing Legislation on Reeducation through Labor*, marking the end of the system of reeducation through labor that had been implemented for more than half a century. The repealing of the system of reeducation through labor was generally recognized by all sectors of society and is a major advancement in China's judicial protection of human rights. After this system was repealed, all reeducation-through-labor camps nationwide were transformed into compulsory isolation centers for drug rehabilitation and sites for education and correction of minor criminal offenders.

2. Reforming the Mechanism for Litigation Termination and Itigation-Related Complaints by Letters and Visits

The 4th Plenary Session of the 18th CPC Central Committee proposed implementing the mechanisms to separate litigation from complaints by letters and visits and ensuring that the parties concerned exercise their right to appeal in accordance with the law. For appeals due to dissatisfaction with effective judgments or decisions by judicial organs, a system of representation of appellants by lawyers will be gradually implemented. Appellants unable to hire a lawyer will be brought within the scope of legal aid.

Litigation-related complaints by letters and visits account for a large proportion of complaints by letters and visits and have a serious impact on social order and social stability. To resolve conflicts and disputes within the framework of the rule of law, in March 2014, the General Office of the CPC Central Committee and the Office of the State Council jointly issued the *Opinions on Handling Complaints by Letters and Visits Involving Laws or Litigations in Accordance with the Law*, proposing the general ideas on reforming the working mechanism for complaints by letters and visits involving laws or litigations and handling complaints by letters and visits involving laws or litigations in accordance with the law. That is, judicial and public security organs must change the working methods of frequent centralized

[15]Huang wenyi, "Analysis of the basic principles of China's judicial reform", Law and social development, issue 2, 2017.

assignment, excessive reliance on administrative promotion, and initiation of legal procedures through complaints by letters and visits and solve the problems related to complaints by letters and visits involving laws or litigations on the track of the legal system. The judicial and public security organs should handle these problems and correct law enforcement errors in accordance with the law, protect the legitimate rights and interests of persons making complaints, and stop complaints that disrupt the public order to effectively resolve conflicts concerning complaints by letters and visits and safeguard the legitimate rights and interests of the people and judicial authority. The specific reform measures proposed in the *Opinions* include establishing a system for separating litigations from complaints, establishing a mechanism for introducing complaints by letters and visits involving laws or litigations into judicial procedures, strictly implementing the system for handling complaints in accordance with the law, establishing a legal system for terminating complaints by letters and visits involving laws or litigations, improving the national judicial assistance system, and improving the leadership system and mechanism, etc. It is expected to unblock channels for complaints by letters and visits and enhance judicial credibility through reform measures. To broaden the channels of acceptance and handle complaints under the proper jurisdiction, the Supreme People's Court has also formulated and issued the *Opinions on Further Promoting the Reform of the Work Mechanism for Complaints by Letters and Visits Involving Litigations*, requiring the people's courts to receive visits through the complaint reception halls, accept letters of complaints, and handle complaints online to make smooth the channels for filing complaints by letters and visits. In June 2016, the Supreme People's Court issued *the Opinions on Several Issues concerning People's Courts' Handling of Cases regarding Complaints by Letters and Visits about Enforcement* to offer opinions on the assignment and supervision of the handling of cases regarding complaints by letters and visits about enforcement, the implementation of separation of litigations from complaints by letters and visits and several other issues in a bid to implement the guiding spirits of the CPC Central Committee and the State Council on resolving litigation-related complaints by letters and visits on the track of rule of law, separating litigations from complaints by letters and visits, and establishing and improving the termination system for complaints by letters and visits.

In November 2015, the Committee of Political and Legal Affairs of the CPC Central Committee issued the *Opinions on Establishing a System for Participation in Resolving Cases Regarding Complaints by Letters and Visits Involving Laws or Litigations and Representation of the Complainants by Lawyers (for Trial Implementation)*, which clearly stated that we should give full play to the role for the legal service team in safeguarding the legitimate rights of the people, resolving conflicts and disputes and promoting social harmony and stability, and further reform the system for complaints by letters and visits involving laws or litigation. This reform helps safeguard the legitimate rights and interests of the parties concerned, and it also helps resolve social conflicts, effectively solving the common problem that "the people would rather resort to petitions rather than legal procedures for resolving disputes" to ensure that the judiciary truly becomes the last line of defense to safeguard social fairness and justice.

3. Strengthening Judicial Protection of Disadvantaged Groups

This round of judicial reform focused on strengthening the judicial protection of minors, women, and disabled persons among disadvantaged groups, which is mainly reflected in the following two aspects.

First, procuratorial organs should strengthen the judicial protection of minors. In May 2015, the Supreme People's Procuratorate issued *Eight Measures for Procuratorial Organs to Strengthen the Judicial Protection of Minors*. First, for minors suspected of crimes, we should implement special procedures and regulations such as professional handling, legal aid, social investigations, suitable adult presence, social investigations, family meetings, conditional nonprosecution, social observation and protection, assistance and education, and criminal record sealing etc., to help the minors involved in crimes return to society. Second, we should strengthen the criminal judicial protection of juvenile victims, apply special procedures that better suit the psychological characteristics of juveniles to assist them in accordance with the law, and protect their legitimate rights such as right of privacy and reputation. Third, the procuratorial organs should give procuratorial recommendations and urge the relevant departments to strengthen the protection of left-behind children in rural areas, migrant child beggars in urban and rural areas, and children of prisoners. In March 2016, the *Opinions of the Supreme People's Procuratorate on Strengthening the Professionalization of Juvenile Procuratorial Work* was issued. It states that prosecuting departments specializing in cases involving minors should implement an integrated work mode of "arrest, prosecution, supervision, and prevention," require provincial-level people's procuratorates to establish prosecuting departments specializing in cases involving minors before the end of 2016 and urges prefecture-level people's procuratorates and basic-level people's procuratorates in areas where cases involving minors have occurred frequently to establish prosecuting departments specializing in cases involving minors. It clarifies that prosecutorial departments specializing in cases involving minors should not take punishment, conviction and sentencing and dispute settlement as the ultimate goal but should explore the causes of problems, carry out necessary interventions, improve their psychological conditions, family education and social environment, and help minors with difficulties return to society. Minors Prosecution is for the purpose of protecting their rights and interests, preventing re-commitment of crime, and offering assistance and education, prosecutorial departments specializing in cases involving minors undertake social functions such as assistance, education and crime prevention. We should establish a special evaluation mechanism for prosecution involving minors cases and set up a reasonable list of prosecutor quotas and powers of prosecuting departments specializing in cases involving minors.

Second, the judicial organs should disclose typical cases to strengthen the judicial protection of several types of vulnerable groups, such as minors, women, children, and the disabled. The Supreme People's Procuratorate has disclosed typical cases to strengthen judicial protection of minors from the aspects of protection of minors involved in crimes or victimized minors and severe punishment of crimes against minors. The Supreme People's Court has disclosed typical cases to severely punish violations of the rights of women and children and typical cases of judicial protection for thc disabled to strengthen judicial protection of them.

4. Regulating the Examination of Custody Necessity

The *Provisions on the Handling of Cases about Examination of Custody Necessity by People's Procuratorates (for Trial Implementation)* issued by the Supreme People's Procuratorate in January 2016 requires that the procuratorial department of criminal execution of the people's procuratorate may adopt a public examination handling method and set specific criteria for score addition or subtraction, and rejection items based on the factors such as criminal facts, subjective malignancy, behavior of repentance, physical conditions, case progress, possible penalties, and whether there is any risk of harming society again, etc. of the arrested criminal suspect or defendant and adopt quantitative methods as the reference for comprehensive assessment of custody necessity. The *Provisions* enumerates 16 circumstances in which the case-handling organ should or may release the criminal suspect or defendant or change the compulsory measure and promptly notify the applicant in writing of the examination opinions. If continued custody is unnecessary, the people's procuratorate shall suggest that the case-handling organ should release the criminal suspect or defendant or change the compulsory measure. This is of great significance to safeguarding the legitimate rights and interests of arrested criminal suspects or defendants.

5. Improving the Legal Aid System

Legal aid is conducive to safeguarding the legitimate rights and interests of the parties concerned, ensuring the correct enforcement of laws, safeguarding social fairness and justice, effectively resolving social conflicts, and maintaining harmony and stability.

The 12th Meeting of the Central Leading Group for Comprehensively Deepening the Reform adopted the *Opinions on Improving the Legal Aid System*, pointing out that legal aid is an important undertaking related to people's livelihood. First, regarding criminal cases, it requires providing legal aid to more parties, carrying out trial work in criminal appeal cases and speedy trial procedures, establishing a working mechanism for participating in handling cases regarding criminal reconciliation and death penalty review, establishing a duty lawyer system, and establishing and improving mechanisms for notification of defense. Second, regarding civil administrative cases, it requires expanding the coverage of legal aid to gradually include labor security, marriage and family, food and drugs, education and medical care and other matters closely related to people's livelihood; gradually relaxing the criteria for identifying financial difficulties and lowering legal aid thresholds to gradually expand the coverage of legal aid to low-income groups; and exploring to establish a system for participation and representation of petitioners by lawyers in petition cases. Third, it requires focusing on providing legal aid to groups such as migrant workers, laid-off workers, women, minors, the elderly, the disabled, and servicemen and their family members. Fourth, it requires achieving full coverage of legal aid consulting services.

6. Protecting Litigation Rights and Implementing a Case Filing Registration System

The 4th Plenary Session of the 18th CPC Central Committee proposed reforming the system for case acceptance by courts and changing the case-filing review system to the case-filing registration system. For cases that shall be accepted by People's Courts for processing in accordance with law, they shall be filed as long as they are in existence, and the suits in them shall be processed as long as they are in existence to protect the right of action of the parties concerned. Meanwhile, we will increase the intensity of punishment for false and malicious litigation and acts of unreasonably vexatious litigation.

In April 2015, the 11th meeting of the Central Leading Group for Comprehensively Deepening the Reform adopted the *Opinions on Promoting the Reform of the Case Filing Registration System of the People's Courts*, proposing to change the system for case acceptance by courts from the case filing review system to the case filing registration system and increase the intensity of punishment for false and malicious litigation. The *Provisions of the Supreme People's Court on Several Issues Concerning the Registration and Filing of Cases by the People's Courts* issued in the same month requires prohibiting the circumstances involving violation of law or discipline such as not receiving the complaint for a lawsuit or private prosecution, not issuing a written document after receiving for a lawsuit or private prosecution, neither filing a case that should be file nor making a ruling or decision etc.

While implementing the case filing registration system, supporting systems should also be established. First, we should improve diversified dispute settlement mechanisms such as mediation, arbitration, administrative adjudication, administrative reconsideration, and litigation. Second, we should establish and improve pretrial preparation procedures to promote efficient settlement of disputes through mediation, reconciliation, speedy trial, and judgment.

After implementing the case filing registration system, the parties' right to prosecution is fully safeguarded, the phenomena that a case should be filed was not filed and the filing of a case is under the control of some organizations or individuals were eliminated, and difficulties in filing cases were significantly eased. In 2015, when the case filing registration system was introduced, the courts across the country accepted 19.527 million cases, and the year-on-year increase in newly accepted and concluded cases reached a record high, of which the number of accepted cases increased by 24. 68%. In 2016, the courts across the country accepted a total of 23.056 million cases, an increase of 18.07% year-on-year, and the rate of case registration on the spot reached 95%. However, the case filing registration system has also caused a rapid increase in the number of court cases. Some parties abused their right of action. The cases that did not comply with the procedural law and should not be accepted by the courts also flooded to the courts in large numbers, resulting in high pressure on judicial resources.

3.4 Outlook of the Judicial Reform

To date, the measures of the latest round of judicial reform in China have been fully rolled out and implemented. In the future, judicial reform will focus more on the implementation and supervision of various judicial reform measures. In the future, China's judicial reform will advance continuously, and judicial reform will further develop in the direction of depth, breadth and institutionalization.

3.4.1 Consolidating the Achievements of Reform

To ensure that judicial activities are more in line with judicial laws, bold breakthroughs have been made in some measures of the latest round of judicial reform on the basis of the original laws and regulations. For example, in judicial delocalization, a key point of the judicial reform is to push forward the unified management of personnel, funds and properties of judicial organs below the provincial level, which conflicts with the relevant provisions of the Chinese *Constitution*, the *Organic Law of the People's Courts*, and the *Organic Law of the People's Procuratorates*. This is manifested in the conflict between the provincial-level management of personnel, funds and properties and the mode of appointment and removal of the National People's Congress. The selection committees for judges and prosecutors established during the quota system reform to strengthen the professional security of judicial personnel and the disciplinary committees for judges and prosecutors established to implement the judicial accountability system were not specified in the original *Organic Law of the People's Courts*, *Organic Law of the People's Procuratorates*, *Judges Law* and *Prosecutors Law*. Some good practices and experiences in the reform should also be fixed in the form of legislation or law amendments. For example, the current measures to ensure the courts and procuratorates to exercise judicial power independently and strengthen the guarantee the security of judicial personnel in lawfully performance of their duties are only specified in the documents of the General Office of the CPC Central Committee and the General Office of the State Council.

The *Organic Law of the People's Courts* and the *Organic Law of the People's Procuratorates* have been amended now, and the amendments to the *Judges Law* and the *Prosecutors Law* are also in full swing. When amending the abovementioned laws, we should follow the direction and path of judicial system reform determined by the 18th CPC National Congress and the 4th Plenary Session of the

18th CPC Central Committee, fully absorb the results of this round of judicial reform, and fix the mature contents of the results in the form of law amendments. For example, the *Provisions on Protection of Judicial Personnel in Lawful Performance of Their Legal Duties* and other documents have breakthrough provisions on in job security and personal security for judges. The important contents that have been gradually promoted in practice in this judicial reform, such as the quota system for judges, the selection committee of judges, the specialist job ranks and salary systems for judges, and the disciplinary committee for judges, etc., are fixed through amendments to the laws. Some conflicts with the basic legal system can also be discussed and amended at the level of the *Constitution*. For example, court presidents and chief prosecutors will be appointed and removed of office by the standing committees of provincial people's congresses rather than by local people's congresses and their standing committees. The voting system of the work reports of courts and procuratorates will be replaced by the recall system in which those who fail to meet the qualification requirements will be dismissed. Meanwhile, China's *Civil Servants Law* should also be amended to separate judges and prosecutors from the ranks of civil servants and free them from the management of administrative departments.[16]

3.4.2 Adopting Detailed Implementation Measures for the Reform

Although various judicial reform measures have been fully rolled out and a series of policies, documents and regulations have been issued, many judicial reform measures still need to be further implemented and refined.

First, although there are principled provisions on some systems, specific operating measures and implementation guarantees have not yet been formulated. This requires formulating guarantee measures in the next step to ensure the effectiveness of the reform measures.

In judicial reforms, we cannot rest on our laurels indefinitely once existing problems are solved. The latest round of judicial reform starting at the 18th CPC National Congress has made great strides in promoting independent exercise of judicial power, bringing the exercise of judicial power more in line with judicial laws, and striving to achieve fairness and justice. Some problems and challenges appearing in the reform need to be gradually resolved through continuously deepening the reform, creating a judicial environment that guarantees the independent exercise of judicial power, improving laws and regulations, and implementing reform responsibilities. The report to the 19th CPC National Congress

[16]Chen Weidong and Zheng Bo, "Judicial Reform: Issues and Prospects," published in *The Blue Book on the Rule of Law: Report on Development of the Rule of Law in China No. 13 (2015)* edited by Li Lin and Tian He, Social Sciences Academic Press (China), 2015.

proposed carrying out comprehensive and integrated reform of the judicial system and enforcing judicial accountability in all respects so that the people can see in every judicial case that justice is served. This puts forward new expectations and requirements for judicial reform and gives the direction of development of the entire judicial system. In the future, China's judicial system is expected to move one step further towards the goal of fairness, transparency, honesty and high efficiency.

Chapter 4
The Rule of Law in Civil and Commercial Matters: Building the Cornerstone for Safeguarding Rights

Hongfei Xie and Xiaoxiong Xia

4.1 Overview of the Rule of Law in Civil and Commercial Matters in China

China's civil law system mainly regulates two types of basic social relations: personal relations and property relations. The areas it regulates mainly include marriage, family and market areas. The first law promulgated by the PRC was the 1950 *Marriage Law*, which confirmed the fruits of the most successful revolution in Chinese society—the family revolution. In 1985, the *Inheritance Law* was promulgated. This kind of legislative pattern made the law of identity relations stay outside civil law and placed the focus of the development of Chinese civil law on property law. The *General Principles of Civil Law* promulgated in 1986 awakened for the first time the modern concept of rights in China as a vast country, and the rule of law genes such as equality and freedom were deeply rooted in the hearts of the people, which was of epoch-making significance. After the establishment of the market economy system in 1992, China's reforms can be roughly summarized as a see-saw process between the state and the market. The overall trend was that state power was gradually withdrawn from the market, but so far, there is still some distance from striking a balance between state regulation and market autonomy. The basic context of the development of Chinese civil law is also to gradually establish and improve the legal rules of the market economy, and its basic spirit is to protect property rights and promote private law autonomy.

Since the 1990s, China has continuously improved its civil law system. Presently, China's civil and commercial law system has been basically established, with 34 civil and commercial laws promulgated. In the field of property relations,

H. Xie (✉) · X. Xia
Institute of Law, CASS, Beijing, China

H. Tian and Y. Lv (eds.), *The Chinese Path of Rule of Law Construction*,
China Insights, https://doi.org/10.1007/978-981-16-4130-5_4

the *Guaranty Law*, the *Land Contracting Law*, the *Contract Law*, the *Real Right Law* and the *Tort Liability Law* have been promulgated, and the civil laws in the field of market economy have been fully established. In the field of personal relations, the *Marriage Law* and the *Adoption Law* have been revised, and judicial interpretations and some laws and regulations involving marriage, family relations and personality rights have also set the complete rules in this field. The 4th Plenary Session of the 18th CPC Central Committee proposed compiling a civil code. In 2015, China started to compile the *General Provisions of Civil Law*. In 2017, the foundation of the compilation of the Civil Code—the *General Provisions of Civil Law*—was promulgated, which was of milestone significance. This indicates that China has taken the most important step in compiling the civil code. China will soon have its own civil code, and China's "Civil Code Dream" would soon come true.

A market economy is an economy under the rule of law. The development of a market economy requires that commercial activities be carried out under the rule of law, and especially in the aspects of protecting property rights, upholding contracts, unified markets, fair exchange, fair competition and effective supervision, the commercial law system must be improved. Without a sound legal system for commercial matters, there will be no effective development of the market economy.

Looking back at the history of the development of commercial law in Western countries, we can find that the development and prosperity of commercial law has a crucial impact on economic development. In the cities on the Mediterranean coasts in the Middle Ages, it was precisely the relatively sound commercial legal system that had promoted the development of maritime trade and the prosperity of commercial transactions. During the period of absolute monarchy, the commercial prosperity of the maritime powers was also attributed to their comparatively sound commercial legal systems. With the development of the industrial revolution, the commercial laws of European countries were further codified, and the rules of commercial law were further improved. In particular, the development of legal systems for corporations, bankruptcy, insurance, and negotiable instruments provided strong guarantees for the development of commercial trade and the advancement of industrial production, promoting the economic development of these countries. In the twentieth century, with technological advancement and innovation, a large number of new types of commercial transactions and commercial entities emerged, and the systems and institutions of commercial law were further enriched and developed. The United States was leading the world in this respect. Its well-developed corporate law, securities law, bankruptcy law and other legal systems have supported the rapid development of the US economy. The US commercial law system has also exerted extensive influence worldwide. It goes without saying that the development of the market economy is inseparable from the guarantee of the rule of law in commercial matters. Commercial law itself has a certain degree of internationality and convergence. The rule of law in commercial matters in economically developed countries and regions often has a leading position, and it often has an important impact on other countries and regions.

The development history of Chinese commercial law is not long. At the end of the Qing Dynasty and the early years of the Republic of China, China tried to introduce the commercial legal system in the Western sense, formulated basic commercial laws such as corporate law, insurance law, bankruptcy law, and negotiable instruments law, and introduced the terminology system and institutional structure of commercial law. In this way, the commercial law system in the Western sense took root in China, and the ideas of commercial law were born and bred. During the period of the Republic of China, the commercial law system was further improved, and corporate law, bankruptcy law, insurance law, negotiable instruments law and other systems became mature. After the founding of the PRC, with the abolition of all six laws enacted by the previous regime, the original commercial legislation was basically abandoned. Since the reform and opening up, with the gradual transformation of the planned economic system to the market economic system and the practical needs of reform and opening up, China has reconstructed a relatively sound commercial law system. From the early institutional exploration to the formulation of corporate law, insurance law, bankruptcy law, negotiable instruments law, securities law, maritime law, trust law, partnerships law and other separate commercial laws since the 1990s, a relatively sound commercial law system that met the development needs of market economy had basically been formed. The development of the commercial legal system plays an important role in guaranteeing the development of the market economy and the advancement of reform and opening up in China. The establishment of the commercial law system provides a normative basis for regulating various commercial behaviors of business entities, confirming the legality of various business activities and settling various commercial disputes in a timely manner. This is an important institutional basis for the success of China's economic and social development in the past 40 years since the reform and opening up.

4.2 The Rule of Law in Personal Relationship

After 1949, the *Marriage Law* was the first law enacted in the rule of law in civil matters in China. Since the 1950s, China's *Marriage Law* has established the principles of freedom of marriage, equality between men and women, and monogamy and has good implementation effects. The 1980 *Marriage Law* reiterated these principles. In 1998, in response to the influence of social development on marriage, China revised the *Marriage Law*. The key points of the amendments include the following: first, it specified the circumstances in which marriage is invalid or dissolved, including committing bigamy; second, it improved the marital property system; third, it improved the provisions on divorce, listing the legal reasons for divorce in detail.

In terms of judicial interpretations, the Supreme Court has issued a total of three important judicial interpretations. The *Interpretations on Several Issues Regarding the Application of the Marriage Law of the People's Republic of China (I)* (2001) is the first systematic judgment experience summary made 20 years after the promulgation of the *Marriage Law*, focusing on interpreting the main legal application issues in case trials. In 2003, the Supreme People's Court issued the *Interpretations on Several Issues Regarding the Application of the Marriage Law of the People's Republic of China (II)*, which focused on typical legal disputes in trials in family matters, tried to respond to the new challenges brought by social changes to the application of law, and further clarified issues such as invalidity of marriage, identification of community property of spouses, division of property at the time of divorce, and handling of debts. The *Interpretations on Several Issues Regarding the Application of the Marriage Law of the People's Republic of China (III)* (2011) gives interpretations on issues concerning paternity testing, reproductive rights, intramarital loans or property division, and determination of ownership of immovable property purchased by spouses or their parents. It is worth mentioning that Article 7 stipulates that immovable property purchased by a spouse's parents for that spouse during a couple's marriage, if the property right is registered in the recipient spouse's name, may be deemed a gift to that spouse and s that spouse's separate property; in the case of immovable property purchased by the parents of both spouses, where the property right is registered under the name of one spouse, the immovable property may be regarded as community property according to the share of the contribution made by each spouse's parents, unless otherwise agreed upon by the spouses. This provision has caused heated controversy. One ground for objection is that this provision violates the Chinese people's view of marriage and family: "The affect of relatives and family relations are more reliable than an agreement. The righteous things forming over thousands of years will live longer than the law."[1]

4.3 The Rule of Law in Civil Property Matters

4.3.1 Contracts

A very important notion in China's *Contract Law* is to encourage transactions. Legislators believe that the more transactions are successfully concluded, the more benefits they will bring to the state, society, and contractual subjects. The state will increase its fiscal revenue; funds and goods will be fully circulated thanks to the contracts, and resources will be fully utilized; the contractual subjects will also obtain benefits from the contracts. The starting point of the *Contract Law* is to encourage transactions, that is, to encourage the parties to conclude contracts and make them effective and fully performed. Encouraging transactions is reflected in many legal systems and rules. For example, a contract can be concluded in written, oral, and behavioral forms (a contract is concluded through behaviors); the scope of

[1]Zhao Xiaoli, "Backfeeding Model and Marriage Law," *Legal Daily*, August 20, 2011, 7th edition.

invalid and revocable contracts is minimized; and the applicable scope of contract rescission is limited.

In the year when the *Contract Law* was promulgated, the Supreme People's Court issued the *Interpretations on Several Issues Concerning the Application of Contract Law of the People's Republic of China (I)*. It involves not only issues concerning the application of the Contract Law such as the retroactive effect but also the interpretation of specific rules, especially new rules, such as the right of subrogation and revocation for creditors. Since then, the Supreme People's Court has successively issued judicial interpretations on specific contract areas, such as the *Interpretations on Several Issues Concerning the Application of Law in the Trial of Cases Involving Commercial Housing Sales Contract Disputes* (2003), the *Interpretations on the Application of Law in the Trial of Cases Involving Disputes over Construction Contracts for Construction Projects* (2004), the *Interpretations on Several Issues Concerning the Application of Law in the Trial of Cases Involving Technical Contract Disputes* (2004), the *Interpretations on Several Issues Concerning the Application of Law in the Trial of Cases Involving Contract Disputes over State-owned Land Use Rights* (2005), the *Interpretations on Several Issues Concerning the Application of Several Law in the Trial of Cases Involving Urban House Rental Contract Disputes* (2009), and the *Interpretations on Several Issues Concerning the Application of Law in the Trial of Cases Involving Sales Contract Disputes* (2012), etc. The judicial interpretations of the Supreme People's Court have not only improved the contract rules but also cleverly avoided the impact of certain unreasonable administrative controls on economic life based on the situation of social and economic development and expanded the scope of application of contract freedom. The most typical example is that in 2015, the Supreme People's Court legalized private lending to a certain extent from the perspective of judicial trials and indirectly confirmed the legality of some part of China's informal finance. Based on various social policy considerations, it adopted the objective adjustment method of "two lines and three zones" (annual interest rate between 24 and 36%) for private loan interest rates. It has alleviated the two major problems that have existed since China's reform and opening up: high household savings, but almost no way to get money invested; difficulties and high-cost of financing for small- and medium-sized enterprises.

4.3.2 Land Contracting

Rural land contracting is arguably one of the most important issues in rural areas in China. Although the Chinese Constitution and other laws have relevant provisions on the rural land contracting system, there was a lack of detailed legal norms to adjust it. In practice, it was not rare that farmers' land contract rights were not effectively safeguarded and were even arbitrarily violated. To solve this problem, China promulgated the *Law on Contracting of Rural Land* in 2002. It grants farmers long-term and guaranteed right to right to rural land contractual management in the form of law and establishes provisions on many detailed issues concerning land contracting, embodying the spirit of the 3rd Plenary Session of the 15th CPC Central Committee. It has great practical and far-reaching historical significance in effectively safeguarding the legitimate rights and interests of farmers, further mobilizing the enthusiasm of farmers, promoting agricultural and rural economic development, and maintaining rural social stability.[2] Article 4 of the *Law on Contracting of Rural Land* clearly stipulates that the State protects the long-term stability of the relationships of the contracting of rural land. Article 20 stipulates that the duration of a contract for cultivated land shall be 30 years. The duration of a contract for grassland shall be between 30 and 50 years. The duration of a contract for forestland shall be between 30 and 70 years. The duration of a contract for special forestland may be extended upon approval of forestry administration departments under the State Council. Meanwhile, in response to infringement on women's rights in rural land contracting, Article 6 specifically stipulates that men and women shall have equal rights to contract rural land. The women's lawful rights to land contracts shall be protected. No organizations or individuals shall exploit or infringe upon the right to operate contracted land that women shall enjoy. To safeguard the right to contractual management of rural land, it also clearly stipulates the party that undertakes the contract shall acquire the right to operate the contracted land when the contract becomes effective; within the duration of the contract, the party that lets the contract shall not withdraw the contracted land or readjust the contracted land. However, the *Rural Land Contracting Law* did not clarify whether the nature of farmers' right to the operation of contracted land is a kind of real right or a kind of creditor's right. This issue was resolved by the subsequent *Real Right Law*.

4.3.3 Real Rights

The promulgation of the *Real Right Law* was a milestone event in the civil rule of law in 2007. In the process of its promulgation, great controversies arose from all walks of life in society, and some even wrote to the central government that the draft was unconstitutional. Although notions such as "those who have permanent property have perseverance" and "when the granaries are full, the people follow appropriate rules of conduct" have been deeply rooted in the hearts of the people, and it is also recognized by the public that the definition of real right is important to the country, society and individuals, the promulgation of the *Real Right Law* has also exposed many social contradictions and demands of different interest groups in China since the reform and opening up, supporters and opponents clashed fiercely

[2]"Safeguarding the Lawful Rights and Interests of the Parties to the Land Contracts to Maintain the Long-Term Stability of the Party's Basic Rural Policies—Answers by Liu Jian, Deputy Minister of Agriculture, to Questions from the Reporter of the Journal on Issues Related to the Rural Land Contract Law," *Newsletter About Work in Rural Areas*, Issue 1, 2002.

over the draft.[3] The *Real Right Law* also set a record for the number of deliberations in the legislative history of the People's Republic of China: the NPC Standing Committee carried out seven rounds of deliberation on the draft real right law, plus one round of deliberation by the NPC, totaling eight rounds of deliberations. The legislature fully coordinated the opinions of all parties, and the NPC also fully deliberated and made amendments.[4] The *Real Right Law* is of great significance in improving the rules of China's market economy, strengthening the protection of private property, advancing law-based government administration, and promoting political progress. It also helps to promote the promulgation of the civil code.

In 2016, after 9 years of deliberation and precipitation, the Supreme People's Court adopted the *Interpretations on Several Issues Concerning the Application of the Real Right Law of the People's Republic of China (I)*. It is the outcome of judicial experience and practical rationality since the promulgation of the *Real Right Law*, which eliminates ambiguities or discrepancies in the trial of various cases involving real rights. The interpretations cover many aspects of the real right system, such as the effectiveness of forenotice registration and demurrer registration, statutory changes in real rights, requirements for changes in real rights, right of first refusal and bona fide acquisition system, etc. For example, Article 2 stipulates that "Where a party has evidence that the information recorded in a register of immovable property is inconsistent with the true status of a right and the party is the true holder of the real right in the immovable, the party's request for confirmation of the party's real right in the immovable shall be supported." This has changed the wrong practice that the real estate register is deemed equal to the only basis for confirmation of right.

Although the *Real Right Law* specifies a unified real estate registration system, because unified real estate registration involves administrative management systems and many other factors, it has encountered many difficulties in the enforcement process and has advanced slowly in practice. To completely solve the problem of unified registration of real estate and establish a unified registration authority, unified registration basis, unified real estate register, etc., the State Council issued the *Interim Regulations on Real Estate Registration* in 2014. It defines real estate registration as the act of recording real estate ownership and other statutory matters in the real estate register by the real estate registration authority in accordance with the law. Real estate means land, sea area and fixtures such as buildings and woods. The state applies a uniform registration system for real estate. The competent department of land and resources of the State Council shall direct and supervise real estate registration across the country. Presently, the unified registration of urban housing and real estate in China has basically been completed.

[3]For related controversies, see Tong Zhiwei's "How the *Real Right Law* (Draft) Makes Use of the Constitutional Gate—Comments on the Controversies over Unconstitutional and Constitutional Interpretations Arising from An Open Letter," *Open Journal of Legal Science*, Issue 3, 2006.

[4]Chen Liping, "Real Right Law is Coming in the World's Concern," *The People's Congress of China*, Issue 4, 2017.

Although the *Real Right Law* specifies the principle of property rights protection, in practice, there exist problems such as insufficient protection (especially the frequent occurrence of improper infringements by state power) of property rights, especially insufficient protection of private property rights, and failure to implement equal protection. To this end, on November 4, 2016, the CPC Central Committee and the State Council issued the *Opinions on Improving the Property Rights Protection System and Protecting Property Rights in accordance with the Law*, clearly stating that the property rights system is the foundation of the socialist market economy and protecting property rights is the inevitable requirement of adherence to the basic socialist economic system. Whoever has permanent property is firmly confident. The effective guarantee and realization of the property rights of economic entities are the foundation of the sustainable and sound development of the economy and society. It requires further improving the modern property rights system, advancing the legislation of protection of property rights, and embodying the notion of rule of law in all aspects and parts such as legislation, law enforcement, justice and law observation with regard to protection of property rights.

4.3.4 Torts

Tort means that the acts that the actor illegally infringes upon personal rights and property rights of others intentionally or by fault and should assume civil liability in accordance with the law, and other acts that cause damages for which the actor should assume civil liability in accordance with the special provisions of the law. Prior to the enactment of the *Tort Liability Law*, the provisions of the *General Principles of Civil Law* concerning tort acts were the main basis for judgment in the field of tort law. In 2009, the 11th Session of the Standing Committee of the 11nth National People's Congress adopted the *Tort Liability Law*, which is the first separate law in the field of civil torts in China. Its promulgation also means that the basic system of China's civil legal system has been established.

After the *Tort Liability Law* was enacted, the Supreme People's Court adopted the *Notice on Several Issues Concerning the Application of Tort Liability Law of the People's Republic of China* (2010), clarifying how the *Tort Liability Law* should be applied in judicial practice. Since then, the Supreme People's Court has issued a series of judicial interpretations to clarify the adjudication rules for special tort disputes, including the *Regulations on Several Issues Concerning the Application of Law in the Trial of Cases Involving Tourism Disputes* (2010), the *Interpretations on Several Issues Concerning the Application of Law in the Trial of Cases Involving for Railway Transport Personal Injury Compensation Disputes* (2010), the *Regulations on Several Issues on the Trial of Cases Involving Ship Oil Pollution Compensation Disputes* (2011), the *Interpretations on Several Issues Concerning the Application of Law in the Trial of Cases Involving Road Traffic Accident Damage Compensation Disputes* (2012), the *Regulations on Several Issues of the Application of Law in the Trial of Cases Involving Civil Disputes over*

Infringement on Personal Rights and Interests Using Information Networks (2014), and the *Interpretations on Several Issues Concerning the Application of Law in the Trial of Cases Involving Environmental Tort Liability Disputes* (2015). In addition, regarding the public interest litigation stipulated in the new *Civil Procedure Law*, the Supreme People's Court adopted the *Interpretations on Several Issues Concerning the Application of Law in the Trial of Cases Involving Environmental Civil Public Interest Litigation* (2015) and the *Interpretations on Several Issues Concerning the Application of Law in the Trial of Cases Involving Consumer Civil Public Interest Litigation* (2016).

4.4 Compilation of the Civil Code

The 4th Plenary Session of the 18th CPC Central Committee proposed compiling a civil code. Since 2015, China has initiated the compilation of the *General Provisions of Civil Law* because it is the opening chapter of the Civil Code and lacks existing separate laws. After 1949, China successively initiated the compilation of the civil code four times, but all ended in failure due to immature conditions. Based on the experience of the comparative method, the compilation of civil code should be supported by at least political will, market economy, rights culture, and civil law theory. Otherwise, even if the civil code is reluctantly promulgated, it could hardly be truly enacted. In 2017, the *General Provisions of Civil Law* as the foundation for compiling the civil code was promulgated. This indicates that China is about to enter the era of civil code and the era when China did not have its civil code as a vast country has gone forever.

Among various chapters of the Civil Code, the *General Provisions of Civil Law* is the opening chapter and plays a leading role in the Civil Code. It is most difficult to compile the *General Provisions of Civil Law* because it extracts the common rules of the individual chapters of the Civil Code, with the most abstract contents. 它规定 It stipulates the basic principles and general rules to be followed in civil activities and governs the other chapters of the Civil Code. Each chapter gives specific and operable provisions for various civil systems on the basis of the general provisions. It is based on the *General Principles of Civil Law* enacted in 1986, adopts the method of "extracting common factors," and incorporates universally applicable and leading contents in the civil law system into the general provisions.[5] In addition, it also depicts the values and basic principles of the entire Civil Code, constituting the cornerstone of the entire Civil Code. On the basis of the *General Principles of Civil Law* and other separate laws, the *General Provisions of Civil Law* conforms to the social reality of the dual transformation of the country and society since the reform and opening up, meets the new requirements of China's

[5]Li Shishi, "The General Provisions of Civil Law is the Basic Law for Establishing and Improving the Basic Civil System," *The People's Congress of China*, Issue 4, 2017.

national and social governance, and responds to the new challenges to laws in technological and economic development. It has many new bright spots in the value concept and institutional system.

The *General Provisions of Civil Law* highlights the important characteristics of Chinese society and reflects the efforts of legislators to respond to social needs. First, it highlights the characteristics of the Internet society in the era when the Chinese Civil Code was formulated. For example, in response to the frequent infringement on personal information in practice, Article 111 clearly stipulates that the personal information of natural persons shall be protected by the law. Any organization or individual shall legally obtain the personal information of other persons when necessary and ensure the safety of such personal information, and shall not illegally collect, use, process or transmit the personal information of other persons, or illegally buy or sell, provide or make public the personal information of other persons. Article 127 also provides provisions on the protection of data and virtual network properties. Second, it responds to the reality of Chinese society's transition from a rural society to a market economy society and emphasizes the integration of civil and commercial laws in legislative technology. For example, it recognizes that business practices can be a source of law and classifies legal persons as profit-making legal persons and nonprofit legal persons. Finally, it responds to the reality that both the country and society are stronger after the dual transformation of the state and society since 1978 and emphasizes the legal protection of disadvantaged groups, such as minors and adults, who cannot fully judge or cannot judge their own behavior. For example, in the field of guardianship, compassionating orphans and the elderly is regarded as an aiding obligation of the state and society.

In terms of values and notions, it takes the protection of private rights, respect for autonomy, protection of the disadvantaged, respect for morality, and care for the environment as its basic notions. To a certain extent, it has broken through the value system of traditional private law and laid a value foundation for the entire civil code. There are two aspects worth mentioning.

4.4.1 Protection of Private Rights

The notion of protecting private rights in the *General Provisions of Civil Law* is first embodied in legislative purposes and basic principles. It takes protecting the legitimate rights and interests of civil subjects as its legislative purpose (Article 1). Article 3 further clarifies the principle of private rights protection, that is, personal rights, property rights and other lawful rights and interests of civil subjects shall be protected by the law; no organization or individual may infringe upon such lawful rights and interests. The draft of the *General Provisions of Civil Law (Draft)* for the 4th round of deliberation places this principle in Article 9. When the *General Provisions of Civil Law (Draft)* was deliberated on the 5th Session of the 12th National Peoples Congress, some deputies proposed that protecting private rights is the basic spirit of civil law, and its status should be highlighted.[6] The *General Provisions of Civil Law* then regards the protection of private rights as the primary principle of the Civil Code, showing that the protection of private rights is the basic spirit of civil law and one of the basic principles of civil law.

Following the *General Principles of Civil Law*, the *General Provisions of Civil Law* also devotes a special chapter to "Civil Rights," which specifies various rights of civil subjects to construct a complete civil rights system, including various personality rights, real rights, creditors' rights, intellectual property rights, right to inheritance and rights based on kinship. Compared with the *General Principles of Civil Law*, the *General Provisions of Civil Law* provides more comprehensive provisions on civil rights. In the field of personality rights, it specifies the general personality rights of natural persons, namely, personal freedom and personal dignity (Article 109), and adds special personality rights such as the rights to body and privacy on the basis of the *General Principles of Civil Law*. It is worth mentioning that it regards the information rights of natural persons as an independent civil right for the first time. In the field of property rights, it includes rights to data and network virtual property, intellectual property rights, equity and other investment rights into property rights for the first time. This not only enriches the contents of civil rights but also highlights the status of the civil code as the basic private law.

The *General Provisions of Civil Law* not only expands the scope of civil rights but also increases the intensity of protection of civil rights. First, on the basis of the *Real Right Law*, Article 113 clearly stipulates that the property rights of civil subjects shall receive equal protection under the law. This eliminates the hierarchical order of property rights, equity, and intellectual property rights enjoyed by different civil subjects and puts them under equal protection of the law. It alleviates the unequal legal status of state-owned property rights, collective property rights, and private property rights, strengthens the protection of private property rights and promotes the formation of a property rights culture that respects wealth. Second, the protection intensity of civil rights in the *General Provisions of Civil Law* has also strengthened on the basis of separate civil laws. Article 130 stipulates that "Civil subjects shall, at their own will, exercise civil rights in accordance with the law without interference. "Without interference" here means freedom from interference by other civil subjects and freedom from interference by public power." Paragraph 2 of Article 179 stipulates that "Where the law contains provisions on punitive compensation, such provisions shall apply." This is the first time that a Chinese law has established general provisions on punitive compensation, which has reserved legal space for establishing more punitive compensation rules in the Civil Code. It can give full play to the function of deterring the intentional infringement of civil rights and reflects the new notion that modern civil laws emphasize the preventive function. In other statutory law countries, punitive compensation is rarely recognized because it breaks through the "make-someone-whole principle" of civil

[6]Yang Lixin, "General Provisions of Civil Law: A Bright Embodiment of Contemporary Rule of Law," *Beijing Daily*, March 20, 2017, 13th edition.

liability (that is, the scope of compensation depends on the scope of legal losses). Finally, Article 187 once again reiterates the notion of "priority in civil liability," including two aspects: first, where a civil subject shall bear civil liability, administrative liability and criminal liability simultaneously for a single act, the administrative liability or criminal liability borne does not affect the civil liability to be borne; second, where the civil subject's property is insufficient to cover the payment, the property shall be used in the first place for civil liability purposes.

Finally, to strengthen the protection of private rights, the *General Provisions of the Civil Law* also devotes a special chapter to civil liabilities as a remedy for civil rights. Therefore, China's civil law is constructed with legal relations as the core, and its logical main line is "civil rights-civil obligations-civil liabilities."[7] This style specifies the consequences of non-performance of civil obligations and infringement of rights and helps to increase the predictability of the actors' own behaviour to make them abandon behaviour that violates their obligations or infringes on the rights of others.

4.4.2 Ecological Protection

One of the stubborn problems of traditional civil law is that it neglects ecological protection, and as the legal basis of free capitalism, its notion of freedom of contract and respect for property rights has also created a social atmosphere that encourages people to chase profits and extract more resources from the environment. Arguably, traditional civil law based on liberalism cannot accommodate the notion of ecological protection. Because of this, some scholars have advocated the notion of "environmental citizenship" and placed it in the perspective of liberal political theory, especially contemporary global political liberalism, to correct the environmental protection problem that cannot be accommodated by liberalism.[8] The only means of traditional civil law for environmental protection is to define violations of the environment as torts and specify the liability for compensation of the actor.

A major innovation of the *General Provisions of the Civil Law* is the establishment of the principle of ecological protection. Article 9 stipulates that "All civil subjects engaging in civil activities shall help save resources and protect the ecological environment." In addition, Article 119 does not list the provision of "Restoring the ecological environment" in the draft separately as a form of civil liability, but the intention of the legislators is to include it in the liability form of "restoration to the original state."

---

[7]Wei Zhenying, "What General Provisions of Civil Law Do We Need—Compare with German Civil Law," *Northern Legal Science*, Issue 3, 2016.

[8][England] Derek Bell, "Justice, Democracy and Environment: A Concept of Liberal Environmental Citizenship," translated by Yang Xiaoyan, *Journal of Nanjing University of Technology* (Social Science Edition), Issue 1, 2013.

In terms of content, the *General Provisions of the Civil Law* extracts the greatest common divisors from the subclauses to form the foundation of the Civil Code Building. Based on the *General Principles of the Civil Law*, separate civil laws and common human legal and cultural achievements, it adds rights to personal information, data, network virtual property and other rights and constructs a comprehensive and open civil rights system based on China's social, economic and cultural conditions. It has also established many systems with unique Chinese elements, such as the national guardianship system, the classification of profit-making legal persons and nonprofit legal persons, etc., which not only reflect the current urgent needs but also reserve legal space for future changes. It has made many important institutional changes in the sources of law, the classification of natural persons, profit-making legal persons and nonprofit legal persons, the system of civil rights, legal acts and limitation of action, etc., promoting communication between the state and society and balancing the interest structure among the parties.

It is foreseeable that the enforcement of the *General Provisions of Civil Law* will have a positive impact on China's national and social governance, economic and social development, and notions of rights. On its basis, the promulgation of the Civil Code as the basic law of society is just around the corner.

4.5 Construction of the Rule of Law in Commercial Affairs

The development of the market economy is inseparable from a sound commercial rule of law system. The development experience of countries with a mature market economy has proven that a sound commercial rule of law system is a prerequisite for the healthy development of the market economy, and the deepening of the market economy will continue to promote the development and optimization of the rule of law in commercial affairs. For the development of China's socialist market economy, advancing the rule of law in commercial affairs is also of vital importance.

Since the reform and opening up, with the establishment of the socialist market economic system, China's commercial rule of law system has gradually been established and improved, providing a good institutional foundation and environment for the development of the market economy. Without the efforts to advance the rule of law in commercial matters, China's market economy would not be able to develop in an orderly manner, and economic and social reforms focusing on the socialist market economic system would not be effectively promoted. To understand China's economic miracle, you need to have a thorough understanding of the rule of law in commercial affairs in China.[9]

[9]Jiang Ping and Wu Jinglian, "The Market Economy and the Economy under the Rule of Law—A Dialogue Between Economists and Jurists," *Journal of China University of Political Science and Law*, Issue 6, 2010.

Without doubt, while affirming the achievements, it is undeniable that there are still many problems in the rule of law in commercial affairs in China, such as imperfect legislation, untimely supervision, and low judicial efficiency. The existence of these problems has affected the development of China's socialist market economy to a certain extent and made it hard to effectively solve some long-standing and fundamental institutional problems.

On occasion of the 40th anniversary of the reform and opening up, it is necessary to summarize the progress China has made in the rule of law in commercial affairs since the reform and opening up, especially in the past two decades, and analyze the existing problems in the development of the rule of law in commercial affairs so as to improve the commercial rule of law system to better meet the needs of the development of the socialist market economy.

4.5.1 Commercial Law System

A market economy is an economy under the rule of law. The development of a market economy requires a sound commercial rule of law system, and the first essential element is to establish a sound commercial law system. In the historical development of commercial law, many countries have formulated commercial codes to provide comprehensive legal rules for commercial transactions and constantly updated and improved commercial law systems according to the needs of commercial practice. For example, in the nineteenth century, France, Spain, Italy, Germany and other European countries formulated independent commercial codes to regulate commercial transactions. From the perspective of promoting the development of a market economy, it is undoubtedly the best practice to establish "comprehensive" commercial laws and regulations through the "one-step" legislative mode of codification, but this kind of legislative mode did not conform to the actual situation of China's economic and social development since the reform and opening up.

Since the reform and opening up, in the process of transitioning from a planned economy to a market economy, China has not adopted the "one-step" legislative strategy in commercial legislation but has continuously been improving commercial legislation based on practical needs. After more than 30 years of legislative accumulation, a relatively sound commercial law system was initially formed.

In terms of legislation for commercial entities, in the early stages of reform and opening up, the laws on foreign-funded enterprises (*Law on Sino-foreign Equity Joint Ventures*, *Law on Chinese-Foreign Contractual Joint Ventures* and *Law on Foreign-Capital Enterprises*) were formulated to meet the needs of attracting foreign investment, creating a suitable commercial organization form for business operation of foreign capital in China. In March 2019, the second session of the 13th National People's Congress deliberated and passed the Foreign Investment Law of the People's Republic of China, which ushered in a new era in the promotion, protection and management of foreign investment. China has continuously explored the direction and path for reforming state-owned enterprises and formulated the *Law on Industrial Enterprises Owned by the Whole People*, the *Regulations on Rural Collectively Owned Enterprises* and other laws and regulations, laying the foundation for the gradual transformation of traditional state-owned enterprises to modern enterprises. After long-term practical preparations, the *Company Law* in a unified sense was promulgated in 1993, formally confirming the legitimacy of the corporate system through legislation and providing an organic law basis for the development of the socialist market economy. In 1997, the *Partnership Enterprise Law* was enacted to fully regulate partnership enterprises. In 2005 and 2013, the *Company Law* was revised to make major adjustments and restructures to the corresponding systems in the law. In 2006, the *Partnership Enterprise Law* was revised to introduce limited partnership enterprises as an important type of commercial organization into the commercial law system. In addition, in terms of legislation for individual commercial subjects, China has promulgated laws and regulations such as the *Regulations for Individual Industrial and Commercial Households* and the *Sole Proprietorship Enterprise Law* to ensure that individuals as commercial subjects can effectively carry out commercial activities.

In terms of legislation for commercial behaviors, regarding the establishment of general rules for commercial transactions, in the early stage of reform and opening up, China promulgated the *Economic Contract Law*, the *Foreign Economic Contract Law* and the *Technical Contract Law* in accordance with the needs of market economy development. In 1999, China promulgated the unified *Contract Law* on the basis of previous practice and experience, providing the normative basis for various commercial transactions and the performance of commercial contracts.[10] In terms of legislation for special commercial activities, in the past two decades, China has successively formulated the *Negotiable Instruments Law*, the *Insurance Law*, the *Bankruptcy Law*, the *Securities Law* and the *Trust Law* to provide complete legal rules for commercial activities in negotiable instruments, insurance, securities issuance, securities trading, trusts, etc.

Admittedly, although the existing commercial laws still have many problems and need to be further revised and improved, as far as legislative form is concerned, China's commercial law system is comparatively perfect, with a comparatively comprehensive institutional structure. It can comprehensively regulate commercial subjects and their commercial activities and effectively support the development of the market economy since the reform and opening up, which is of vital importance to the improvement of the efficiency of commercial transactions and the guarantee of the safety of commercial transactions.[11]

---

[10] Liang Huixing, "Uniform Contract Law: Successes and Shortcomings," *China Legal Science*, Issue 3, 1999.

[11] Zhao Xudong, "Thirty Years of Chinese Commercial Law," *China Law*, Issue 3, 2012; the Commercial Law Research Center of Central China Normal University, "Analysis about China's Thirty Year Commercial Law & Commercial Jurisprudence," *Law Science Magazine*, Issue 2, 2009.

4.5.2 Commercial Law System Structure

The institutional arrangements of commercial law should aim to promote transaction efficiency and ensure transaction security. For a country such as China that has transitioned from a planned economy to a market economy, in addition to establishing a basic system that conforms to the principles of efficiency and safety, it is of greater importance to weaken administrative power's improper interference in market transactions and respect the autonomy of will and transaction arrangements of merchants to ensure that commercial subjects can carry out commercial transactions efficiently and conveniently so that the creativity of merchants can be brought into full play.

In advancing the rule of law in commercial affairs, China has been trying to establish a convenient and efficient commercial system and a free and relaxed commercial operating environment, constantly adjust the relationship between the market and the government in accordance with the inherent requirements of the market economy, and adjust the logic of autonomy and control to ensure that the market mechanism can give full play to the basic role of resource allocation. Regarding the admittance of commercial subjects, China has been continuously lowering the admittance conditions and restricting and reducing the areas that should be subject to admittance conditions so that commercial subjects can be easily established. In terms of commercial transaction activities, China has been continuously strengthening merchant autonomy and weakening administrative control to ensure that various transactions can be carried out efficiently. In terms of the regulation of commercial competition, China will effectively regulate all kinds of unfair competition and monopolistic behaviors to ensure that commercial subjects can carry out business activities freely and equally. In each specific field of commercial law, the abovementioned notions are reflected at the institutional level. The specific systems in different fields of law will be briefly analyzed as follows.

In the field of contract law, restricting the applicable fields of illegal and invalid contracts is an obvious example. When the *Contract Law* was enacted in 1999, the legislators narrowed down the reasons for invalidity of contracts to "violation of mandatory provisions of laws and administrative regulations." In principle, contracts that violate departmental rules and local regulations should not be identified as invalid.[12] In the subsequent practice of the rule of law in commercial affairs, to better protect the freedom of business transactions and limit the interference of administrative powers in private autonomy, in judicial practice, mandatory provisions are generally reduced to "provisions on effectiveness," and contracts that violate "management rules" should not be deemed arbitrarily invalid.[13]

---

[12] Wang Liming, "On the Judgment Standards for Invalid Contracts," *Journal of Law Application*, Issue 7, 2012.

[13] Article 14 of the *Interpretations on Several Issues Concerning the Application of the Contract Law of the People's Republic of China (II)* promulgated by the Supreme People's Court on February 9, 2009, stipulates that "Mandatory provisions" under the provision of Clause 5 of

In the field of corporate law, the adjustment of the corporate capital system also follows the same theoretical logic. When the *Company Law* was enacted in 1993, the legislators adhered to a strict legal capital logic, which not only established higher minimum legal capital thresholds but also required entrepreneurs who were dedicated to start-ups to make a one-off payment in full. There were also stricter restrictions on the form of capital contribution. When the *Company Law* was revised in 2005, the legislators eased the requirements for the legal capital system to a certain extent, lowered the minimum registration capital limits, and allowed payment in installments, making it easier to set up a company than before. The *Company Law* revised in 2013 completely changed the previous structure of the registration capital system and did not set requirements for minimum capital limits and capital contribution periods. The company registration reform makes it very convenient to set up companies and greatly promotes people's entrepreneurial enthusiasm, so the number of start-ups increases significantly.[14]

In addition, in the field of securities law, control over the public issuance of securities has also undergone a logical transformation from "a censorship-based system" to "an approval-based system." Regulators no longer impose strict quantitative controls on securities issuance censorship but have gradually shifted to a market-oriented logic. In recent years, the reform has moved towards the direction of a "registration-based system." In the field of bankruptcy law, a market-oriented reorganization mechanism was introduced, and the autonomy space of the parties was strengthened to enable enterprises in difficulties to be reborn through the reorganization mechanism.

In terms of optimizing the business environment, reducing approval items in the field of commercial transactions and reducing administrative power's intervention in commercial subjects and transactions have become important goals for advancing the rule of law in commercial affairs. In particular, commercial registration reform has been promoted in recent years. Companies seeking registration can have their business licenses issued to them before receiving administrative permits, and the annual inspection conducted by industry and commerce administration departments on companies has been replaced by open annual reports submitted by companies, creating favorable conditions for citizens' investment in entrepreneurship and optimizing the business development environment.[15] These reform measures have effectively unleashed market vitality, promoted the spirit of market innovation, and provided the guarantee for achieving such outstanding results in the development of the market economy.

Article 52 of the Contract Law refers to the provisions specifically addressing the validity of contracts."

[14]Liu Kaixiang and Zhang Qijian, "Legislative Changes of China's Corporate Capital System and Solutions to the Problems," *Journal of Henan University of Finance, Economics and Law*, 2014, Issue 5.

[15]Jiang Daxing, "'Getting Business Licenses Before Getting Administrative Permits' and Regulatory Innovation—Reshaping the 'Creditable Country' with a Coordinated Regulatory Model," *Study on China Administration for Industry & Commerce*, Issue 11, 2015.

4.5.3 Commercial Supervision System

Modern commercial transactions have intrinsic capital and financial attributes. Especially for special business activities that focus on financial borrowing, commercial insurance, securities trading, commercial trust, and asset securitization, we should pay attention not only to the risk of a single transaction but also to the overall impact of these transactions on commercial transactions and economic order. For these special commercial transactions, it is necessary to establish a corresponding transaction supervision system to prevent overall systemic risks.

In the process of transition from a planned economy to a market economy, it was particularly important to establish a modern commercial regulatory system. On the one hand, government power's intervention in economic life under the planned economy system was almost ubiquitous, but in the development of a socialist market economy, government power is not allowed to intervene in economic activities arbitrarily, and the influence of government power on the market economy must be limited to a reasonable range. On the one hand, even if reasonable supervision of the government over market operations is recognized, the exercise of these supervision powers must be regulated to ensure that the legitimate rights and interests of market entities must not be arbitrarily infringed on. Looking back at the economic development since the reform and opening up, we can find that to ensure the healthy development of China's market economy, on the one hand, it is necessary to prevent abuse of government power, and on the other hand, it is necessary to guide the reasonable exercise of government power. To achieve the above two goals, China has continuously adjusted the components of the regulatory system in accordance with the internal needs of the socialist market economy and finally established a corresponding commercial regulatory system, thus changing the relationship between the government and the market from the mode of "restricting the market and unleashing the government" to the mode of "restricting the government and unleashing the market."[16]

Taking supervision over the securities market as an example, after the securities market was established in China, the People's Bank of China was initially responsible for supervision over the securities market. In 1998, the China Securities Regulatory Commission (CSRC) was established on the basis of the Securities Committee of the State Council to take full charge of supervision over the securities market. After more than 20 years of practice, the CSRC has conducted comprehensive and in-depth supervision over securities issuance, securities trading, listed companies, and securities companies, ensuring the orderly and healthy development of the securities market. Meanwhile, China has established corresponding professional regulatory agencies, such as the China Banking Regulatory Commission and the China Insurance Regulatory Commission, to conduct comprehensive and in-depth supervision of the development of the banking and insurance industries. In

[16]Chen Su, "The Functional Positioning of the Government and the Market in the Commercial Law Mechanism," *China Legal Science*, Issue 5, 2014.

addition, to maintain the orderly development of the market and fair competition, China has also established a corresponding regulatory system to regulate unfair market competition. Administrative agencies have also conducted comprehensive supervision over illegal subjects and illegal behaviors in the operation of the market economy, effectively maintaining the order of the socialist market economy.

It is worth mentioning that, in addition to administrative supervision, to maintain the modern commercial law order, it is also necessary to improve the self-regulatory system. Self-regulation in various commercial fields in China has also been developed and improved. Similarly, taking the securities industry as an example, the supervision of stock exchanges and the self-regulation of securities industry associations and associations for listed companies have also played an important role in regulating the operation of the securities market.[17]

The rule of law in the use of government supervision power has prevented the abuse of government power that was common under the conditions of a planned economy and reasonably delimits the scope and method of the use of supervision power. This not only guarantees the structural safety of the market economy but also maintains the autonomy of market subjects. The establishment of a modern commercial regulatory system is an important result of China's advancement of the rule of law in commercial affairs.

4.5.4 Commercial Trial Mechanism

The development history of commercial law shows that a sound commercial trial mechanism is of vital importance to the development of commercial law. Independent commercial courts, efficient trial procedures, and unique trial concepts have always been important signs that commercial laws are independent of civil laws.

Since the reform and opening up, no independent commercial court has been established in the process of advancing the rule of law in commercial affairs in China. In early judicial practice, there was strict distinction between civil trials and commercial trials, and few discussions had been carried out on issues such as commercial trial thinking and concepts. With the deepening and development of the market economy, judicial organs and judicial personnel have become increasingly aware of the uniqueness of commercial trials and have gradually begun to explore the establishment of a mechanism for commercial trials.[18]

At the conceptual level, the concept of commercial trials has been highly valued by courts and judges. The concept of commercial trial advocates promoting

[17]Huang Xiangping, "The Development Process and Trends of Self-Regulatory Organizations in China's Securities Industry," *China Finance*, Issue 11, 2010.

[18]Li Houlong, "The Evolution of the Concept of Commercial Trial in China," *Nanjing University Law Review*, Spring, 2006.

transaction efficiency, protecting transaction security, and stressing the implementation of the principle of appearanceism and the protection of good-faith reliance interests. Both the theoretical and practical circles advocate the implementation of the concept of commercial trial in practice to highlight the particularity of commercial transactions and commercial trials and emphasize the protection of system benefits such as transaction efficiency and transaction security under the premise of respecting merchants' autonomy, efficiently and fairly dealing with corresponding commercial disputes and effectively maintaining the order of the market economy.[19]

At the institutional level, to compensate for the shortcomings of commercial legislation, courts at various levels, especially the Supreme People's Court, continue to concretize and substantialize the concept of commercial trial and "evolve" it into adjudication policies, measures and rules that guide adjudication practices.[20] The most important institutional form is the promulgation of various judicial interpretations and the disclosure of typical cases. Based on judicial practical experience, the Supreme People's court has issued a series of judicial interpretations, laying a solid foundation for the orderly advancement of commercial trials. Among them, two judicial interpretations were promulgated in the field of contract law, four judicial interpretations were promulgated in the field of company law, three judicial interpretations were promulgated in the field of insurance law, three judicial interpretations were promulgated in the field of bankruptcy law, and three judicial interpretations were promulgated in the field of negotiable instruments law. The promulgation of these judicial interpretations has enriched and developed the existing commercial law system to a certain extent, effectively made up for the loopholes and insufficient regulation of the existing commercial law system and provided a normative basis for solving related problems in practice. Meanwhile, to further promote the unification of judicial adjudication standards, the Supreme People's Court has also introduced a guiding case system and issued a series of guiding cases. The main points of the judgments extracted from these cases have important reference significance for solving related problems in practice. The higher people's courts of various provinces, municipalities and autonomous regions have also continuously summarized their experience in commercial trials and summarized the judgment rules through the publication of trial minutes and other forms, providing more comprehensive guiding rules for the commercial trials of the basic-level courts.

In terms of institutions, although China has not established a special commercial court, in some local reforms and innovative practices, some special commercial trial institutions have been established. For example, in the reform and innovative practice of the Shanghai Free Trade Zone, China's first financial court was established, where professional judges efficiently handled cases involving financial disputes, with good adjudicative results having been achieved.

---

[19]Wang Baoshu, "Concept and Thinking of Commercial Trial," *Shandong Justice*, Issue 2, 2010.

[20]Li Zhigang, "A Brief Discussion on the Practice and Application of the Concept of Commercial Trial," *People's Justice*, Issue 15, 2014.

Chapter 5
The Rule of Law in Economic Affairs: Escorting a New Normal of China's Economy

Jia Yao

5.1 Overview of the Rule of Law in Economic Affairs in China

Compared with Western developed countries, China is a late-developing country in terms of the economy and the rule of law. Since the reform and opening up, China's socialist market economy has roughly experienced the embryonic stage, the growth stage, and the accelerating development stage, and the rule of law in China's market economy has also gradually been constructed and developed in response to social reality. In China's law systems, market economy laws with a very important position have established important rules of conduct and legal systems in China's market economy. On the basis of the aforementioned civil and commercial laws, economic laws mainly include laws for market regulation, fiscal, taxation, and finance.

The laws for market regulation are the legal rules for the state to intervene in misconduct in the market through the "visible hand," regulate market behaviors, maintain the market order, protect and promote various economic relations emerging in the process of fair competition, mainly including the *Anti-monopoly Law*, the *Anti-unfair Competition Law*, the *Consumer Rights Protection Law*, the *Product Quality Law*, and the *Standardization Law*. So far, China has enacted the *Anti-monopoly Law* (2007), the *Anti-unfair Competition Law* (enacted in 1993, revised in 2017), the *Consumer Rights Protection Law* (enacted in 1993, revised in 2013), the *Product Quality Law* (enacted in 1993, revised in 2009), the *Standardization Law* (enacted in 1988, revised in 2017), etc.

The fiscal and taxation laws mainly include fiscal law and taxation law. Fiscal law is the body of law that regulates the relations between the state's fiscal revenue and expenditure; tax law is the body of law that governs the relations between the

J. Yao (✉)
Institute of Law, CASS, Beijing, China

H. Tian and Y. Lv (eds.), *The Chinese Path of Rule of Law Construction*, China Insights, https://doi.org/10.1007/978-981-16-4130-5_5

state and taxpayers in terms of the rights and obligations related to tax payment. So far, China has enacted the *Corporate Income Tax Law* (enacted in 2007 and revised in 2017), the *Individual Income Tax Law* (enacted in 1980, and the latest amendment in 2011), the *Interim Regulations on Value Added Tax* (enacted in 1993 and revised in 2017), etc.

Finance law is the body of laws that govern financial relations, mainly including financial supervision and financial transaction laws. The financial supervision law mainly refers to the state's laws and regulations on the supervision and management of financial institutions, financial markets, financial products and financial transactions; the financial transaction law mainly refers to the body of legal rules and norms regulating various financial markets such as the money market, securities market, insurance market and foreign exchange market, and financial transaction relationships between financial institutions and transaction entities, and between transaction entities. So far, China has enacted the *Law on the People's Bank of China* (enacted in 1995 and revised in 2003), the *Law on Commercial Banks* (enacted in 1995 and revised in 2015), the *Securities Law* (enacted in 1998 and revised in 2014), *Insurance Law* (enacted in 1995, revised in 2015), the *Trust Law* (enacted in 2001), the *Deposit Insurance Regulations* (enacted in 2015), the *Regulations on the Foreign Exchange System* (enacted in 1996, revised in 2008), etc.

Since 2000, China's economy has been developing rapidly and healthily. Although the financial crisis occurred worldwide in 2008, China was not seriously affected by the crisis and has since placed more emphasis on healthy and rapid development. The rule of law in China's market economy has also advanced vigorously simultaneously with the rapid development of the market economy. The competition legal system aimed at maintaining market competition has basically been established, a competitive culture has gradually formed, the rule of law in fiscal and taxation has been advanced steadily, and the rule of law in financial affairs has also been developing sustainably and healthily while breaking traditional restraints, promoting innovations and preventing risks. The rational and regular advancement of the rule of law in China's market economy has become a powerful guarantee for the development of the socialist market economy and even to a certain extent has become an important driving force for economic development.

5.2 The Rule of Law in Market Competitions and Consumer Protection

A market economy is a system where individual initiative and creativity are achieved through free competition. It aims to improve market efficiency and enhance social well-being. The history and experience of the economic development of human beings have proven that competition is the most effective means to achieve and ensure prosperity. In the process of transforming from a planned economy to a market economy, China was keenly aware of the competitive nature of the market economy and has explored different paths and methods to maintain market competition. The final consensus is still the rule of law, i.e. to protect market competition by advancing the rule of law to ensure the vitality of the market economy. Therefore, the competition law is regarded as "the core law of the market economy." Since the reform and opening up, especially since the beginning of the twenty-first century, the development of China's competition law has shown phased, diversified, and systemic features. With the promulgation of the *Anti-Monopoly Law* in 2007 and the revision of the *Anti-Unfair Competition Law* in 2010, China has gradually established a competition law system. Meanwhile, the ultimate goal of competition law to maintain market competition order is to protect consumers, and consumers benefit from a good competition order, so the competition law and the consumer protection law are closely related. The consumer protection law is self-contained. It belongs to a relatively independent legal field and has formed its own perfect track. It was revised in 2013 to complete the mission of system construction. Therefore, looking at the overall situation of the rule of law in the socialist market economy, the "three engines" at the core of the market economy, the anti-monopoly law, the anti-unfair competition law, and the consumer protection law, have basically been systematically established in the past ten years and are playing an important role in promoting and escorting the development of the market economy.

5.2.1 Anti-Monopoly Law System

The anti-monopoly law plays an important role in ensuring the normal operation of the market economy, which is a worldwide consensus. As far as China is concerned, anti-monopoly law is considered to be an effective means to eradicate restrictions on competition in shaping a market economy system and is conducive to guiding and regulating the development of China's market economy. However, due to China's weak economic foundation and its poor economic management capabilities before the reform and opening up, there was still a lack of some elements and an external environment necessary for establishing a rule of law system for competitions. In recent years, there are still various forms of threats to competition, and particularly, various behaviors and phenomena that hinder fair competition, such as setting up administrative barriers, discriminating against products from other places, service market segmentation, industrial monopolies and regional blockades, are still rampant. Therefore, clearly identifying China's problems has become the prerequisite and basis for China to establish a legal system to regulate competitions. In terms of the development of rule of law in anti-monopoly, the promulgation of the 2007 *Anti-Monopoly Law* is an important "time division point." During the period from 2002 to 2007, both scholars and practitioners mainly focused on issues such as whether an anti-monopoly law was needed to combat monopoly and protect market competition in the operation of China's market economy, and later they started to discuss shaping the basic ideas and framework for anti-monopoly legislation. After the *Anti-Monopoly Law* was promulgated in 2007, its interpretations were put on the agenda, and its studies were promoted at different levels.

First, the interpretations of legal norms on traditional issues were continuously promoted to standardize the core concepts. For example, relevant markets were defined, and exemption of application and extraterritorial application systems were discussed; typological analysis of monopoly behaviors was conducted, such as monopoly agreements (horizontal monopoly agreements, vertical monopoly agreements), forgiveness system, and abuse of market dominant position (public enterprises, key facilities, standard-essential patents,[1] Internet industry), concentration of undertakings (safe harbor rules, rule of thirds/dichotomy), and administrative monopoly. Meanwhile, some basic issues and unique Chinese issues were re-examined, such as the enforcement of anti-monopoly law and legal liabilities.

Second, more attention was paid to issues concerning anti-monopoly in new business formats and new behaviors. In recent years, China's Internet industry has developed rapidly and even surpassed its counterparts in European and American countries at the scale and development levels. Meanwhile, it has also encountered unprecedented problems and difficulties, and there is no experience worldwide that can be learned from. Therefore, after 2009, especially in 2012, cases involving monopoly disputes frequently emerged in the Internet industry in China, such as the three lawsuits between Qihoo 360 and Tencent, which aroused reflection and analysis on the localization of definition of relevant markets in the field of anti-monopoly law.[2] The rule of law in anti-monopoly needs to be further expanded to adapt to emerging business formats and problems.

Third, the enforcement of the *Anti-Monopoly Law* was promoted in all aspects. When the *Anti-Monopoly Law* was promulgated, one of the requirements it set for the Anti-Monopoly Committee of the State Council was to formulate and promulgate the implementation guidelines to interpret the basic principles and clarify the vague legal rules in the law. The guidelines that have been promulgated include the *Guide of the Anti-Monopoly Committee of the State Council for the Definition of the Relevant Market* in 2009 and the *Provisions of the Ministry of Commerce on Imposing Restrictive Conditions on the Concentration of Undertakings* in 2014. Some regulations are being formulated, such as the *Anti-monopoly Guidelines for the Abuse of Intellectual Property Rights*. Meanwhile, the typical anti-monopoly cases ruled by the anti-monopoly law enforcement organs also have strong guidance, and their role in the implementation of the anti-monopoly law should not be

[1]The most typical and sensational case is the standard patent dispute between Huawei and ZTE in the EU.

[2]Zhong Chun, "Definition of Relevant Market in the Anti-monopoly Law Enforcement in the Internet Industry," *Legal Science* (Journal of Northwest University of Political Science and Law), Issue 4, 2012; Jiang Yanbo, "Judicial Dilemma and Outlet of Definition of Relevant Market in the Internet Industry," *Jurists Review*, Issue 6, 2012; Huang Yong and Jiang Xiaojun, "The Definition of 'Relevant Markets' in the Internet Industry," *Open Journal of Legal Science*, Issue 6, 2014.

ignored. In addition, the commitment system in administrative law enforcement and international cooperation and private enforcement mechanisms have also strengthened the implementation of anti-monopoly law at different levels. Thus, it can be seen that after years of efforts, China has put in place a relatively sound anti-monopoly legal system and an implementation mechanism with Chinese characteristics.[3]

5.2.2 *Anti-Unfair Competition Law*

China enacted the *Anti-Unfair Competition Law* in 1993 when the socialist market economy was in its early stage of development. The text of the law was mainly formulated with reference to the anti-unfair competition laws of major Western developed countries. However, shortly after the law was promulgated, both scholars and practitioners pointed out that the law had many flaws and should be revised and improved. In 2003, the State Administration for Industry and Commerce began to amend the law. In 2006, the Supreme People's Court promulgated the *Interpretations on Several Issues Concerning the Application of Law in the Trial of Civil Cases Involving Unfair Competition.* Since then, discussions on the revision of the law have never ceased among both scholars and practitioners. Since the promulgation of the *Anti-Unfair Competition Law*, after more than 20 years of efforts, the degree of marketization of the Chinese economy has increased significantly, and the economic aggregate, market size, degree of market competition, and competition conditions have undergone extensive and profound changes. To give full play to the decisive role of the market in resource allocation, establish fair, open and transparent market rules, build a unified, open, and orderly competitive market system, and better protect the legitimate rights and interests of consumers, the State Administration for Industry and Commerce, based on the opinions of all parties, initiated the procedures of amendment to the *Anti-Unfair Competition Law.* In February 2016, the Legislative Affairs Office of the State Council promulgated the *Anti-Unfair Competition Law (Revised Draft for Review)*, and in February 2017 and September 2017, the NPC Standing Committee conducted the first and second rounds of deliberation over the *Anti-Unfair Competition Law (Revised Draft),* respectively. The prolonged and fruitful revision of the law is about to come to a successful conclusion.

Article 2 is the "focal point" in the *Anti-Unfair Competition Law*, which has caused great controversy among both scholars and practitioners and attracted much attention during the revision of the law. Paragraph 2 of Article 2 stipulates that "'unfair competition' means a business operator's conduct that damages the lawful

[3]For the text of this part about the anti-monopoly law, the author is in acknowledgement of associate researcher Jin Shanming at the Institute of Law of the Chinese Academy of Social Sciences for providing relevant information.

rights and interests of the other business operators and disturbs the order of social economy in violation of the provisions of this law." Some scholars believe that an unfair competition act should include three elements. (1) It is an act in market transactions. This emphasizes that a competition act regulated by the *Anti-Unfair Competition Law* is economic competition for profit-making purposes that occurs in business relations or market transactions. (2) It is an act for the purpose of competition. This is because the *Anti-Unfair Competition Law* is not directed against all infringements of business operators in the market but only against infringements in market competition. (3) It is an act in violation of business ethics. Business operators should follow the principles of free will, equality, fairness, and good faith. If a business operator unfairly grabs competitive advantages in the market by impairing other competitors, then it violates business ethics.[4]

As there has been much controversy among both scholars and practitioners over Article 2 of the *Anti-Unfair Competition Law* as an umbrella article, this article has been repeatedly adjusted during the revision of the law. Paragraph 1 of Article 2 of the *2017 Anti-Unfair Competition Law (Revised Draft)* (Draft for Second Deliberation) stipulates that "business operators shall adhere to the principles of free will, equality, fairness, and good faith, as well as generally accept business ethics, in their market transactions." Paragraph 2 of this article stipulates that "'unfair competition' means a business operator's conduct that damages the lawful rights and interests of the other business operators and disturbs the order of social economy in violation of the provisions of the preceding paragraph." Some scholars have pointed out that such expression clearly combines the general principles stipulated in the preceding paragraph with the specific enumerations in Chapter 2 to ensure the unity of form and spirit and has injected life and vitality to the adjustment of economic order, which is undoubtedly an important progress in legislative design. Meanwhile, it also leaves enough space for the "application" and judicial interpretation of the law and has greatly enriched the scope of adjustment of the *Anti-Unfair Competition Law*.[5]

This revision of the *Anti-Unfair Competition Law* has mainly solved three issues: first, solving the issue concerning the status and guiding role of the general provisions of the law; second, adjusting the treatment of specific systems; and third, how to deal with issues brought about by the development of new technologies. In terms of specific systems, first, it has refined the provisions on commercial bribery. It stipulates that business operators shall not bribe the other party to a transaction or the third party that may affect a transaction by property or other means, and it clarifies the scope of "third parties that may affect the transaction." Second, it has amended the text regarding trade secrets. Third, based on the provisions of the *Trademark Law* and the *Patent Law*, it has increased the statutory compensation for

---

[4]Wang Xiaoye, *The Studies of Competition Law*, Social Sciences Academic Press (China), 2007, pp. 51–53.

[5]"The Revision of the Law Should Leave Space for the "Application" of the Law: Interview with Liu Chuntian, Chairman of the China Intellectual Property Law Association," *Legal Daily*, September 26, 2017, 10th edition.

acts involving confusion and infringement of trade secrets. In addition, it adds provisions on unfair competition behaviors by making use of the Internet.[6] Thus, it can be seen that in the past 10 or 20 years, the anti-unfair competition law has attracted attention from various fields such as legislation, justice, law enforcement, scholars and practitioners, its legal text has been continuously improved, and its implementation law has been continuously promoted.

5.2.3 Consumer Protection

Since its promulgation, the *Law on Protection of Consumer Rights and Interests* has a different path from the consumer protection laws of Western developed countries. The consumer protection laws of European and American countries were created on the basis that private laws had been fully developed and private subjects had sufficient right consciousness. However, China's consumer protection law was born under the background that private subjects and private rights have not been fully developed, and the legal rules mostly follow the "regulatory approach" and protect consumer rights through administrative means. When the *Law on Protection of Consumer Rights and Interests* was enacted in 1993, China's market economy was still in its early stage of development, and in fact, there was no relatively mature market. Therefore, at that time, the legal text was formulated based on the texts of the relevant laws of Western developed countries. However, after more than two decades of economic and social development, the legal text of the law has lagged behind the social facts. Therefore, in 2013, the National People's Congress revised the *Law on Protection of Consumer Rights and Interests*. This revision improved the relevant provisions and added provisions on consumer personal information protection, consumers' repentance rights, information disclosure systems for online and other off-site shopping, consumer associations' right to initiate public interest litigation, and an increase in consumer fraud compensation. In terms of legal text, the *Law on Protection of Consumer Rights and Interests* is more perfect.

In terms of law enforcement, the effect of consumer rights protection in China is not satisfactory, but both law enforcement and judicial practice aim to solve practical problems.

On the one hand, consumer rights infringement events have occurred frequently, and in some events, business operators have almost flouted the law. In recent years, although no official statistical data were published or disclosed on consumer rights infringement events or cases throughout the country each year, there were official comments on consumer protection events or cases, and statistical data in some

[6]"The Revision of the Law Should Leave Space for the "Application" of the Law: Interview with Liu Chuntian, Chairman of the China Intellectual Property Law Association," *Legal Daily*, September 26, 2017, 10th edition.

regions and industries were disclosed. Based on the data disclosed, it is almost impossible to fully protect the rights and interests of consumers. Even if their rights were safeguarded, the costs were very high. According to statistics, in 2011, the courts in Jiangsu Province accepted 8,986 first-instance civil cases involving disputes over consumer rights and interests, an increase of 9.21% from 8,228 cases in 2010. However, compared with cases involving other civil disputes, such cases only accounted for a small proportion. For example, in 2010, among the 597,505 first-instance civil cases accepted by the courts in Jiangsu Province, this kind of case accounted for only 1.37%. In 2011, among the 650,198 first-instance civil cases accepted by the courts in Jiangsu Province, this kind of case accounted for only 1.38%.[7] Taking the statistical data of the Supreme People's Court and the China Consumers' Association from 2010 to 2013 as an example, local courts across the country accepted a total of 482,545 first-instance cases involving the protection of consumer rights, while local courts across the country accepted 28,785,173 civil and commercial first-instance cases. Cases involving the protection of consumer rights accounted for only 1.68%. Meanwhile, from 2010 to 2013, consumers' associations at various levels across the country accepted as many as 2,519,340 cases involving consumer complaints, and first-instance cases involving consumer rights protection accepted by the courts accounted for only 19.15%. Admittedly, the majority of consumers choose to give up protecting their rights when their legitimate rights and interests are infringed upon. A survey with 2012 respondents conducted by chinanews.com.cn on consumers' awareness to protect their own rights in 2009 showed that when the legitimate rights and interests of consumers were infringed upon, the respondents who chose to "endure silently" accounted for up to 63.82%, while those who chose to "to ask for help from consumers' associations" only accounted for 5.467%. If the aforementioned survey data are in line with the actual situation of consumer rights protection in China, then the probability of consumers filing consumer rights protection lawsuits is only 1%.[8]

On the other hand, in implementing the new systems as prescribed by the *Law on Protection of Consumer Rights and Interests*, various problems have been encountered, effective relief for consumers could hardly be achieved, and typical problems such as "professional extortioner for fraud fighting" could hardly be solved.

First, consumers' right to rescission can hardly be guaranteed, and the system for the return of goods without reasons can hardly be effectively implemented. As the highlight of the newly revised *Law on Protection of Consumer Rights and Interests*, Article 25 of the law establishes a system for return of goods without reasons for new shopping modes such as the Internet. It stipulated that consumers have up to seven days from the date of receipt of the goods to send back items bought on the internet or by TV, phone or mail order without being charged. This system has

[7]The Research Group of the First Civil Division of the Higher People's Court of Jiangsu Province, "Guiding Consumers to Protect Their Rights and Strengthening Judicial Protection," *Jiangsu Legal News*, March 13, 2012, edition A07.

[8]Huang Zhongshun, "The Second Order Structure of Consumers' Collective Damage Compensation Litigation," *Global Law Review*, Issue 5, 2014.

attracted widespread attention from society. However, as the provision in the article is too rough and does not give specific operating procedures, it is hard to operate in practice. Business operators often attach many restrictive conditions when performing the so-called "obligation to return goods without reason," which makes it difficult for consumers to enjoy the real right to return goods without reason.[9] Therefore, the State Administration for Industry and Commerce and consumer associations have also adopted various means to urge business operators to fulfill this obligation.

Second, consumers' collective compensation for damages currently can hardly be achieved. Pursuant to Article 55 of the *Civil Procedure Law* and Article 47 of the *Law on Protection of Consumer Rights and Interests*, the China Consumers' Association and the consumers' associations established in the provinces, autonomous regions and centrally administered municipalities may bring litigations against acts that are detrimental to consumers' legitimate rights and interests. In terms of its interpretation, consumers' associations have the right and responsibility to initiate public interest litigations. In April 2016, the Supreme People's Court promulgated the *Interpretations of the Supreme People's Court on Several Issues concerning the Application of Law in the Trial of Civil Public Interest Actions regarding Consumption*, which provides a basis for the trial of public interest actions regarding consumption in China. However, the practice in recent years shows that the data on the number of public interest actions filed by consumers' associations and the industries and the consumer rights and interests involved were far below public expectations.

Third, the problem of a "professional extortioner for fraud fighting" has become a typical "Chinese problem." The *Law on Protection of Consumer Rights and Interests* and the *Food Safety Law* establish a punitive compensation system aiming to protect consumers' rights and interests against fraudulent conduct by business operators, such as the production or sale of foods that do not meet food safety standards. However, in reality, it has become a profit-making tool for "the persons who buy false goods with intention" and "the professional extortioners for fraud fighting", causing huge losses to enterprises and posing huge challenges to judicial practice. People's courts in various regions have different attitudes towards "the professional extortioners for fraud fighting." In May 2017, the Supreme People's Court issued *Response to Recommendation No. 5990 of the 5th Session of the 12th National People's Congress* (FBH No. [2017] 181), which clearly states that the behaviors of professional extortioners for fraud fighting should not be supported and that the profit-making anti-counterfeiting behaviors of professional extortioners for fraud fighting should be curbed gradually by timely use of judicial interpretations, guiding cases and other forms, indicating that it is necessary to safeguard the legitimacy of law and authority of the rule of law through judicature.

---

[9] China Jiangsu Net, "Return of Goods Bought Online Can still Hardly be Achieved Pursuant to the New *Law on Protection of Consumer Rights and Interests*," http://jsnews.jschina.com.cn/systeni/2014/04/14/020768616.shtml, access time: September 10, 2017.

Generally, the text of the *Law on Protection of Consumer Rights and Interests* has been constructed and gradually improved, but it still faces many problems in implementation. Therefore, the real objective of the law is to realize legal expectations and strike a balance of interests between consumers and business operators.

5.3 The Rule of Law in Fiscal and Taxation System

5.3.1 The Rule of Law in Fiscal and Taxation Systems Since the Beginning of the Twenty-First Century

In the 15 years from 2002 to 2017, the advancement of the rule of law in fiscal and taxation systems in China can roughly be divided into two major stages.[10] The first stage was the ten-year tax reform period from 2002 to 2012. This round of tax system reform was actually initiated in 2001, starting from the shift of transportation and vehicle tax to vehicle purchase tax, mainly aiming to establish a more standardized and sound tax law system, partially adjust the tax system,[11] and explore structural tax cuts. The second stage aimed to further implement structural tax cuts and gradually implement the principle of law-based taxation under the background that the Party made the decision to comprehensively deepen reforms in 2012. The launch of the pilot program for the reform to replace the business tax with a value-added tax (VAT) in Shanghai and the proposal of "implementation of the principle of law-based taxation" at the 3rd Plenary Session of the 18th CPC Central Committee were the milestones in the reform. Tax system reform or tax system evolution is a concentrated embodiment of China's political, economic, social, and legal development, with distinctive characteristics of the times.

In terms of the scope of the reform, the second stage focused on reforming the tax system mode within the tax category (one of the significant goals of the tax system reform is to establish an individual income tax mechanism that combines the classified and comprehensive taxation systems) and exploring the merger of tax systems between different tax categories (such as advancing the reform to replace the business tax with a VAT and exploring the real estate tax system, etc.).

---

[10]Since 2002, some scholars have begun to sort out the studies of China's fiscal and taxation laws on a regular basis. Ding Yi, "Summary of the 2002 Annual Meeting of the Fiscal and Taxation Law Research Association of the China Law Society," *China Legal Science*, Issue 6, 2002; Li Jianren, "Summary of Finance and Taxation Law Research in China in 2002," in *Finance and Taxation Law Review* Vol. 4, edited by Liu Jianwen, the Law Press, 2004; Guo Weizhen et al,. "Summary of Finance and Taxation Law Research in China in 2004," in *Finance and Taxation Law Review* Vol. 7, edited by Liu Jianwen, the Law Press, 2005; Zhai Jiguang, "The Present Status and Future of China's Fiscal and Taxation Law," in *Finance and Taxation Law Review* Vol. 13, edited by Liu Jianwen, the Law Press, 2013.

[11]Zhang Shouwen, "Tax System Changes and the Modernization of Rule of Law in Taxation System," *Social Sciences in China*, Issue 2, 2015.

In terms of the degree of reform, both the first and second stages were actually the reform of "structural tax cuts," but the intensity of "structural tax cuts" varied in the two stages. In the first stage, the concept of structural tax cuts was proposed. Exploration of the direction of tax reform actually did not start until the 2008 financial crisis.[12] The structural tax cuts in the second stage were the gradual implementation of various reform measures under the direction of the tax reform.

In terms of the driving force of reform, the tax system reform in the first stage was closely related to China's accession to the WTO in 2001. The tax system reform showed a clear sign of "integration," mainly focusing on unifying the tax laws for domestic and foreign enterprises and implementing national treatment, such as amendment of tariff regulations and unifying the income tax for domestic and foreign enterprises. The tax system reform was mainly driven by external factors. However, the tax system reform in the second stage was a response to the problems in China's political, economic, and social development. It has distinctive characteristics of "basing on China's reality, solving China's problems, and exploring the characteristics of the Chinese model." The tax system reform was mainly driven by internal factors.

In terms of the path of reform, the tax system reform in the first stage focused on how to make use of international experience.[13] In this stage, China was considering whether to levy inheritance taxes, social security taxes, stamp taxes on securities trading, etc. which were practiced in the developed countries. It involved explorations on tax cuts, while there were also actual demands for tax increases. The tax system reform in the second stage focused on localized reforms. With the attitude of combining experience and lessons from foreign tax system reforms, China clearly proposed a reform path that did not introduce new taxes, such as inheritance taxes, and continuously summarized and began to introduce and promote the experience of China's tax reform to the world.

Without doubt, the tax system reform was not completely different in the two stages but instead had inherent logical consistency and continuity. First, the tax system reform in the two stages was a response to the Party's reform decisions. The decision of the 3rd Plenary Session of the 16th CPC Central Committee in 2003 and the decision of the 3rd Plenary Session of the 18th CPC Central Committee in 2013 established the political basis for the tax system reform in the two stages. The endeavors of the state and the government to promote the reform have always been a main line that cannot be ignored in the process of tax system evolution.[14] Second, both stages focused on alleviating distribution pressure and solving distribution problems to properly handle the multisubject and multilevel distribution relationship between countries, state powers at different levels, residents and nonresidents

---

[12]Yan Kun and Yu Shuyi, "On China's Structural Tax Cuts under the Global Financial Crisis," *Taxation Research*, Issue 1, 2011.

[13]Yu Guangyuan, "30 Years of the Rule of Law in Fiscal and Taxation Systems in China," *China Taxation*, Issue 12, 2008.

[14]Zhang Shouwen, "Reform Decisions and Consensus of Economic Law," *Law Review*, Issue 2, 2014.

in tax law, and market entities. Third, protecting taxpayers' rights was also a very important part of the tax system reform in the past 15 years. The rights of taxpayers (announcement in 2009) were clarified and implemented in the design of specific systems (some tax preferences were changed from an approval system to a filing system, etc.). Fourth, the fiscal and taxation system reform in the second phase is the inheritance and development of the fiscal and taxation system reform in the first phase. The second phase focused on implementing and realizing the goals proposed and determined in the first phase through various measures.

5.3.2 Typical Legal Systems of Fiscal and Taxation

In the past 15 years, China's fiscal and taxation system reform has achieved remarkable results. Among them, the reform of some important systems has shown a clear development course, mainly including the following aspects.

Firstly, the reform of goods and services tax. In the reform of goods and services tax, the most important events were the 2008 amendments to the provisional regulations on VAT, consumption tax, and business tax and the reform to replace the business tax with a VAT in 2012. The pilot program for the reform of the VAT transformation initiated in some industries in the three eastern provinces in 2004 was comprehensively expanded in 2009, and China's VAT has realized the transition from a production-based VAT system to a consumption-based VAT system. The expansion of the VAT reform and VAT legislation are the most important aspects of the reform of goods and services taxes. The design of the tax system elements in VAT legislation is particularly important. The pilot program to replace the business tax with a VAT in 2012 was expanded nationwide on May 1, 2016, and the construction industry, real estate industry, financial industry, and life service industry were all included in the scope of value-added tax. Without doubt, there were also many problems in the VAT reform. During the reform process, the State Administration of Taxation issued a series of regulatory documents to support it, especially the VAT policy in the financial industry.

Second, the reform of property and behavior taxes. The reform of property and behavior taxes focused on merging different tax categories in the early stage. In 2007, vehicle and vessel usage tax and vehicle and vessel usage license plate tax were merged into vehicle and vessel tax. From 2008 to 2009, urban land usage taxes, farmland use taxes and property taxes were levied internally and externally in a unified manner. In recent years, reforms have mainly focused on the design of the housing property tax system and the reform of resource taxes. The reform of resource taxes mainly included the reform to include salt tax in the taxation scope in 2011, the reform to replace charges by taxes in 2010–2016, the reform to apply ad valorem rates to all resource taxes, and the pilot reform to introduce the water resource tax. The reform of the housing property tax system mainly included the pilot reform of the housing property tax in Shanghai and Chongqing in 2011, aiming to combine the housing property tax and urban land use tax and comprehensively design the elements of the housing property tax system.

Third, the tax collection administration system was reformed. The reforms mainly include the reform of the tax registration administration system in 2003, the separation of the taxation function from the financial department in 2009, the deepening of the reform of state and local tax collection administration systems in 2015, the reform of the social insurance premium collection administration system, and the reforms in administration over tax evasion in recent years, such as international mutual administrative assistance in tax matters. Among them, deepening the reform of state and local tax collection administration systems and the reforms in administration over tax evasion are the most critical ones. After the *Law on Administration of Tax Collection* was revised substantially in 2001, it was adjusted only slightly in 2013 and 2015. The revised draft was published in 2013, 2014, and 2015, but the legal revision process has not yet been completed.

Fourthly, the budget reform. The reform of the budget management system was initiated in 2004 and was basically completed in 2014 when the Budget Law was revised. The reform contents mainly include budget disclosure, full-caliber budgetary administration, exploration of provinces directly governing counties, compilation of four budget reports (general public budget, government-managed fund budget, state-owned capital management budget and social insurance fund budget), division of budget power, democratic budget participation, and the government procurement system.[15] In addition, China issued a number of documents from 2011 to 2015 to strengthen the administration of local debt to prevent fiscal risks.

Fifth is the development and implementation of the principle of law-based taxation. The legal basis for most current tax categories in China is the interim regulations promulgated by the State Council under the authorization of the National People's Congress in 1985. With the formation and improvement of the socialist legal system with Chinese characteristics, China has basically put in place a multilink and multilevel taxation system covering a wide range of tax categories.[16] The 3rd Plenary Session of the 18th CPC Central Committee clearly proposed to "implement the principle of law-based taxation," and the 4th Plenary Session of the 18th CPC Central Committee also took "fiscal and taxation" as the key areas where legislation should be strengthened. The amendment to Article 8 of the 2015 *Legislation Law* took major steps in implementing the principle of law-based taxation. In March 2015, the CPC Central Committee reviewed and adopted the *Opinions on the Implementation of the Principle of Law-based Taxation*, which specified the timetable and road map for the implementation of the principle of law-based taxation. The *Environmental Protection Tax Law*, the *Vessel*

[15]Liu Longheng, "The Basic Concepts, Basic Features and Implementation Suggestions of the New Budget Law," *Law Science Magazine*, Issue 4, 2015.

[16]Refer to "Answers from the Person in Charge of the Legislative Affairs Committee of the Standing Committee of the National People's Congress to the Questions of Xinhua News Agency's Reporters on the Implementation of Legal Principle of Taxation," http://news.xinhuanetcoiw/politics/2015-03/25/c_1114763794.htm, access time: September 28, 2017.

Tonnage Tax Law (Draft for Comments), the *Tobacco Tax Law (Draft for Comments)* promulgated in December 2016, the *Cultivated Land Occupation Tax Law (Draft for Comments)* and the *Vehicle Purchase Tax Law (Draft for Comments)* promulgated in 2017 are concrete implementations of the principle of law-based taxation.

5.4 The Rule of Law in Financial Affairs

Compared with Western developed countries, China's financial industry started relatively late, but it has developed very rapidly. In just over 30 years since the reform and opening up, China's foreign exchange reserves have ranked first in the world for many years, China's A-share market capitalization also stands in the front rank in the world, and many economic data and indicators are far ahead. The driving force for the development of the financial industry comes from the innovation and development of products and technologies that serve the real economy. It is also affected by factors such as the economic and social development of a country, the world's financial market environment, and changes in the international political structure. The rule of law is an inherent requirement of the market economy system. As an important part of the market economy, the financial system is combined with the rule of law to form a relatively independent financial rule of law system to provide ideas and rule support for the healthy and orderly development of the financial industry. After the beginning of the twenty-first century, China joined the WTO and established the Qualified Foreign Institutional Investor (QFII) system in 2002 to open wider to the outside world. The global financial crisis in 2008, ignited by the subprime mortgage crisis in the United States, severely frustrated Western developed countries, but China was not seriously affected by the crisis, and China has since paid more attention to preventing systemic financial risks. In recent years, with the support of the Internet and other technologies, China's financial innovation has accelerated, but it is also facing more challenges. Improving or changing financial supervision methods and patterns, strictly controlling risks and protecting individual financial service recipients have become the requirements of the rule of law in financial affairs.

5.4.1 Systematic Improvement of Financial Law

China has always placed equal emphasis on development and risk prevention in its financial macrocontrol system, financial supervision system and financial market system since the reform and opening up. In recent years and since the abnormal volatility of the stock market in 2015, China has placed particular emphasis on the construction of a corresponding rule of law financial system based on the requirement of "preventing systemic financial risks."

The *Decision of the CPC Central Committee on Several Major Issues Concerning Comprehensively Deepening the Reform* adopted at the 3rd Plenary Session of the 18th CPC Central Committee proposed improving the financial market system. We will open the financial industry wider and allow qualified nongovernmental capital to set up, in accordance with law, financial institutions such as small- or medium-sized banks on the precondition that this comes under stronger oversight. We will push ahead with the reform of policy financial institutions. We will improve the multilayer capital market system, promote reform toward a registration-based stock-issuing system, promote equity financing through diverse channels, develop and regulate the bond market, and increase the proportion of direct financing. We will improve the compensation mechanism for the insurance industry and establish an insurance system for catastrophic risks. We will develop inclusive finance. We will encourage financial innovations and enrich the financial market with more levels and more products. We will improve the mechanism for market-based Renminbi exchange rate formation, accelerate interest-rate liberalization, and improve the national debt yield curve that reflects the relationship between market supply and demand. We will promote the opening of the capital market in both directions, raise the convertibility of cross-border capital and financial transactions in an orderly way, establish and improve a management system of foreign debt and capital flow within the framework of macromanagement, and accelerate the realization of Renminbi capital account convertibility. We will carry out reform measures and stability standards for financial oversight, improve the mechanism for oversight and coordination in the financial sector, and define the oversight functions and risk management responsibilities at both the central and local levels. We will build a deposit insurance system and improve the market-based exit mechanism for financial institutions. We will strengthen financial infrastructure construction to ensure that the financial market operates in a safe, efficient and stable way.

The State Council promulgated the *Regulations on Deposit Insurance* in October 2014. Deposit insurance is an important measure to protect the interests of depositors under the conditions of a market economy and an important part of the financial safety net. It plays an important role in deepening the financial reform, maintaining financial stability, and promoting healthy development of the financial system in China. The CBRC is currently drafting the *Regulations on the Disposal of Bankruptcy Risks of Commercial Banks*. The regulations will be drafted in accordance with the relevant requirements of the Financial Stability Board and *Key Attributes of Effective Resolution Regimes for Financial Institutions* and will fully consider suspending the close-out netting power for financial derivatives contracts related to the ISDA Agreement in risk disposal to provide adequate guarantees for handling banks in crisis in a rapid and orderly manner.

It is particularly worth mentioning that at the National Financial Work Conference held in Beijing from July 14 to 15, 2017, Xi Jinping delivered an important speech, emphasizing the need to resolutely deepen financial reforms. The State Council's Financial Stability and Development Committee was established to strengthen the PBoC's macroprudent management and systemic risk prevention responsibilities.[17] The Financial Stability and Development Committee has transformed the previous regulatory competition into regulatory coordination to a certain extent, which is conducive to preventing systemic financial risks.

5.4.2 Promoting Innovation and Opening of the Traditional Financial Industry

The rule of law is the most powerful guarantee for the development of industries, and emphasizing the regularity, objectivity and local path of development is the top priority. Meanwhile, it is given effect at the legal and policy level and fixed as the rules that must be observed, which is the contribution and influence of the rule of law to the development of the industry. In recent years, the financial industry has intended to promote the development and innovation of the traditional financial industry and escort the development of the financial industry in all aspects by revising important laws and issuing important regulations and policies.

In 2015, the National People's Congress revised the *Law on Commercial Banks*, which was the first major revision since the law was promulgated in 2003. In particular, "the ratio of the outstanding balance of loans to that of deposits should not exceed 75% in Article 39" and "the ratio of loan to deposit" in Article 75 were deleted. To a certain extent, it has increased the lending scale of banks, which has a positive impact on banks when the demand for loans is relatively large.

On September 30, 2017, the People's Bank of China announced the implementation of a targeted RRR cut policy for inclusive finance, which was implemented in 2018. The relevant person in charge of the central bank stated that the implementation of the targeted RRR cut policy for inclusive finance would not change the overall orientation of the prudent monetary policy. The policy establishes a positive incentive mechanism to increase loans to the inclusive financial sector and helps allocate more financial resources to inclusive finance and optimize the credit structure, which is a structural policy. In the next step, the People's Bank of China will continue to implement a prudent and neutral monetary policy, encourage an appropriate increase in monetary credit and nongovernmental financing, and create a sound monetary and financial environment for stable economic growth and supply-side structural reforms.[18]

[17]"What Role Will Be the Important Committee Proposed by Xi Jinping Play?," http://www.china.com.cn/news/2017-07/17/content—41226326.htm, access time: September 28, 2017.

[18]"The Person in Charge of the People's Bank of China Answered the Questions from the Reporters on the Implementation of Targeted RRR Cuts for Inclusive Finance," http://www.pbc.gov.cn/goutongjiaoliu/113456/113469/3393337/index.html, latest access time: October 1, 2017.

5.4.3 Risk Prevention for Financial Innovation

In recent years, China's Internet technology has developed vigorously. New financial business formats based on Internet technology are also emerging and developing rapidly, such as equity crowd funding and P2P online lending. However, many of these new products have grown so quickly that they exist in a regulatory "gray zone" where supervision responsibilities are not yet clearly defined. In recent years, Internet finance has become a relatively concentrated high-risk area. How to regulate Internet finance has become a key and difficult issue in recent years.

In July 2015, ten departments, including the People's Bank of China, issued the *Guiding Opinions on Promoting the Healthy Development of Internet Finance*, which defines Internet payment, Internet lending, equity-based crowd funding, Internet fund sale, Internet insurance, Internet trust, and Internet consumer finance. Internet finance has developed rapidly in recent years. These financial innovations have had a positive impact on the promotion of economic and social development, but there are also greater risks. Failing to stick to the baseline of morality, Internet finance has been severely alienated. The relatively sensational e-zubao incident is a typical case; other P2P online loan platforms are also suspected of illegal fundraising or even the owners have run away with the investors' assets. The *Guiding Opinions* stated that direct lending and borrowing on individual online lending platforms belonging to the category of private lending and borrowing must be governed by laws and regulations such as the *Contract Law*, the *General Principles of Civil Law*, and the relevant judicial interpretations of the Supreme People's Court.

To prevent the risk brought about by equity-based crowd funding, the *Guiding Opinions* pointed out that "equity crowd funding" mainly means small equity financing activities conducted publicly via the Internet. Crowd-funding transactions take place through equity crowd-funding intermediaries (Internet websites or other similar electronic media). The financier should be a small and micro enterprise, should truthfully disclose key information about the enterprise's business model, operation management, finance, and capital use through equity crowd-funding intermediaries to investors, and should not mislead or defraud investors. Investors should fully understand the risks of equity crowd-funding activities, have the corresponding risk tolerance, and make small investments.

The problem of private lending, which has long been a hard nut to crack in economic reality and judicial practice, has also found its way out in recent years. Private lending was not recognized previously. In fact, this was because of insufficient respect for citizens' right to dispose of property, which has led to the phenomenon of financial repression. In particular, insufficient respect for citizens' lending behaviors has long kept private finance in the gray area.[19] The *Provisions of*

[19]Wu Xiaoling, "Spending Your Own Money at Will, Spending Others' Money Subject to Strict Supervision," http://finance,ifeng.coiw/news/hXj/20081013/177326.shtml, latest access time: September 28, 2017.

the Supreme People's Court on Several Issues Concerning the Application of Law in the Trial of Private Lending Cases promulgated in 2015 provides judicial norms and standards for private lending litigation in practice. More importantly, it limits the maximum interest rates while legalizing private lending to a certain extent.

However, objectively speaking, China's financial legislation currently still lags behind the new requirements of financial supervision, and some financial supervision behaviors have a low level of legal effect. Therefore, we should further enhance the effect of laws on which supervision and regard this a fundamental requirement. Mixed financial operations will become the development trend of the financial industry in the future, which will pose challenges to the existing divided operation and supervision system. Functional supervision and behavioral supervision will become inevitable, and this will also entail a large number of legal and regulatory amendments.

Chapter 6
The Rule of Law in Social Affairs: Alleviating the Problems Related to People's Livelihoods

Yanjie Li

The rule of law in social affairs in China is an important part of the rule of law in promoting economic, political, cultural, social, and ecological progress. It aims to protect the social rights of citizens, adjust the relationship between the government and society and between the government and citizens through the rule of law, promote the establishment of systems for social insurance, social assistance, social special care and pension, employment promotion, protection of disadvantaged groups, charity, etc. to solve social problems, maintain the normal operation of the entire social safety net, and ensure the healthy and sustainable operation and development of the entire society. To implement social law, the state has given full consideration to the establishment of administrative organs. At the central level, the Ministry of Human Resources and Social Security under the State Council is responsible for the implementation of social insurance laws and regulations nationwide.[1] The Ministry of Civil Affairs coordinates the implementation of legal systems for social assistance, charity and welfare, and the National Council for Social Security Fund is responsible for the investment and operation of social security funds.[2] Departments for health and family planning,[3] education, housing and urban-rural development, finance, auditing, and taxation are responsible for the management and implementation of corresponding social laws in accordance with

[1]Among them, the functions of basic medical insurance and maternity insurance for urban employees and urban residents were integrated into the newly established National Healthcare Security Administration after the institutional reform in 2018.

[2]After the institutional reform in 2018, the National Council for Social Security Fund would no longer be administered by the State Council, but by the finance ministry, and the administrative level was no longer specified.

[3]After the institutional reform in 2018, its main function related to social law is integrated into the newly established National Health Commission.

Y. Li (✉)
Institute of Law, CASS, Beijing, China

H. Tian and Y. Lv (eds.), *The Chinese Path of Rule of Law Construction*, China Insights, https://doi.org/10.1007/978-981-16-4130-5_6

their respective responsibilities.[4] At the local level, local competent departments for social insurance, civil affairs, taxation and so on take on their respective responsibilities.[5] Township governments and sub-district offices also assume part of the functions in this respect. In addition to these administrative organs, labor unions, women's federations, disabled persons' federations, youth leagues and other people's organizations, social organizations, and basic-level autonomous organizations such as villagers' committees and residents' committees also assume part of the functions for the implementation of social laws.

Since the reform and opening up, China has entered a new era of comprehensive and profound changes in the social field, and the social law system has gradually entered a new stage of finalized stable and sustainable development. Social legislation and its implementation provide solid legal support for China's social construction. Since 2012, the income of urban and rural residents has grown faster than the economy, and the middle-income groups have continued to expand. A social security system covering urban and rural residents has basically been established, people's health and medical standards have been greatly improved, and the construction of indemnificatory housing has been steadily advanced. From 2013 to 2018, decisive progress was made in the fight against poverty: more than 68 million people were lifted out of poverty, and the poverty headcount ratio dropped from 10.2 to 3.1%. Social pension insurance covers more than 900 million people, and basic medical insurance covers 1.35 billion people, forming the world's largest social security network.[6] In November 2016, the government of the People's Republic of China received the prestigious Award for Outstanding Achievement in Social Security (2014–2016) at the 32nd Global Conference of the International Social Security Association (ISSA). This important international honor not only reflects the international community's recognition toof the achievements China has made in social security, but also means that China's experience in the reform and construction of the social security system will definitely have a positive impact on

[4]It should be noted that the institutional reform of the State Council was initiated in March 2018. Those closely related to the advancement of the rule of law in social affairs include: the Ministry of Veterans Affairs was established to be responsible for preferential treatment and resettlement of retired military soldiers and officers, which was previously the responsibility of the Ministry of Civil Affairs and the Ministry of Human Resources and Social Security; the National Health Commission was established, as a department under the State Council, and the National Health and Family Planning Commission is dissolved; the National Healthcare Security Administration was established to integrate the following functions: basic medical insurance for urban employees and urban residents and maternity insurance of the Ministry of Human Resources and Social Security, new rural cooperative medical care of the National Health and Family Planning Commission, drug and medical service price management of the National Development and Reform Commission, and medical assistance of the Ministry of Civil Affairs; the Ministry of Emergency Management was established to be responsible for disaster relief.

[5]After the institutional reform in 2018, various social insurance premiums, such as basic old-age insurance premiums, basic medical insurance premiums, and unemployment insurance premiums, were collected from collected by the taxation authorities in a unified manner.

[6]For the data, please refer to the *Government Work Report—at the 1st Meeting of the 13th National People's Congress on March 5, 2018*.

other countries in the world. The report to the 19th CPC National Congress called for strengthening the social security system, and required "developing a sustainable multi-tiered social security system that covers the entire population in both urban and rural areas, with clearly defined rights and responsibilities, and support that hits the right level." Social governance systems have been improved, law and order have been maintained, and national security has been fully enhanced.

6.1 Overview of the Rule of Law in Social Affairs in China

In recent years, China has achieved remarkable results in advancing the rule of law in social affairs. More than 20 laws and more than 40 administrative regulations have been enacted, and even more departmental and local regulations have been promulgated. In general, the basic structure of social law has taken shape, and the effect of law enforcement has been increasingly enhanced. The specific results are described below by different fields.

6.1.1 Social Insurance

The *Labor Insurance Regulations* promulgated in 1951 was the first official legal document on social insurance of the PRC. After the reform and opening up, especially after the beginning of the twenty-first century, the social insurance system entered a period of rapid reform. After the 2010 *Social Insurance Law* was promulgated, the State Council and relevant departments formulated and promulgated more than 40 supporting regulations, rules and policy documents, further consolidating the foundation for improving the social insurance system.

The old-age insurance system has been fully established. The old-age insurance for urban residents was piloted in 2011, together with the old-age insurance for rural residents which as previously launched, the old-age insurance system has achieved full coverage of urban and rural residents. By the end of 2014, the basic old-age insurance systems for urban and rural residents were integrated, and the unified old-age insurance for urban and rural residents became an important part of the multitiered old-age insurance system. As of the end of 2013, 31 provinces, autonomous regions, municipalities directly under the Central Government and the Xinjiang Production and Construction Corps had established a basic old-age insurance system at the provincial level.[7]

[7]See the *2013 Statistical Bulletin of the Development of Human Resources and Social Security* by the Ministry of Human Resources and Social Security, http://www.moliES.gov.cn/SYrlzyhshbzb/zwgk/szE/tjgb/201405/t20140529_131147.htmlm, latest access time: May 20, 2017.

The basic old-age insurance system for specific groups is advancing steadily. The *Civil Servants Law* clearly stipulates that "the state shall establish a civil service insurance system." However, China's social insurance system for civil service has been piloted in localities for a long time, but the establishment of a unified national system has been delayed. In January 2015, the State Council issued the *Decision of the State Council on the Reform of the Old-age Insurance System for Employees of State Organs and Public Institutions*, which initiated the reform of the old-age insurance system of state organs and public institutions at the national level and established the same basic old-age insurance system of Party and government organs as that of enterprises. The reform of old-age insurance of state organs and public institutions was implemented simultaneously, occupational annuities and basic old-age insurance were established simultaneously, the reform of old-age insurance system and improvement of the wage system were simultaneously advanced, benefit adjustment mechanism and calculation and payment methods were simultaneously reformed, and various reform measures were implemented simultaneously across the country. In April 2012, the *Military Personnel Insurance Law* was adopted, and the military personnel insurance system with mandatory legal effects and institutional guarantees was formally established in an all-round way. After yeas of development, China's social security system for military personnel covers insurance, pensions and occupational benefits for military personnel, veterans' employment security, and other benefits for military personnel and their families. In 2015, the *Notice on Issues Concerning the Transfer and Continuation of Basic Old-age Insurance Relations for Veterans* and the *Notice on Issues Concerning the Transfer and Continuation of Military Occupational Annuity* were promulgated, clarifying that the financial departments of military logistics organs at various levels are responsible for the establishment and transfer of basic old-age insurance relations for veterans, as well as the calculation, review and transfer of basic old-age insurance benefits.

The basic medical insurance system has been increasingly improved. In 1952, China established a publicly funded medical care system. After the reform and opening up, to meet the needs of the development of the market economy, a basic medical insurance system for urban formal sector workers was established in 1998, requiring that all employers and their employees in cities and towns be covered by insurance. In 2003 and 2007, China established a new rural cooperative medical scheme and a basic medical insurance system for the rural population and urban non-employed population. These two systems were established to meet the basic medical needs of the people and improve the health of all the people in the country. However, in their implementation, the negative effects of the separation of the two systems gradually emerged, and the problems of repeated insurance, repeated investment, and unequal treatment became increasingly serious. Therefore, some localities started to promote the integration of the two systems, and local explorations have provided a useful reference for nationwide integration. In 2016, the State Council promulgated the *Opinions on Integrating the Basic Medical Insurance Systems for Rural and Non-working Urban Residents*, which integrated the basic medical insurance system for urban residents and the new rural cooperative medical system into a unified basic medical insurance system for urban and rural residents. In this way, urban and rural residents enjoy consistent treatment in medical reimbursement, so the medical security system is fairer. In 2012, the National Development and Reform Commission and five other ministries and commissions jointly promulgated the *Guiding Opinions on Conducting the Work on Critical Illness Insurance for Rural and Nonworking Urban Residents* to ease the burden of critical illnesses for participants under basic medical insurance, and China has thus established a critical illness insurance system. In August 2014, the Ministry of Human Resources and Social Security issued the *Opinions on Further Strengthening the Supervision over Basic Medical Insurance and Medical Services*, including medical personnel in the objects of supervision, which is conducive to overcoming illegal expenditures, defrauding medical insurance funds and other serious misconducts in the medical insurance field in recent years. In March 2018, the National Healthcare Security Administration was established to integrate the functions that were previously scattered among the departments of human resources and social security, health and family planning, civil affairs, and finance. In accordance with the requirements of the documents of the central government, the administration is responsible for formulating policies, plans, and standards on healthcare systems in terms of medical insurance, maternity insurance, and medical assistance and ensuring their implementation. The administration also supervises and administers related Medicare funds, improves a platform for transregional medical services and expense settlement, organizes related parties to fix and adjust prices for drugs and medical services, formulates bidding and purchase policies for drugs and medical consumables, supervises their implementation, and supervises and administers medical service behaviors and medical expenses that are included in the scope of medical insurance expenditures.

The functions of the unemployment insurance system have been significantly expanded. The report to the 18th CPC National Congress proposed strengthening the role of unemployment insurance in promoting employment. The 3rd Plenary Session of the 18th CPC Central Committee further clarified that we will strengthen the functions of the unemployment insurance system in preventing unemployment and boosting employment. In November 2014, the Ministry of Human Resources and Social Security, other ministries and commissions jointly promulgated the *Notice on Issues concerning Granting Support in Respect of Unemployment Insurance to Enterprises for Stabilizing Employment*, stating that subsidies for stabilizing employment shall be granted from unemployment insurance funds to enterprises that adopt effective measures to conduct no layoffs or fewer layoffs and stabilize employment. Subsidies for stabilizing employment shall be used for expenses such as employee living allowances, payment of social insurance premiums, job transfer training, and skills upgrading training. Subsidies for stabilizing employment shall be paid once a year and distributed once a year after receiving the applications. In 2017, the Ministry of Human Resources and Social Security and the Ministry of Finance issued the *Notice on Issues concerning Granting Support in Respect of Unemployment Insurance to Insured Workers for Improving Vocational Skills*, specifying the conditions, review, standards, and supervision for employees participating in unemployment insurance to receive subsidies for skill improvement. It is conducive to motivating workers to upgrade their skills, improving employment competitiveness, stabilizing employment, easing employment structural contradictions, and thus reducing unemployment risks.

The management of social insurance handling has been gradually standardized. Since the release of the *Guiding Opinions on the Work for Standardization of Social Insurance* in 2010 (RST/F No. [2010] 41), the formulation of social insurance standards has proceeded in an orderly manner. With the continuous enrichment of standards, the work priority in the standardization of social insurance has shifted from formulation to implementation. In 2015, the Ministry of Human Resources and Social Security issued the *Opinions on Promoting the Implementation of Social Insurance Standards* (RSB/F No. [2015] 63), requiring that by the end of 2017, social insurance handling organs in provinces, cities, and pilot counties shall gradually realize unified business terminology, a unified service image, and a unified service process in the implementation of standards. Among various types of social insurance, there are many bright spots in the promotion of standardization. In 2014, the Ministry of Human Resources and Social Security, the National Health and Family Planning Commission, and the Standardization Administration distributed a series of documents, promulgated the *Administrative Measures for Assessing the Work Capacity of Employees Sustaining Work-Related Injuries*, revised the national standard of *Standard for Identifying Work Ability—Gradation of Disability Caused by Work-related Injuries and Occupational Diseases*, and promulgated the *Operational Specifications for Occupational Rehabilitation of Work-related Injury Insurance (for Trial Implementation)*, to further promote the standardization of work-related injury management. The Ministry of Human Resources and Social Security, the Ministry of Housing and Urban-Rural Development, the State Administration of Work Safety, and the All-China Federation of Trade Unions jointly promulgated the *Opinions on Further Improving Work on Work-related Injury Insurance in the Construction Industry*. Based on the characteristics of the construction industry, it improves the insurance participation method, promotes insurance participation, expands insurance coverage, clarifies the source of payment funds, improves the collection method, scientifically determines the premium rates, simplifies the work-related injury identification and labor ability appraisal procedures, and ensures payment of benefits, etc., laying an institutional foundation for promoting construction enterprises to participate in work-related injury insurance.

The supervision and operation of the Social Security Fund are moving towards legalization. The social insurance fund is the material basis to ensure effective operation of the social insurance system. In 2016, the State Council promulgated the *Regulations on the National Social Security Fund*. As the national social security reserve fund, the funding sources of the national social security fund (NSSF) include budget allocation from the central government, transfer of state-owned capital, fund investment proceeds and funds raised by other means as approved by the State Council. The NSSF assets should be independent from the assets of the National Council for Social Security Fund, the investment management institution or the custody institution and independent of other properties invested by the investment institution and managed by the custodian institution. A strict firewall was built to ensure the safety of the NSSF at the legal level. The operation of the NSSF should try to realize its value preservation and appreciation under the premise of ensuring its safety. In terms of supervision, the National Audit Office is required to audit the NSSF every year, disclose the results to the public, publish on its official website (http://www.ssf.gov.cn/) and nationally circulate newspapers the income and expenditure, management and investment operation of the NSSF every year to accept the supervision of all sectors of society. The regulations clarify that no unit or organization should embezzle or misappropriate the NSSF or engage in its investment operation in violation of the relevant rules.

Fund investment is becoming institutionalized. In August 2015, the State Council promulgated the *Measures for Administration of Basic Pension Insurance Fund Investment*. Pursuant to the Measures, pension fund investment shall be made under the principles of market orientation, diversity and professionalism. Centralized operation by the central government and market-oriented investment operations should be practiced for pension funds. The provincial government collects investable pension funds from various areas into the provincial special-purpose financial account for social security funds and entrusts them to the institutions authorized by the State Council for investment operation. To ensure the safety of pension fund assets, the *Measures* specifies the rights and responsibilities of the trustor, trustee, custody institution and investment management institution and establish a mechanism for mutual checks and balances. The *Measures* also clarifies the independence of pension fund assets. Pension fund assets shall be independent from the assets of and other property managed by the trustor, trustee, custody institution or investment management institution. The trustor, trustee, custody institution and investment management institution shall not incorporate pension fund assets into their own property. To strengthen the management and supervision of the social security fund and straighten out the relationship of functions and duties between relevant departments to ensure the security and steady value preservation and appreciation of the social security fund, after the institutional reform in 2018, the National Council for Social Security Fund was no longer administered by the State Council but by the finance ministry. No administrative level is defined for the National Council for Social Security Fund as China's national social security fund investment operator.

In addition to the sound system brought about by institutional building, the outstanding achievements of the social insurance system are also reflected in the following aspects.

First, the standards for social insurance premium rates are more reasonable. From 2015 to 2017, the Ministry of Human Resources and Social Security and the Ministry of Finance successively promulgated policy documents for adjusting unemployment insurance premium rates, reducing the unemployment insurance premium rate from 3 to 1%.[8] In July 2015, the Ministry of Human Resources and Social Security and the Ministry of Finance promulgated the *Notice on Adjusting the Policy for Work-related Injury Insurance Premium Rates*, which lowered the rate of work-related injury insurance and classified industrial work-related injury risks into one to eight categories. By 2019, the proportion of social insurance paid by companies was steadily and orderly reduced. Timely adjustment of social insurance premium rates is conducive to reducing the burden on participating enterprises and individuals and is also an important move to improve the social insurance system and the dynamic premium rate adjustment mechanism.

Second, the problems left over from the past have been mostly resolved. After the promulgation of the *Social Insurance Law*, we solved longstanding problems concerning pensions for more than five million retirees of collectively owned enterprises and included 3.12 million persons who suffer from past work-related injuries and dependents of employees who lost their lives in work-related accidents in workers' compensation insurance. We have solved the problem concerning pensions for "May 7th workers" and "family workers," the problem of medical insurance for 5.96 million retired workers from closed and bankrupt state-owned enterprises and the problem of medical insurance for more than 2 million other retirees from closed and bankrupt enterprises and employees of enterprises in difficulties.

6.1.2 Social Assistance

Social assistance is the most basic and oldest institutional arrangement in the rule of law system for social affairs. The bottom line of social assistance is to adhere fairness, and its institutional building and implementation level reflect the country's minimum responsibility for people's livelihood and the conscience of the entire society. The Communist Party of China and the Central People's Government have a fine tradition of attaching great importance to social assistance and insist on investing considerable manpower and material resources to protect those groups in difficulties.

In 2014, the State Council promulgated the *Interim Measures for Social Assistance*, which was China's first central administrative regulations to coordinate various social assistance projects. The *Measures* specifies "the principle of holding the baseline, responding to emergencies and difficulties, and being sustainable" for China's social assistance system and stipulates that China's social assistance covers minimum subsistence guarantees, support for the especially poor, medical assistance, education assistance, housing assistance, employment assistance, temporary

[8]Refer to *The Notice of the Ministry of Human Resources and Social Security on the Phased Reduction of Unemployment Insurance Premium Rates* (RSB/F No. [2017] 14), and *The Notice of the Ministry of Human Resources and Social Security on the Phased Reduction of Social Insurance Premium Rates* (RSB/F No. [2016] 36) and other documents.

assistance and disaster relief, etc., and its goal is to bridge the urban-rural gap in social assistance in the past.

In terms of minimum subsistence guarantees, in 2012, the State Council promulgated the *Opinions on Further Strengthening and Improving the Work of Rural and Urban Minimum Subsistence Guarantee* (GF No. [2012] 45), and the Ministry of Civil Affairs and the Ministry of Finance jointly promulgated the *Measures for the Administration of Rural and Urban Minimum Subsistence Allowances* (CS No. [2012] 171), which clearly specifies the raising, distribution, granting and supervision of urban and rural subsistence allowances. In the same year, the Ministry of Civil Affairs promulgated the *Measures for Examination and Approval of Minimum Subsistence Allowances (for Trial Implementation)* to regulate the examination and approval procedures of the subsistence allowance. On this basis, many localities started to make active explorations. For example, Zhejiang Province has established a system of avoidance of social assistance examination and approval, Tianjin City has improved the examination and approval mechanism for subsistence allowances with separation of registered and actual residences, Chongqing City has implemented regular announcement of households receiving urban and rural subsistence allowances, and Jilin Province has fully implemented the minimum subsistence allowance approval and management mode characterized by "two-tiered management, three-tiered joint review, and one-hall services."

In terms of medical assistance, in 2012, the Ministry of Civil Affairs, the Ministry of Finance and other departments promulgated the *Opinions on the Pilot Work of Medical Assistance for Major and Critical Diseases* to launch trials to provide medical assistance to eligible people suffering from serious diseases. In 2015, the *Notice of the General Office of the State Council on Forwarding the Opinions of the Ministry of Civil Affairs and Other Departments on Further Improving the Medical Assistance System and Comprehensively Carrying out the Work of Medical Assistance for Major and Critical Diseases* (G/F No. [2015] 30) was promulgated, which combined the urban and rural medical assistance systems into the urban-rural medical assistance system. In terms of recipients, family members living on minimum subsistence allowances and the especially poor are the major recipients, and the elderly, minors, severely disabled and severely ill people from low-income families, and other special especially poor people are gradually included in the scope of assistance. The assistance methods include outpatient assistance and hospitalization assistance. Outpatient assistance is mainly targeted at patients with chronic diseases who need long-term medication or patients with critical disease who need long-term outpatient treatment, which leads to high out-of-pocket expenses. Hospitalization assistance is targeted at those who have higher personal burdens among hospitalization expenses incurred by designated medical institutions after reimbursement for basic medical insurance, major illness insurance for urban and rural residents, various supplementary medical insurances, and commercial insurance.

In terms of education assistance, receiving education is a basic right granted to citizens by the Constitution. However, due to factors such as family economic status and their own disabilities, there are still school-age students who have dropped out of school in reality. The 2015 *Decision of the CPC Central Committee and the State Council on Winning the Tough Battle Against Poverty* requires that children from poverty-stricken families receive fair and quality education to block the intergenerational transmission of poverty. In addition, to guarantee the basic right to receive education, it is necessary to provide education assistance to the poor. The *Interim Measures for Social Assistance* promulgated by the State Council in 2014 stipulates that the State should provide educational assistance to students in the compulsory education stage who are members of families receiving minimum subsistence allowances and extremely poor families. For students in high school education (including secondary vocational education) and general higher education stages who are members of families receiving minimum subsistence allowances and extremely poor families and disabled children who are unable to attend compulsory education, appropriate education assistance should be given according to the actual situations. Based on the needs of different stages, the government supports the students by reducing or exempting tuition fees, granting aid and providing living allowances to ensure that students' basic needs in life and study can be met.

Temporary assistance is an emergency and transitional assistance rendered by the state to families or individuals who have fallen on hard times due to emergencies, accidental injuries, major illnesses, or other special causes, and other social assistance systems are temporarily unable to cover or who still have serious difficulties in basic life after assistance. The establishment of a temporary assistance system is of great significance to fill the gaps in the social assistance system and ensure that the bottom of the social assistance safety net is not broken. Regarding temporary assistance, on the basis of the *Interim Measures for Social Assistance*, the State Council promulgated the *Notice on Comprehensively Establishing the Temporary Assistance System* in October 2014, clarifying that the civil affairs department of the State Council should coordinate the establishment of a national temporary assistance system, and local governments at various levels should be responsible for its implementation to ensure that assistance is rendered timely and appropriately to all people in need of their sudden, urgent, and temporary life difficulties.

Assistance and support for the extremely poor is an assistance system for persons who are aged, disabled or under the age of 16 and have no ability to work, no source of income, and no statutory obligors to provide for them, bring them up or support them, or whose statutory obligors have no ability to provide for them, bring them up or support them. Assistance and support for the extremely poor is a continuation and development of the previous systems for rural residents eligible for the "Five Guarantees" and urSban residents without income, the ability to work, or support by family.[9] Approximately 5.91 million people live in extreme poverty in urban and rural areas nationwide. In 2016, the State Council promulgated the

[9]Urban "sanwu" people means persons with non-agricultural registered permanent residence in urban areas who are aged, disabled or under the age of 16 and have no ability to work, no source of income, and no statutory obligors to provide for them, bring them up or support them, or whose statutory obligors have no ability to provide for them, bring them up or support them.

Opinions on Further Improving the Assistance and Support System for People in Extreme Difficulty, which included all eligible persons in extreme difficulties into the scope of assistance and support, to ensure that assistance and support is rendered to all people in need. Assistance and support to them is divided into two parts: basic life and attendance, including basic subsistence guarantees such as grain and oil, clothing, pocket money, and services such as disease treatment and funerals. The funds required are included in the fiscal budget. To better integrate it with other security systems, the Opinions clarify that the abovementioned people in extreme difficulty can simultaneously enjoy benefits such as basic pension insurance and basic medical insurance for urban and rural residents but should no longer receive minimum subsistence allowances.

6.1.3 Social Welfare

China's legal system for social welfare was initially established and constantly improved. The adoption and implementation of the three major rights protection laws (namely, the *Law on the Protection of Rights and Interests of the Elderly*, the *Law on the Protection of the Disabled*, and the *Law on the Protection of Minors*) have become the cornerstones of the legal system for social welfare. The supporting laws, regulations, and policy systems have also been gradually improved.

Actively responding to population ageing has been raised as a major national strategy. The *Law on the Protection of the Rights and Interests of the Elderly* was revised and adopted in December 2012 and was revised for the second time in April 2015. The two legal revisions added content such as preferential social treatment and the construction of a favorable inhabiting environment. Later, more than ten provinces and municipalities, including Jiangsu, Shandong, Shaanxi, Hunan, Jilin, Gansu, Anhui, Shanghai, Jiangxi, Shanxi, Liaoning, etc. revised their local regulations to protect the rights and interests of the elderly.

With rapid social and economic development, an increasing number of migrant workers have moved into cities, but the development of the education and medical security system for the children of migrants in places where their families have relocated is not synchronized. The common phenomenon of "left-behind children" in rural areas has aroused widespread social concern. "Left-behind children" are in a state of lack of parental care and effective guardianship, and there are some vicious cases in society that have seriously damaged the life and health rights of left-behind children. In response to this, the State Council specifically promulgated the *Opinions on Strengthening the Care and Protection of Left-behind Children in Rural Areas*, clarifying and strengthening the responsibilities of primary-level township governments and villagers' (residents') committees. The opinions require villagers' (residents') committees to conduct regular visits and comprehensive investigations to grasp the basic information on family status, guardianship, and school attendance of left-behind children in rural areas in a timely manner and report it to the township people's governments (subdistrict offices); establish information records for each left-behind child in rural areas; and conduct dynamic management. The Opinion also requires Party members and officials, stationing officials in villages and professional social workers to pay regular visits to left-behind children in extreme difficulties to ensure that they are being properly cared for. In view of the fact that the root cause for the problems of left-behind children lies in the spatial separation of migrant workers as parents and their children, the Opinions also clearly requires the local governments in the places where migrant workers' families have relocated to provide more help and support to migrant workers in household registration, housing security, care and schooling. The above measures will help solve the problems of left-behind children completely.

In recent years, China has constantly strengthened the protection of children's rights and significantly optimized the environment for their subsistence and development. However, there still exist some problems. Some children face difficulties in life due to the poverty of their families, their own disabilities or a lack of effective custody. Children living in difficulty include those who grow up in poverty and thus have poor access to medical treatment or education, those who have difficulties in receiving rehabilitation, nursing and integrating in society due to their disabilities, and those who are subject to maltreatment, abandonment, accidental injuries or infringement that threaten or infringe on their safety for lack of or improper family custody. To strengthen the protection of children in difficulty, the State Council promulgated the *Opinions on Strengthening Security Work for Children in Difficulty* (GF No. [2016] 36), which proposed establishing relevant mechanisms in five aspects: ensuring subsistence, basic medical care, schooling and custody, and strengthening welfare services for children with disabilities. To solve practical problems such as shorter basic-level workers for child welfare, imperfect systems, and lack of departmental collaboration, the Opinions clarifies the responsibilities of county-level people's governments, township people's governments (subdistrict offices), and villagers' (residents') committees in protecting children in difficulty and sets up the system of child welfare supervisors (child rights inspectors). In terms of departmental cooperation, the departments of civil affairs and working committees on women and children are required to take the lead and work with the departments of education, health and family planning, human resources and social security, public security and so on to jointly carry out the work for protection of children in difficulty, and a mechanism of "one-department acceptance, collaborative handling" with strong operability has been established. As a result, child welfare is institutionalized and categorized and expanded from orphans and abandoned infants to children in social difficulties, which will ensure that all children in difficulty have access to supportive policies.

The Ministry of Civil Affairs and the Ministry of Finance have promulgated a series of documents, including the *Notice on the Payment of Basic Living Expenses for HIV-Infected Children,* to include HIV-infected children in the scope of basic subsistence guarantees and have steadily promoted a security system for children in difficulties such as unsupported children, children from single-parent families, and minor children of prisoners and minor children of severely disabled families.

China currently has about 85 million disabled people. How to protect their legal rights and interests, such as the right to education and employment, is an important task for advancing the rule of law in China's society. The *Regulations on Education for the Disabled* promulgated in 1994 has played an important role in the protection of the rights to education of the disabled and the development of educational undertakings for the disabled under the historical background. However, so far, education for persons with disabilities still lags behind education in other aspects. Insufficient and uneven distribution of special education resources, low standards of education and teaching, low education quality, insufficient security support, and relatively lagging educational concepts have restricted the level of protection of the right to education for persons with disabilities. In response, the *Regulations on Education for the Disabled* have been revised and improved in terms of the development goals and concepts of education for persons with disabilities, admission arrangements, teaching standards, teacher team building, and security support. The revised *Regulations on Education for the Disabled* upgraded the policy documents that have been promulgated in recent years for promoting the development of education undertakings for persons with disabilities to a legal system to improve the admission arrangements for persons with disabilities and education and regulate teaching activities on the basis of overall planning and reasonable allocation of special education resources. In terms of security and support, the funds needed for education for persons with disabilities are included in the government budget at the corresponding level, and the employment guarantee funds for persons with disabilities can be used in special education schools to carry out vocational education as prescribed; schools should exempt disabled students with financial difficulties from tuition and reduce sundry fees or exempt them from such fees in accordance with relevant national regulations and prioritize subsidies to them.

The Chinese government has always attached great importance to disability prevention work and has continuously promoted the formulation and improvement of laws and policies related to disability prevention. Some practices have achieved remarkable results. Since 1988, the rehabilitation of the disabled has been incorporated into national plans for economic and social development. China has successively formulated and implemented five 5-year development plans for the cause of the disabled and the supporting implementation plans for rehabilitation. By the end of 2015, the state had provided basic rehabilitation services to 27.97 million disabled persons.[10] On the basis of summarizing existing practices and experience, in response to the challenges at the current stage, the State Council promulgated the *Regulations on Disability Prevention and Rehabilitation of Persons with Disabilities* in 2017, which stipulates that disability prevention work should cover

[10]See "Improving the Prevention Mechanism and Enhancing the Ability of Rehabilitation—Interpretation by Hu Xiangyang, Director of the Rehabilitation Department of the China Disabled Persons' Federation on *Regulations on Disability Prevention and Rehabilitation of Persons with Disabilities*," http://www.gov.cn/xinwen/2017-02/27/content5171461.htm#1, latest access time: June 12, 2017.

the entire population and the entire life cycle, and on the basis of communities and families, universal prevention and control over key objects should be combined. In terms of institutional arrangements, people's governments at or above the county level should take the lead in the work of disability prevention, assess and supervise the work undertaken by relevant departments; strengthen monitoring and information integration, regularly investigate disability status, and implement dynamic monitoring of major disability factors; clarify the division and coordination of responsibilities between departments of health and family planning, education, civil affairs, and disabled persons' federations and other relevant departments.

In the field of social welfare, it is also worth mentioning that the national birth policy is improving. Since the State Council approved and circulated the *Report on Strengthening the Work for Family Planning* in 1971, which emphasized the need for family planning, China's fertility policy has been continuously adjusted and improved in practice. In December 2013, the Standing Committee of the 12th National People's Congress adopted the State Council's proposal on adjusting and improving the fertility policy and agreed to initiate the implementation of the policy that couples can have two children if either spouse is an only child. In December 2015, China revised the *Law on Population and Family Planning* to comprehensively implement the policy that one couple can have two children to promote balanced population development and actively carry out actions to deal with population ageing.

6.1.4 Charity and Others

In recent years, the development of China's philanthropy has ushered in unprecedented opportunities. At the end of 2014, the State Council promulgated the *Guiding Opinions on Promoting the Healthy Development of Philanthropy*, which affirmed the positive role of philanthropy in China's social field, and proposed encouraging and supporting charitable activities focusing on poverty alleviation, cultivating and regulating various charitable organizations. As the first central document dedicated to promoting and regulating philanthropy at the national level, it has strong declarative significance and practical effects.

In 2016, the *Charity Law* was reviewed and adopted at the 4th Session of the 12th National People's Congress. As a basic law promulgated by the National People's Congress, it has established the basic system in the field of charity and improved the institutional mechanism for philanthropy. This law is an important law in the social field and the basic law of the charity system. Its promulgation and implementation signify that China's philanthropy has entered the track of legalization. The law defines the concept of "big charity," covering public benefit actions such as helping the poor and the needy; giving relief to the aged, orphans, the sick, the disabled, and giving special care to disabled servicemen, and to family members of revolutionary martyrs and servicemen; alleviating losses incurred by natural disasters; promoting the development of education, science, culture, health, sports and other undertakings, and preventing and controlling pollution and other public hazards, and protecting and improving the ecological environment, which has greatly expanded the development space of charity. The establishment of charitable organizations establishes the principle of direct registration and recognition; appropriately regulates charitable organizations' fundraising from the public, especially online fundraising; includes equities, houses, intellectual property rights and other tangible and intangible property to donate property; and comprehensively specifies tax reductions or exemptions for donations for charitable purposes to remove policy obstacles to the development of philanthropy. Meanwhile, the Charity Law devotes a chapter to charitable trusts, and the institutional bottleneck of charitable trusts has been broken to a certain extent. For example, it stipulates that charitable trusts are public trusts, and the competent authority is the department of civil affairs; charitable organizations and trust companies can act as trustees of charitable trusts; in terms of the threshold for establishment, the approval system is replaced by the filing system; charitable trust may determine a supervisor as required; and it also gives provisions on tax preferences and legal liabilities for charitable trusts.

In February 2017, the *Red Cross Law* was revised and adopted. This is the first revision of the law in more than 20 years since it was promulgated in 1993. It is a millstone event in the history of the development of red cross cause in China and has great practical significance for the healthy development of red cross cause in China. In terms of missions, the primary mission of the Red Cross Societies in China was usually summarized as emergence response, first aid and humanitarian aid. The revised law also includes unpaid blood donation, donation of bodies and organs, and hematopoietic stem cell donation as another primary mission of the Red Cross Societies and has brought them into the track of rule of law. In terms of internal governance, Red Cross Societies at various levels should establish the council and the board of supervisors to form a new governance structure with separate powers and responsibilities for the council, executive committee and board of supervisors. The chapter "Funds and Property" was renamed "Property and Supervision" to strengthen the supervision over the property of the Red Cross societies from the perspective of concepts and specific systems. For example, the Red Cross societies should establish a system for financial management, internal control, public auditing and supervision of funds and assets. Legally established independent third-party agencies should be hired to audit the sources and use of donated money and materials, and the results should be reported to the council and the board of supervisors of Red Cross societies and disclosed to the public. The Red Cross societies should also establish a sound information disclosure system and disclose the information on the sources and use of donated money and materials to the public on the unified information platform in a timely manner to accept the supervision of the society, and the income and use of property of Red Cross societies should be subject to supervision by the auditing departments in accordance with the law. As a result, the supervision system for Red Cross societies has been improved. A new chapter entitled "Legal Liabilities" specifies the legal responsibilities and consequences of the Red Cross societies and their staff, and it will play a better role in protecting the reputation, brand logo, property and other legitimate rights and interests of Red Cross societies.

6.2 The Achievements of Rule of Law in Social Affairs in China

Under the background that the Party and government attach great importance to social construction and social governance and comprehensively advance the rule of law, China has achieved fruitful results in advancing the rule of law in social affairs, which are demonstrated in the following aspects.

6.2.1 The Level of Security Has Been Continuously Improved

As the main part of social law, the level of development of the legal system for social security is a barometer reflecting the status of a country's social law. As praised by the International Social Security Association while presenting the Award for Outstanding Achievement in Social Security to the Chinese government, during 2008–2015, the Chinese government's investment in social security increased by 20% every year, the average growth rate of pension insurance coverage was 27.7%, and the coverage of medical security reached approximately 95% of the total population.[11] As of the end of the first quarter of 2017, the number of people participating in basic old-age insurance for urban workers reached 383 million, the number of people participating in basic old-age insurance for rural and nonworking urban residents reached 508 million, and the number of people participating in medical insurance was close to 1.012 billion people.

The level of social insurance benefits has been raised year by year. Since 2005, basic pensions for retirees have been raised for many consecutive years. The State Council proposed in the *2017 Government Work Report* that "we will continue to increase the basic pensions for retirees and ensure that they are paid on time and in full." The *2018 Government Work Report* once again proposed that "we will continue to increase the basic pensions for retirees and the basic old-age pension for rural and non-working urban residents." As a result, the basic pension standard for corporate retirees in China has been increased consecutively over the past 14 years, which has not only effectively improved the living standards of corporate retirees but also greatly reduced the gap between the treatment of retirees from enterprises

[11] See "the Ministry of Human Resources and Social Security Holds Briefing on the Chinese Government's Receiving the Award for Outstanding Achievement in Social Security," http://www.gov.cn/xinwen/2016-12/13/content_5147531.htm#1, latest access time: June 14, 2017.

and those from government organs and public institutions. The fairness of the basic old-age insurance system has been improved. Without doubt, while affirming the positive significance of the increase in the basic pension standard, the Chinese government will also comprehensively evaluate factors such as price increases and the wages of employees on duty in the future and gradually establish a scientific and institutionalized basic pension adjustment mechanism.

Basic public services in the social sector are moving towards equalization. The *Interim Regulations on Residence Permits* promulgated by the State Council in 2015 enables the permanent resident population to enjoy similar treatment or even the same treatment as the household registered population without fundamentally changing the household registration system. Thus, "temporary residence permits" are replaced by "residence permits", which means that for permanent residents without local household registration, the government will switch from a management mode to a service mode. First, the regulations highlight the empowerment function of residence permits and the service function and responsibilities of government departments. Specifying the nature and conditions for the application of residence permits provides basic public services and conveniences for holders of residence permits, including basic public services such as compulsory education, basic public employment services, conveniences for handling entry and exit documents, motor vehicle registration, etc. Second, all localities are required to actively create conditions through the gradient empowerment mechanism to gradually expand the scope of public services and conveniences provided to residence permit holders, improve service standards, and disclose them to the public regularly. Third, it clarifies the connecting channels for the holder to apply for permanent residence registration in his or her place of residence and the criteria for various cities to determine the conditions for household registration. Some localities have actively promoted the equalization of basic public services. For example, the Guangzhou Municipal Government adopted the *Integration Action Plan of Guangzhou City for People Coming to Guangzhoug (2016–2020)*, which will form a more sound system for service provision and management of personnel coming to Guangzhou.

6.2.2 The Supervision System is Gradually Improving

Government leadership is an important feature of China's social security. The transition from policy-based governance to law-based governance is an important mode transformation in China's social sector. The establishment and reform of various systems are brought into the track of rule of law, and the reforms and supervision led by the National People's Congress are gradually strengthened, which is fully reflected in the following typical examples.

Pilot work on the integrated implementation of maternity insurance and basic medical insurance for workers has started. As it has broke the relevant provisions of the *Social Insurance Law*, the State Council requested the NPC Standing Committee to temporarily adjust the implementation of relevant laws in the pilot areas during the pilot period. The 25th Meeting of the Standing Committee of the 12th National People's Congress adopted the *Decision on Authorizing the State Council to Temporarily Adjusting the Implementation of the Relevant Provisions of the Social Insurance Law of the People's Republic of China in the 12 Pilot Cities Including Handan City, Hebei Province for Integrated Implementation of Maternity Insurance and Basic Medical Insurance for Workers*. The issuance of the authorization decision fully demonstrates that the reform of the social security system is moving onto the track of rule of law.

In March 2013, the Ministry of Finance submitted budgets for social security funds at the 1st session of the 12th National People's Congress. For the first time, social security funds were included in the scope of central budgets for management to accept the supervision of the highest organ of state power. In December 2014, the 12th meeting of the Standing Committee of the 12th National People's Congress held a joint meeting to deliberate on the report of the State Council on pressing forward in coordinated manner the building of the urban and rural social security system, and carried out special inquiry on issues, such as how to enhance the sustainability of the old-age insurance fund and the top-level design of the old-age insurance system, promote national overall planning of basic old-age insurance, and gradually raise the retirement age. Special inquiry is an important way for the organs of state power in China to perform their duties to supervise the work of the people's government, the people's court and the people's procuratorate according to law, which is conducive to the final implementation of the central government's decisions on social security affairs.

6.2.3 Synchronous Advancement of Supporting Systems

The name "soft law" in Chinese social law has been around for a long time, and the poor effect of law enforcement has become a bottleneck restricting the effect of the rule of law. In recent years, efforts have been redoubled to promote the establishment of legal responsibilities and supporting systems in various fields of social law, actively connect them with criminal law, and promote the disclosure of punishment results to the public to strengthen the enforcement effect of social law.

In 2014, the NPC Standing Committee promulgated the *Interpretation on Article 266 of the Criminal Law of the People's Republic of China*, which includes defrauding the funds of social insurances for old age, medical care, work-related injuries, unemployment and maternity and the benefits of other social insurances through cheating, counterfeit documentary evidence or other means in the offences of swindling public and private money or property in Article 266 of the *Criminal Law*. This provides a criminal law basis for cracking down on insurance fraud and crimes and safeguarding the safety of social insurance funds. In July 2018, in its *Reply of the Supreme People's Procuratorate as to Whether the Embezzlement of the Funds of Social Insurances for Old-age and Medical Care* etc. *Applies to the Provision in Item 1 of Paragraph 2 of Article 1 of the Interpretation of the Supreme*

People's Procuratorate on Several Issues Concerning the Application of Law in the Handling of Criminal Cases Involving Embezzlement and Bribery, the Supreme People's Procuratorate clearly stated that the funds of social insurances for old age, medical care, work-related injuries, unemployment and maternity can be recognized as "Specific Money and Property" as specified in Item 1 of Paragraph 2 of Article 1 *of* the *Interpretation of the Supreme People's Procuratorate on Several Issues Concerning the Application of Law in the Handling of Criminal Cases Involving Embezzlement and Bribery*. Thus, embezzlement of social insurance funds has been included in the scope of criminal cases involving embezzlement and bribery that should be severely cracked down. The Ministry of Human Resources and Social Security and the Ministry of Public Security jointly promulgated the *Notice on Strengthening the Investigation, Handling and Transfer of Cases Involving Social Insurance Fraud*, providing the basis for the standards and procedures for investigation and transfer of social insurance violations that constitute crimes. In September 2016, The Ministry of Human Resources and Social Security promulgated the *Measures for the Disclosure of Major Acts in Violation of the Labor Security Law*. The implementation of the *Measures* helps increase the cost of labor and social security violations, strengthen social supervision, and force employers to comply with labor and social security laws and regulations.

In the past, there was generally a lack of supporting mechanisms in social legislation. In recent years, remarkable results have been achieved in the establishment of supporting systems in social legislation. For example, the revised *Law on the Protection of Rights and Interests of the Elderly* was formally enacted in 2013, and the two supporting departmental regulations of the law, namely, the *Measures for Licensing for the Establishment of Elderly Care Institutions* and the *Measures for the Administration of Elderly Care Institutions,* were implemented simultaneously, which has positive significance for the enforcement of the law. After the promulgation of the *Charity Law* in 2016, to improve the charity legal system, the Ministry of Civil Affairs and relevant departments promulgated a series of supporting regulations and normative documents to ensure a good enforcement effect of the law. To achieve convergence with the *Charity Law*, the Ministry of Civil Affairs promulgated the *Measures for the Accreditation of Charitable Organizations* and the *Notice on Related Issues Concerning the Accreditation of Charity Organizations*. In view of the relatively rough provisions of the *Charity Law* regarding fundraising from the public, the relevant departments have promulgated a series of regulations and normative documents, such as the *Administrative Measures for Charitable Organizations' Fund-raising from the Public*, the *Measures for the Administration of Public Fund-raising Platform Services*, and the *Announcement of the Ministry of Civil Affairs on Designating the First Batch of Internet Fund-raising Information Platforms for Charitable Organizations*, to regulate charitable fundraising and fundraising from the public and enable online fundraising to be more operational. In view of the fact that charitable trusts have received extensive attention from charity practitioners and academia during the formulation of the *Charity Law*, the *Charity Law* has been repeatedly revised and finally devotes a chapter to charitable trusts. The Ministry of

Civil Affairs and the China Banking Regulatory Commission jointly promulgated the *Notice on Strengthening the Work for the Filing of Charitable Trusts*, which provides an important basis for the implementation of charitable trusts. To ensure tax reduction or exemption for charity, the Ministry of Civil Affairs and the General Administration of Customs jointly promulgated the *Notice on Issues Concerning the Procedures for Handling Tax Reduction or Exemption for Imported Charitable Donated Materials by Social Organizations and Foundations* (M/F No. [2016] 64), the General Administration of Customs promulgated *Announcement No. [2016] 17 on Interim Measures for the Exemption of Import Duties on Charitable Donated Materials* and other documents, and abolished the *Announcement of the Ministry of Finance and the State Administration of Taxation on Interim Measures for the Exemption of Import Duties on Poverty Alleviation and Charitable Donated Materials* (CS No. [2000] 152). These documents specify the objects, contents and implementation measures of tax deduction or exemption for materials directly used for charitable purposes donated altruistically by donors to recipients. The promulgation of a series of laws and favorable regulations and policies will ensure healthy and sustainable development of philanthropy in the future.

6.2.4 Highlighting the Demand Orientation of the People

Whether the rule of law in social affairs can be deeply rooted in people's hearts and truly implemented, the important factor lies in whether it can overcome the concern for the self-construction of society and whether it can respond to the deep-seated problems in social transformation and social governance. In recent years, the important source of the effectiveness of the rule of law in social affairs in China lies in its increasing responsiveness.

First, remarkable results have been achieved in advancing the rule of law in social affairs. Taking social insurance as an example, the information disclosure system has been established and improved in an orderly manner, and a relatively sound legal system has been put in place. The Ministry of Human Resources and Social Security has successively issued a series of documents to set requirements for the disclosure of social insurance information and government affairs, including the *Implementation Measures for Government Information Disclosure* (RST/F No. [2010] 111), the *Opinions on Promoting the Disclosure of Government Affairs* (RSBF No. [2013] 92), and the *Implementation Opinions of the General Office of the Ministry of Human Resources and Social Security on Comprehensively Promoting the Work of Disclosure of Government Affairs* (RSTF No. [2017] 21). To better meet the information demands of people from all walks of life, at the end of 2014, the Ministry of Human Resources and Social Security promulgated the *Notice on Further Improving the Social Insurance Information Disclosure System* (RSBF No. [2014] 82), making arrangements for the work of social insurance information disclosure in the new era. The Ministry of Human Resources and Social Security has proactively disclosed information on social insurance to the public through various channels, including the news release system, the statistical bulletin on the development of human resources and social security every year, statistical yearbooks and social security yearbooks, and annual reports on China's social insurance development, which are regularly made public.

Second, high efficiency and convenience for the people has become an important orientation for advancing the rule of law in social affairs. To streamline the tedious procedures of business registration, China has implemented the new "Five-in-One" business license by incorporating social insurance registration and statistics registration certificates into the previous "Three Certificates in One" reform (business license, organization code certificate and tax registration certificate), which upgraded the business license to include five certificates and achieve one code for one license. To this end, in June 2016, the General Office of the State Council promulgated the *Circular on Accelerating the Reform of the Registration System of "Incorporating Five Certificates into One and One Code for One License."* To solve the much criticized problem of "call in vain for help" in the field of social assistance, the mechanism of "one-department acceptance, coordinated handling" was promoted at the township and subdistrict levels. For example, many regions represented by Shanghai have constructed social affairs acceptance and handling centers, which accept and handle nearly 200 items of people's livelihood affairs, including employment services, unemployment insurance, endowment insurance, family planning, residence permits, social security cards, etc. in one window and launch innovative reforms such as online reservations, standardization, all-year-round services, and city-wide general handling to provide the people with the most convenient services. Many localities have promoted the "one-stop" settlement mechanism in the field of medical security. For eligible recipients, after reimbursement by basic medical insurance, critical illness insurance for urban residents, and various supplementary medical and commercial insurances, the medical assistance system will provide assistance to the part of individual payment. Specifically, a "one-stop" settlement window is set up in the designated medical institutions, and the medical expenses incurred by the recipients are directly paid to the designated medical institutions through the medical assistance mechanism at the window. As a result, medical assistance procedures have been simplified to better safeguard the right to health of urban and rural residents in need.

Third, the issues that concern the people the most have become the focus of legal system construction. The report to the 19th CPC National Congress stated that "As we work to ensure and improve people's well-being, we must focus on the most pressing, most immediate issues that concern the people the most." A typical example is the initiation of the formulation of the *Charity Law*. Since 2008, more than 800 delegates to the National People's Congress have put forward 27 motions and 29 proposals for enacting the *Charity Law*, reflecting the eager expectations of all sectors of society. In 2014, the NPC Internal and Judicial Affairs Committee established a charity legislation leading group to initiate the legislative process and decided to submit the draft to the 4th Session of the 12th National People's Congress for deliberation; thus, the *Charity Law* was successfully promulgated. To solve the problems of "expensive medical bills and difficult access to quality medical services," in October 2016, the CPC Central Committee and the State Council issued the *Outline of the plan for a Healthy China 2030*, which will become the action plan for promoting a healthy China for more than ten years in the future. The outline stresses the notion of "mass health", shifts the emphasis from "disease treatment to the promotion of public health", and takes "health for all" as the fundamental purpose of building a healthy China. It focuses on the whole population and the whole life cycle, highlights the security role of legislation and legal amendments, strengthens the government's responsibilities in the health field, establishes a supervision and management system that combines government supervision, industry self-discipline and social supervision, and strengthens the enforcement supervision system and capacity building in the health field. At the micro level, interprovincial on-the-spot settlement of medical bills through basic insurance accounts has received widespread public attention. In recent years, with the frequent migration of the population, migrant workers and elderly people living with their children in other places have been constrained by mechanisms such as the level of coordination, payment methods, review mechanisms, and reimbursement ratios. Although they are covered by the national medical security system, they fail to receive the benefits of medical insurance in a timely manner. In November 2014, the Ministry of Human Resources and Social Security issued the *Guiding Opinions on Further Strengthening Interprovincial on-the-spot settlement of Medical Bills through Basic Insurance Accounts*. By relying on the social insurance information system, we will promote interprovincial on-the-spot settlement services for medical bills to realize direct settlement of medical bills within the scope of cities, standardize intraprovincial direct settlement of medical bills, and improve the policies for interprovincial employment. In December 2016, the Ministry of Human Resources and Social Security and the *Ministry of Finance jointly issued the Notice on Direct Settlement of Medical Bills for Interprovincial Medical Treatment and Hospitalization for Basic Medical Insurance* and the *Regulations for Direct Settlement of Medical Expenses for Basic Medical Insurance for Interprovincial Medical Treatment and Hospitalization Expenses* to accelerate the promotion of the national network of basic medical insurance and direct settlement of medical expenses for hospitalization in different places. As of the end of 2016, 30 provinces, autonomous regions, and municipalities directly under the central government had achieved settlement with cards for medical treatment in different places within the province. In the first half of 2017, the direct settlement of hospitalization expenses for retired personnel across the provinces was realized. In the future, the direct settlement of hospitalization expenses for all people who meet the referral conditions will be realized.

Fourth, judicial organs should step up efforts in this regard. In the past five years, since the 18th CPC National Congress, the Supreme People's Court has clarified the standards for work-related injuries and made great efforts to protect the rights and interests of workers. Courts at various levels have promoted the experience of the courts in Henan, Hunan and Sichuan in resolving the difficulties for peasant workers in acquiring their wages, punishing malicious arrears of wages in accordance with the law, and recovering 29.44 billion yuan of "hard-earned money" for migrant workers.[12] The procuratorial organs also play a huge role in labor protection. Procuratorial organs at various levels prosecuted 7,957 people for refusing to pay labor remuneration, supported migrant workers to prosecute 9,176 cases of, issued 370 procuratorial recommendations to relevant departments, supervised the performance of their duties in accordance with the law, and helped more than 20,000 migrant workers recover their owed labor remuneration 340 million yuan.[13]

6.2.5 Multi-subject Co-governance

Extensive participation is of great significance to enhancing the scientific rationality and legality of various systems. In the field of social law, this is first manifested in public participation in the social legislation process. As social legislation involves a wide range of areas, it tends to arouse widespread public concern. For example, when the *Labor Contract Law* was revised in 2012, 550,000 opinions were solicited on the article related to labor dispatch, which is the largest number of opinions solicited by the National People's Congress for legislation so far. Public participation should be strengthened in social legislation. Widespread public participation has become the consensus of all sectors of society and the general trend in social legislation.

In terms of the implementation of social law, the departments of civil affair and human resources and social security will join efforts with other departments to form a new pattern for promoting collaboration. In the *Notice on Comprehensively Establishing a Temporary Assistance System* (G/F No. [2014] 47), the State Council clearly stated that "the civil affairs departments of local people's governments at or above the county level shall make coordinated efforts with other departments in performing temporary assistance work within their administrative areas," requiring that "the departments of health and family planning, education, housing and urban-rural development, human resources and social security and finance must cooperate actively and closely." The *Charity Law* and the *Guiding Opinions of the State Council on Promoting the Healthy Development of Charities* specify the responsibilities of the departments of finance, customs, taxation, public security, broadcasting and television, and supervision in advancing the rule of law in charities and promoting charities. In 2015, the Ministry of Civil Affairs and the China Banking Regulatory Commission issued the *Notice on Banking Financial Institutions' Assisting in the Inquiry of Information on Deposits and Other Financial Assets of Families Receiving Social Assistance* (M/F No. [2015] 61), making a big step ahead in establishing a trans-departmental, multi-tiered, information-sharing mechanism for checking the financial status of families

[12]For the data, please refer to the *Work Report of the Supreme People's Court—At the 1st Meeting of the 13th National People's Congress on March 9, 2018.*

[13]Ibid.

applying for social assistance. This helps the relevant departments objectively judge household income and property status by sharing information on financial assets such as deposits grasped by banking financial institutions.

The participation of social and market forces in advancing the rule of law in social affairs is also a major development trend. This not only helps achieve comprehensive and accurate implementation of social law but also helps ease the government's excessive financial burden and management pressure. In 2015, the Ministry of Civil Affairs issued the *Guiding Opinions on Supporting and Guiding Social Forces to Participate in Disaster Relief*, which affirmed for the first time the importance of the participation of nongovernmental organizations and enterprises in disaster management. The promulgation of the *Charity Law* and a series of supporting regulations and policies will open up channels for enterprises and individuals with goodwill and love to participate in social construction.

6.2.6 Relying on the Internet + Efficiency Improvement

The social construction and modernization of social governance steered by IT application is a distinctive characteristic of social development in China. In advancing the rule of law in social affairs, the government's information-based public service capabilities have been continuously enhanced. As of the end of 2014, 31 provinces, autonomous regions, and municipalities directly under the Central Government, as well as the Xinjiang Production and Construction Corps, had established a unified information system of the old-age insurance for urban and rural residents. As of the end of 2017, the number of holders of the nationwide unified social security card had reached 1088 million, accounting for 78.7% of the population.[14] In terms of IT application in social assistance, the nationwide assistance management information system has been upgraded many times, and the nationwide network for assisting in the search for missing loved ones (http://xunqin.mca.gov.cn/xun-qinweb/index.html) has been launched.[15] As of the end of 2015, the nationwide minimum subsistence guarantee information management system had completed 97% of the data collection. In addition, on December 3, 2014, the military personnel insurance relationship transfer system was officially launched. This signifies that the transfer and continuation of retired old-age insurance relationships of military personnel has been electronically and networked, and the transfer and continuation process is smoother.

[14]For the data, please refer to *The Statistical Communique on Human Resources and Social Security Development in 2017.*

[15]The nationwide network for assisting in the search for missing loved ones is intended to facilitate local rescue management organizations to issue notices to help families organize searches for missing loved ones and to assist the missing persons to return to their homes as soon as possible.

6.3 Prospects for the Rule of Law in Social Affairs in China

Since China started to advance the rule of law in social affairs, it has been facing both opportunities and challenges. In terms of opportunities, with the deepening of reforms and opening up, China attaches increasing importance to social governance and social construction. The *Outline of the 13th Five-Year Plan for National Economic and Social Development* devotes Part 15 to "Support for Public Well-being," Chapter 64 to "Carrying out Social Security Reform," and Part 17 to "Better and More Innovative Social Governance." The report to the 19th CPC National Congress clearly states that "We will improve the basic pension schemes for urban employees and for rural and non-working urban residents, and quickly bring pension schemes under national unified management." "We will improve the unified systems of basic medical insurance and serious disease insurance for rural and non-working urban residents, and improve unemployment insurance and work-related injury insurance." "We will improve our systems for social assistance, social welfare, charity, and entitled groups' benefits and services." In short, "We will act on the policy requirements to help those most in need, to build a tightly woven safety net, and to build the necessary institutions, as we work to develop a sustainable multi-tiered social security system that covers the entire population in both rural and urban areas, with clearly defined rights and responsibilities, and support that hits the right level." Therefore, the institutional norms and the level of right protection in China's rule of law in social affairs are expected to be further improved. In terms of challenges facing a series of problems, such as the new normal of economic and social development, the aging of the population, and the rehabilitation and social integration of the disabled, China is facing severe challenges in advancing the rule of law in social affairs, especially in aspects of legislation, enforcement and institutional building. In the future, while advancing the rule of law in social affairs, we should pay special attention to the following aspects.

6.3.1 Fairer and Unified Institutional Building

Social law is oriented to the whole society, covers all members of society, and safeguards the right to subsistence and development of all members of society. We must ensure that all are equal before the law and eliminate discrimination on grounds of region, household registration, occupation, gender, etc. We must revise and improve the existing legal system based on the concept of equality, and highlighting equality in law enforcement will be the key content of the rule of law in social affairs in China. Equality distinguishes modern social insurance from traditional charities and feudal assistance systems at the levels of conception and implementation.

In the past, in advancing the rule of law in social affairs, especially in the field of social assistance, we were affected to varying degrees by the notion of "efficiency first." For example, the review mechanism for minimum subsistence allowances, the ceiling and deductible lines of medical insurance, and the exclusion of non-registered population still have a large space for improvement in equality. In a series of major political documents, the state has set the goals of "gradually narrowing the gap in basic public services between rural and urban areas" and "accelerating the equalization of basic public services." In recent years, China has achieved some phased results in the integration of rural and urban social legal systems. For example, the basic pension insurance for rural and nonworking urban residents and the new rural cooperative medical system and the basic medical insurance for urban nonworking residents have gradually been integrated. However, the *Social Insurance Law* clearly states that "The basic pension insurance fund will be coordinated on a national basis gradually and the other social insurance funds will be coordinated on a provincial basis gradually." The Report on the Work of the Government (2018) clearly states that "We will establish a central adjustment system for basic pension funds of enterprise employees." However, in practice, the level of coordination is not high, which hinders the uniformity and fairness of the legal system for social insurance. Taking basic medical insurance as an example, it is still common that basic medical insurance is coordinated on a prefecture basis, and in many localities, it is still coordinated at the county level. This has not only led to differences in the types of disease and proportions of reimbursements between the coordinating units but also problems such as difficulty in reimbursement for medical bills in different places, low medical insurance anti-risk capabilities, and poor enthusiasm for migrant workers to participate in medical insurance.

Confucius once said, "A nation is not troubled by poverty, but by disparity." In the future, with the rapid advancement of urban-rural integration and other reforms in China, equality will be stressed while advancing the rule of law in social affairs. The barriers between local and departmental standards should be broken, and the level of coordination should be improved. Taking social insurance as an example, the legal system for social insurance should fairly satisfy the safety needs of members of society, and this is prominently manifested in the equality of social insurance rights and interests. It includes not only the equality of enjoyment of social insurance benefits but also the equality of social insurance obligations (especially premium payment obligations).

6.3.2 Arduous Task of Law Making and Revision

Although remarkable results have achieved social legislation in China in recent years, there are still many shortcomings. For example, only a small number of laws have been made and there are legislative gaps in some areas; the overall level of legislation is low, laws and regulations are relatively scarce, but rules and red-head documents are rampant; some laws and regulations are too rough and have difficulties in enforcement; the legislation ideas emphasize management but neglect services, and the supporting mechanisms are insufficient; more than one or two decades after their promulgation, some laws and regulations, such as the *Labor Law* and the *Unemployment Insurance Regulations*, have not even been revised and improved to keep pace with the times. Therefore, for a long period of time in the future, China is facing an arduous and formidable task in social legislation regardless of filling in the gaps or amending the old laws.

As stated in the *Implementation Outline for Advancing the Rule of Law in Human Resources and Social Security (2016–2020)*, we should revise the *Labor Contract Law*, the *Social Insurance Law* and other laws and carry out argumentation for legislative necessity and scientific justification on matters such as promoting employment and entrepreneurship, corporate wage payment security, basic labor standards, labor security supervision, and supervision of social insurance funds and supplementary insurance funds. The laws and supporting administrative regulations, such as the *Social Insurance Law*, the *Labor Contract Law*, and *Regulations on the Human Resources Market*, should also be amended to abolish the provisions that do not meet the requirements of reform and economic and social development, and the interpretations on specific issues in the implementation of the laws and regulations should be strengthened. This shows that we are facing an arduous task in legislation in the social sector. In the future, we should pay particular attention to the following aspects of legislation in the social sector.

First, we should put the formulation of the *Social Assistance Law* on the agenda as soon as possible. Social assistance is the security of the basic life needs of the social security system. Although the State Council has issued the *Interim Measures for Social Assistance*, the word "*interim*" determines that its contents are still uncertain. Legal hierarchy has an obscure relationship with the preceding legal documents, such as the *Regulations on Guaranteeing Minimum Subsistence for Urban Residents*, the *Regulations on the Work of Providing Five Guarantees*, and the *Regulations on the Relief of Natural Disasters*. As these are all administrative regulations promulgated by the State Council, the *Interim Measures for Social Assistance* may prevail in accordance with the principle that new law prevails over old law, but other separate and special administrative regulations may also prevail in accordance with the principle that special law prevails over general law. This contradiction in application has a negative impact on the institutionalization of social assistance. Improving the social assistance system has been included in the report to the 19th CPC National Congress. Therefore, it is necessary for the National People's Congress and its Standing Committee to come forward and formulate the *Social Assistance Law* as a comprehensive basic law. In terms of institutional building, the recipients of social assistance should be expanded from the recipients of minimum subsistence allowances to all kinds of low-income groups and groups temporarily caught in difficulty.

Second, we should start to revise the *Social Insurance Law* as soon as possible. As one of the most important laws in China's social legal system, the *Social Insurance Law* plays an important role in promoting the improvement of the social insurance system. However, under the current background and from the perspective of future demand, many contents of the law have lagged behind the reform and development of social insurance. For example, the *Social Insurance Law* clearly establishes the old-age insurance system for rural residents and the old-age insurance system for nonworking urban residents, but these two systems have been merged in the reform. This means that the two systems in the legal sense no longer exist in practice. The positive prevention functions of work-related injury insurance and unemployment insurance are not reflected in the law, which limits the current reforms. Long-term care insurance is being explored in many places, which has positive significance in dealing with the aging of the population. Therefore, legal gaps urgently need to be filled. To meet the needs of reform and development, it is imperative to carry out a comprehensive revision and improvement of the *Social Insurance Law*. In addition, it must be pointed out that many institutional designs of the Social Insurance Law are actually impossible to operate because they are too principled. This is also something that should be overcome in its revision.

Third, the *Regulations on Unemployment Insurance* should be revised to meet the needs of the new situations. The *Regulations on Unemployment Insurance* promulgated in 1999 was not revised in time after the promulgation of the *Social Insurance Law* in 2010 to ensure their consistency. As of 2019, many of its contents seriously lagged behind the economic and social situation and failed to adapt to the requirements of the new normal of economic growth. Many local reforms have gone far beyond the existing institutional arrangements. The function of unemployment insurance has changed from "guaranteeing the basic livings of the unemployed during unemployment period and promoting their re-employment" to the functional positioning of "guaranteeing livelihood, preventing unemployment and promoting employment," which was affirmed in the *Decision of the CPC Central Committee on Several Major Issues Concerning Comprehensively Deepening the Reform* promulgated in 2013. Therefore, the *Regulations on Unemployment Insurance* should be substantially revised to normalize the function of "prevention of unemployment and employment promotion" of unemployment insurance, establish special institutional arrangements for migrant workers and urban flexible employees such as "one-off unemployment subsidies" and "unemployment insurance savings account" include the provincial-level coordination of fund management into the regulations, and include civil servants in government organs in the unemployment insurance system.

Fourth, legislation for social organizations is gathering pace. In recent years, reforms and innovations in the field of social organizations in China have been in full swing. The 4th Plenary Session of the 18th CPC Central Committee proposed to "strengthen legislation for social organizations, and standardize and guide the healthy development of all kinds of social organizations." In 2015, the Central Office of the CPC Central Committee and the Central Office of the State Council issued the *General Plan for Decoupling Industrial Associations and Chambers of Commerce from Administrative Organs*, canceling administrative approval for the establishment of social organizations. However, in sharp contrast, legislation for social organizations did not keep pace with the reform and failed to fully reflect the results of exploration. Therefore, the revision of the three major regulations, namely, the *Regulations on the Registration Administration of Social Organizations*, the *Regulations on the Administration of Foundations*, and the *Interim Regulations on the Registration Administration of Private Non-Enterprise Units*, were initiated. In the *Decision of the State Council on Amending Certain Administrative Regulations* (GWYL No. 666) promulgated in 2016, some provisions in the *Regulations on the Registration Administration of Social Organizations* have been amended. The three major regulations should be amended as soon as possible, and unified social organization legislation should be initiated on this basis.

6.3.3 Strengthening Social Law Enforcement Supervision

Admittedly, many laws and regulations in the social sector in China remain at the level of the declaration of rights, contain many principled provisions with poor operability, fail to clearly define the responsibilities of relevant departments, and lack guarantees in funding and other aspects. For example, the implementation of mechanisms for advance payment of work-related injury insurance funds and compulsory collection of social insurance premiums under the *Social Insurance Law* proceeded slowly. The advance payment mechanism has fund risk, moral risk, and administrative risk, while the compulsory collection mechanism has not been effectively implemented due to the high cost of compulsory implementation and the relatively low level of cooperation between relevant departments and courts. For example, due to the high social insurance premium rate, especially the basic old-age insurance premium rate, some employers are trying to reduce the contribution base. The contribution bases are far lower than the actual salaries, and the actual payment rates are far lower than the nominal payment rates. This not only impairs the social insurance rights and interests of insured workers and brings serious hidden dangers of disputes but also causes difficulties in collection inspection and damages the stability of the legal order.

Correspondingly, in the future, we should take abiding by the law and enhancing execution power as an important task of advancing the rule of law in the social sector. We must be keenly aware that we still face an arduous task to "ensure that everyone abides by the law" in the field of social law. In terms of medical insurance, we should strengthen publicity, education and training to ensure that public health departments, medical staff, and insured persons have a correct understanding of medical insurance laws and regulations, thereby reducing the difficulty of implementing the medical insurance legal system and forming a good atmosphere in which all parties respect the law, abide by the law, and act in accordance with the law. In terms of social insurance, we should improve the law enforcement supervision system and take "strict law enforcement" as an important goal. Specifically, the administrative law enforcement power of social insurance agencies in collection, auditing, and inspection should be clarified, their corresponding administrative enforcement measures and administrative enforcement power should also be made clear, and the mechanism of work division and coordination between various agencies for administrative law enforcement for social insurance should be improved and fully reflected in their lists of powers and responsibilities to avoid the problems of mutual prevarication and inefficient enforcement. Finally, we should strengthen the effective connection between administrative law enforcement and criminal justice in the field of social law. For serious violations that constitute a crime, criminal responsibility should be investigated to overcome the dilemma of "high cost of compliance but low cost of violation" and insufficient deterrence of legal enforcement.

Inefficient law enforcement will lead to the frustration of legal responsibilities, and even lead to the strange phenomenon of "high cost of compliance but low cost of violation," Taking social insurance as an example, many local social insurance authorities are responsible for social insurance work for a large number of enterprises and a large number of insured persons, and the building of the contingent of law enforcement personnel is lagging behind, and their law enforcement investigation, evidence collection, and enforcement personnel and equipment are all lacking in manpower and equipment. The implementation of the rule of law in the social sector should take the transformation of government functions as an opportunity to further promote the reform to streamline administration and scale back administrative power, lift or exercise regulation where necessary and provide better services, and accelerate the construction and improvement of the interim and ex-post supervision system.

6.3.4 Primary-Level Handling

Primary-level governance is an important task of China's social construction, and the basic content of modernizing China's system and capacity for governance is also an important guarantee for people to live and work in peace and contentment.

In the future, efforts should be made to improve the management level. Insufficient handling capacity has become an important obstacle restricting the implementation of China's social assistance, social insurance, social welfare and other systems and the realization of people's social rights. For example, in many places, social assistance is part of the work of the office for civil affairs at the township and subdistrict levels, and the social assistance handling personnel are also in charge of a large number of other tasks. Due to low work efficiency and poor service quality, household surveys, censorship and other links and mechanisms necessary for social assistance become a mere formality, and the targeting rate and effectiveness of social assistance are greatly reduced. To this end, on the one hand, we should ensure that there are enough social assistance handling personnel, establish a long-term training mechanism, improve the mechanism for grassroots personnel to serve temporary positions and communication, and form the mechanism for training and appointment of grassroots personnel; on the other hand, financial investment should be increased to improve guarantee capabilities. All aspects of the implementation of social law require funding guarantees, and in particular, subsidies should be provided to handling personnel for loss of working time and transportation, and the benefits of social assistance-related staff should be included in the fiscal budget.

6.3.5 Improving the Dispute Settlement System

The level of social construction and social governance is closely related to the efficiency and authority of the social conflict resolution mechanism. In the new normal of economic growth, there is a growing number of labor and social security disputes caused by de-capacity, difficulties in business operation, shutdown, suspension of operation, merging with others or shifting to different lines of production. In general, as the adjustment of the interest pattern becomes increasingly profound and complex, social conflicts and disputes will inevitably occur frequently and tend to be more diversified, complicated, and acute. In this context, mobilizing all positive factors to form a set of social conflict resolution systems is an inherent requirement for the effective enforcement of social law. From the perspective of the realization of the rule of law in social affairs, it is necessary to shape a diversified dispute settlement mechanism with reasonable allocation, cohesion and coordination of judicial trial, mediation, arbitration, reconsideration, and petitions. In particular, two aspects should be considered. One is to give full play to the high-efficiency advantages of informal dispute settlement mechanisms other than litigation, and the other is to highlight the final, fair and authoritative value of judicial trial.

Admittedly, in the enforcement of social law in China, informal dispute settlement mechanisms have been highly evaluated and emphasized, while the role of judicial trials is relatively weak. Here, while affirming the diversification of social dispute settlement mechanisms, we should emphasize that the courts have irreplaceable functions for the effective implementation of the social law system and the improvement of rules through litigation and enforcement mechanisms. This is mainly manifested as follows: (1) The court ensures the enjoyment of social rights and the performance of obligations through the judgment and enforcement system and ensures that all parties act in accordance with the law (including enforcement of litigation judgments and non-litigation administrative enforcement). (2) The courts endow various systems, mechanisms, and rules of social law with enforceability to ensure their effective implementation. (3) The institutional rules and operations were improved through trial activities. However, in China's reality, although the number of social law-related disputes is increasing, they have not been resolved mainly through the courts, so the function of the courts to protect the legal rights of all parties through trials and enforcement has not been effectively brought into play. Under pretexts such as "falling into the category of policy adjustment", "strong policy nature", high social sensitivity, and proneness to cause group disputes, it is not uncommon for courts to give up or passively exercise judicial power. The function of the court is not yet properly exercised, which not only leads to the lack of the ultimate guarantee of the judicial system in the operation of social insurance but also makes it impossible for people whose social insurance rights and interests are impaired to make complaints and lose their right to relief. Obviously, the court should proceed from the case registration system, cancel unreasonable restrictions and open the door to social insurance disputes. Furthermore, public interest litigation in the social insurance field should also be piloted and implemented as soon as possible. Illegal behaviors in the field of social insurance should be punished.

6.3.6 Clarifying Government Responsibilities and Strengthening Guarantees

The enforcement of social law entails a sound guarantee mechanism. First, the government's responsibilities in the enforcement of social laws should be clearly defined. In recent years, the "soft law" hue of the legal system in the social sector has been reduced to a certain extent. In the future, we should continue to improve the guarantee system and highlight the government's guarantee responsibilities.

First, fiscal guarantee. The government's fiscal responsibilities for social security are not only the important responsibilities of the government but also the responsibilities of the government in social security. Paragraph 1 of Article 13 of the Social Insurance Law stipulates, "The basic pension insurance premiums that shall be deemed to have been paid during the payment period before the workers of the state-owned enterprises and institutions participate in the basic pension insurance shall be borne by the government." Paragraph 2 of Article 13 stipulates, "In case the amount in the basic pension insurance fund is insufficient to make payment, the government shall provide the subsidy." However, it is also necessary to clarify the proportion of financial subsidies for the enforcement of social law by the central and local governments through law making, amendment or other institutionalized means.

Secondly, handling guarantee. For specific social security projects, the government should be responsible for organizing, managing, and providing relevant benefits and services. For example, for the implementation of the social assistance system, the government should be responsible for the organization, final review and determination, and provision of benefits.

Thirdly, guarantee by extensive IT application. Although initial results have been achieved in IT application in social construction, there are still problems in social assistance, such as a low targeting rate and incomplete, untrue, and out-of-date social insurance information. Therefore, it is necessary to strengthen top-level design and departmental sharing, adhere to unified leadership, unified planning, and unified standards, and promote the rule of law in social affairs through extensive IT application. We should strengthen information sharing among different regions and government departments, especially departments of public security, civil affairs, human resources and social security, industry and commerce, etc., to lay a solid foundation for the enforcement of social law. A social law enforcement pattern will be formed in the future that integrates online and offline services in an orderly manner and makes the information fully open and shared.

In short, as an important part and guarantee of China's social construction, social law has profound significance in promoting the construction and improvement of the socialist legal system with Chinese characteristics and safeguarding and improving people's rights to subsistence, development, and health. Despite the remarkable results in recent years, China will continue to advance the rule of law in social affairs to contribute to the prosperity of the country and the revitalization of the nation and better satisfy our people's yearning for a better life.

Chapter 7
The Rule of Law in Human Rights: For the Purpose of Safeguarding Human Dignity

Jianwen Zhao, Qian Sun, Renwen Liu, Huawen Liu, and Yiming Wang

7.1 Overview of Human Rights in China

The term "human right" did not originate in China but was introduced into China in modern times from Japan and the West, but there were similar concepts in Chinese culture, such as "Renxing (humanity)," "Rendao (humanism)" and "Renai (benevolence)", which contain the idea of human rights and are rich soil nourishing the contemporary human rights system. The appearance of the "human right" as a terminological phrase in China is indeed an outcome of the influence of foreign civilizations in modern times, but talking about so-called universal value by transcending the specific historical culture is bound to fall into the trap of nihilism. The ideas of "humanism" and "benevolence" are rooted in traditional Chinese culture. In the continuation and evolution of Chinese civilization, these ideas have played the same role as the theories and practices of human rights without any prejudice or presupposition. Since the founding of the PRC, the human rights situation in China has undergone fundamental changes. Under the leadership of the Communist Party of China, the Chinese government has led people across the country to make great progress in China's human rights cause. The report to the 18th CPC National Congress clearly states that "human rights should be fully respected and protected." This is one of the goals of building a well-off society in all respects and deepening reform and opening up. Since the 18th CPC National Congress, under the strong leadership of the CPC Central Committee and the joint efforts of all sectors of society, China's human rights cause has been developing steadily, and the achievements China has made in this regard are universally recognized. Since the reform and opening up, especially after "human rights were written into the

J. Zhao (✉) · R. Liu · H. Liu · Y. Wang
Institute of Law, CASS, Bejing, China

Q. Sun
China University of Political Science and Law, Bejing, China

H. Tian and Y. Lv (eds.), *The Chinese Path of Rule of Law Construction*,
China Insights, https://doi.org/10.1007/978-981-16-4130-5_7

Constitution"[1] and "human rights were written into the law,"[2] China has embarked on a path of advancing the rule of law in human rights with Chinese characteristics in line with its national conditions. Human rights protection institutions in China, including government agencies and nongovernment organizations, form a joint force to promote the development of China's human rights cause. Among them, the government agencies are mainly the National People's Congress and the system of people's congresses under its leadership, the multiparty cooperation and political consultation system under the leadership of the Communist Party of China, and the Chinese People's Political Consultative Conference. In addition, the leading organs for science, education, culture, health, and justice have all established special subordinate institutions for human rights or responsibility systems for human rights coordination. The State Council may have established various departments for human rights. Among them, those most closely related to human rights work are the State Council Leading Group Office of Poverty Alleviation and Development, the State Council Working Committee on Women and Children, the State Ethnic Affairs Commission, and the State Religious Affairs Administration. There are a considerable number of nongovernmental organizations dedicated to the protection of human rights, such as the All-China Women's Federation, All-China Youth Federation, and China Disabled Persons' Federation, etc. Organizations specializing in human rights research take an important position in many universities and research institutions, such as the China Society for Human Rights Studies, China Foundation for Human Rights Development, Research Center for Human Rights and Humanitarian Law of Peking University, Research Center for Human Rights of Party School of the Central Committee of the CPC, Human Rights Research Center of the Renmin University of China, and Wuhan University's Center for the Protection of the Rights of the Disadvantaged Groups. These research institutions have made outstanding contributions to the development of human rights theories in China. To date, China has achieved the first and second goals proposed by the *National Human Rights Action Plan of China* as scheduled. The *National Human Rights Action Plan of China (2016–2020)* is progressing steadily, and China's human rights cause is bound to march towards new glory. Behind the glorious achievements, the advancement of the rule of law has contributed to the development of human rights. In 2017, China proposed its direction for the development of the rule of law in the new era. That is, we should uphold the unity, sanctity, and authority of China's legal system and strengthen legal protection for human rights to ensure that the people enjoy extensive rights and freedoms as prescribed by law.

---

[1]In March 2004, the 2nd Session of the 10th National People's Congress adopted an amendment to the Constitution, which includes "the state respects and protects human rights." It was for the first time that "human rights" were upgraded from a political concept to a legal concept, and the subject of human rights protection and was changed from the Party and government to "the State."

[2]In March 2012, the 5th Session of the 11th National People's Congress adopted a draft amendment to the *Criminal Procedure Law*, which includes "respect and protect human rights" in its General Provisions.

The rule of law and human rights are complementary to and inseparable from each other. The rule of law is the way and process of state governance, while the protection of human rights is the goal and ultimate destination of the rule of law. Protecting human rights is the core value of good law and good governance. Human rights need to be protected in accordance with the law, and any rights that depart from the rule of law will eventually go to extremes and even impair social fairness and justice. In the present stage, China placed greater emphasis on putting people first, promoted coordinated and sustainable economic, political, cultural, social, and ecological advancement, and promoted social harmony and equality. China's human rights and legal construction have yielded fruitfulness results.

Both the advancement of the rule of law and the protection of human rights are currently in a new historical stage in China. The rule of law in human rights in China is being advanced steadily, and new progress has been made. First, China's legal system for human rights protection as the foundation and prerequisite has been continuously improved. At present, China has put in place a socialist legal system with Chinese characteristics composed of seven legal departments and three levels of laws and regulations: the constitution, laws, administrative regulations, local regulations and other regulatory documents. The formation and continuous improvement of the socialist legal system with Chinese characteristics have provided a solid theoretical foundation and institutional guarantee for the development of China's human rights cause. Second, the Chinese government places great importance on regulating the use of power, vigorously promotes law-based administration, clarifies the boundaries of government power, standardizes administrative law enforcement, continuously expands citizens' right to participate in administrative affairs, and safeguards citizens' right to exercise supervision in accordance with law. Finally, the judiciary is the last line of defense to protect human rights. The government has introduced a number of moves focusing on judicial reform to ensure that the people can see in every judicial case that justice is served. Owing to these efforts, China has basically fostered a good social atmosphere where people have developed an awareness of human rights, respect for human rights, and consciously protect human rights.

7.2 Narrowing the Gap Between Rural and Urban Areas and Promoting Integrated Development

7.2.1 Equal Representation of Deputies to the people's Congresses

When the *Election Law* of the People's Republic of China was enacted in 1953, China's urban population accounted for 13.26% of the country's total. Workers as the leading class were concentrated in cities and towns. Therefore, in the specific historical conditions, to reflect the leadership of the working class, the *Election Law* stipulated that the ratio of urban to rural population for electing a deputy to a people's congress should be 8:1. After the reform and opening up, the urbanization process in China accelerated, and the urban-rural population structure underwent tremendous changes. When the *Election Law* was revised in 1995, this ratio was changed from 8:1 to 4:1. In 2007, the report to the 17th CPC National Congress stated that "The position of the people as masters of the country is the essence and core of socialist political democracy." "We propose that both rural and urban areas gradually adopt the same ratio of deputies to the represented population in elections of deputies to people's congresses." "We propose that both urban and rural areas gradually adopt the same ratio of deputies to the represented population in elections of deputies to people's congresses." The 3rd Session of the 11th National People's Congress deliberated and adopted an amendment to the *Electoral Law*. Article 16 of the revised *Election Law* clearly stipulates that "The numbers of deputies to the National People's Congress shall be allocated by the Standing Committee of the National People's Congress, based on the populations of all provinces, autonomous regions and municipalities directly under the Central Government, under the principle of equal number of population represented by each deputy, whether urban or rural, and according to the requirement of ensuring every region, every nationality and every walk of life have an appropriate number of deputies."

On February 27, 2013, the NPC Standing Committee announced 2,987 deputies to the 12th National People's Congress. They were deputies to the NPC, China's highest organ of state power, elected for the first time after the *Election Law* was revised in 2010 to eliminate the difference between rural and urban populations and implement the principle of equal number of population represented by each deputy, whether rural or urban. This marks that equal representation of rural and urban voters in China has been achieved in the election of NPC deputies, and a new step has been taken in ensuring equal political rights of rural and urban residents.

It is an indisputable fact that the most distinctive difference between rural and urban areas lies in the economic field. Undoubtedly, economic development in rural China lags behind its urban counterpart, which is a stage on the road of China's social development and a problem encountered in the process of urbanization in any country. However, this is not the fundamental reason why Chinese farmers were in an unfavorable position in the election of deputies to the organs of state power. As mentioned above, the phenomenon of "inequal representation" of rural and urban residents in the election process was a deliberate arrangement based on the special consideration of the value orientation in a specific historical period. Based on a dialectical understanding of the power structure and the objective conditions of Chinese society at that time, the distribution of the number of deputies to the National People's Congress in the past was rational, and the urban-rural disparity could also be understood as a choice among different distribution standards. As the concepts of democracy and the rule of law advance with the times and take root in the hearts of the people, it seems to have a causal relationship with the economic disparity between rural and urban areas, but in fact, the disparity in identity and political power between rural and urban residents that coexist with the economic disparity have become even greater, so the Party and the state are taking actions to narrow the disparity between rural and urban areas in both the economic and political spheres. The realization of equal voting rights in the political sphere allows farmers to timely and properly air their opinions and thereby enhances urban-rural equality in economic and other fields. The *Election Law* twice adjusted the ratio of deputies to the represented population to grant equal representation in legislative bodies to rural and urban people. On the surface, this is due to the objective reason of China's urbanization process, but in fact, the criteria for the allocation of deputies to people's congress has been leaning towards the subjects of right. To date, farmers still account for more than half of the Chinese population. Chinese leaders and legislators are well aware of this fact and have adjusted the law in due course, eliminating the phenomena that violate the basic provision of the *Election Law* and the *Constitution* that "All citizens of the People's Republic of China are equal before the law" to highlight the people-oriented nature of Chinese law.

7.2.2 Reform of the Household Registration System

The dual household registration or "hukou" system in China was formed in the planned economy era due to some complicated causes. In January 1958, the NPC Standing Committee adopted the *Regulations on Household Registration of the People's Republic of China*, which divided registered residents into agricultural and non-agricultural groups based on residence registration and established the approval system for the change of registered residence and the system for household registration by presenting the required certificates. Article 10 of the Regulations stipulates that "If a citizen is to move out of the area under the jurisdiction of its registration authority, he or the householder shall apply for the moving-out registration to the household registration authority before moving out, get the proof for migration, and cancel the household registration." "If a citizen is to move from a rural area to an urban area, he should hold an employment credential of an urban labor department, an admission credential of a school, or a certificate of residence permit of an urban residence registration authority, and apply to the household registration authority for handling the procedures for moving out." The *Provisions of the Ministry of Public Security on Handling the Change of Household Registration (Draft)* promulgated in August, 1964 proposed two "strict restrictions", namely strict restriction on moving from rural areas to cities and market towns, and strict restriction on moving from market towns to cities.

China's policy orientation of overly strict restriction on household registration actually did not last for a long time. After the reform and opening up, the household registration system itself was adjusted successively to relax restrictions on new migrants to meet the real needs of social life. The *Circular of the State Council on the Issues Concerning the Settlement of Rural Residents in Market Towns* promulgated in October 1984 stipulated that farmers were allowed to settle in market towns based on legal and permanent residence by self supply of rations and should enjoy the same rights and obligations as residents of market towns. Thus, China began to relax restrictions on household registration. In July 1985, to meet the need for management of the growing temporary population in urban areas, the Ministry of Public Security issued the *Interim Regulations on the Management of Temporary Population in Urban Areas*, establishing an urban temporary population management system. In September 1985, the resident ID card system was introduced, state policies and laws gradually relaxed the restrictions on population movement, and the policy orientation began to shift toward maintaining the social order through population management.

The *Circular of the State Council on Approving and Transmitting the Pilot Program of the Ministry of Public Security for Reforming the Management System of Household Registration in Small Cities and Towns and Opinions on Improving the Rural Household Registration Management System* was issued in June 1997, and the *Circular of the State Council on Approving and Transmitting the Opinions of the Ministry of Public Security on Resolving the Serious Issues Concerning the Current Household Registration Management Work* was issued in July 1998. These policies have further relaxed restrictions on household registration in small cities and towns. The *Circular of the State Council on Approving and Transmitting the Opinions of the Ministry of Public Security on Promoting the Reform of the Management System of Household Registration in Small Cities and Towns* issued in March 2001 stipulated that planned quota management would no longer be implemented for persons who intended to handle permanent household registration, marking that the reform of the household registration system was in full swing in small cities and towns.

In February 2012, the *Circular of the General Office of the State Council on Actively and Steadily Promoting the Reform of the Household Registration Management System* pointed out that it is necessary to guide the orderly transfer of non-agricultural industries and rural populations to small and medium-sized cities and designated towns, gradually meet the needs of eligible rural populations for settlement and gradually realize the equalization of basic public services in rural and urban areas. This circular shows that in a new stage of China's urbanization process, the country's attitude towards the rational flow of rural population to cities has changed gradually. Since then, China's household registration reform has gathered pace.

The *Decision of the CPC Central Committee on Several Major Issues of Comprehensively Deepening the Reform* promulgated in November 2013 stated that "We will introduce new population management methods, accelerate the reform of household registration system, completely lift restrictions on new residence registration in administrative townships and small cities, relax restrictions on new residence registration in medium-sized cities in an orderly manner, lay down appropriate conditions for new residence registration in large cities, and strictly control the population size of megacities." The *Opinions of the State Council on Further Promoting the Reform of the Household Registration System* promulgated on July 30, 2014 states that we will completely lift restrictions on new residence registration in administrative townships and small cities, establish a unified household registration system for rural and urban areas and a residence permit system, establish and improve the public service provision mechanism linked to the conditions such as length of residence, and establish and improve a basic public service supply mechanism linked with residence period, and steadily promoted the complete coverage of basic public services for permanent urban residents. For example, the State Council issued the *Opinions on Establishing a Unified Basic Pension Insurance System for Rural and Non-working Urban Residents* in the same year, establishing a unified basic pension insurance system nationwide, which solved the problem of laborers, especially migrant workers participating in the basic pension insurance system for urban workers or non-working people.

The household registration reform has increased the mobility of people and made the distribution of population resources more reasonable. It enhances the inclusiveness of the dividend of reform and opening up and reduces the inequality of income distribution. All institutional barriers and identity discrimination that affect equal employment, equal pay for equal work, equal access to social security and public services have been basically removed. Therefore, the reform of the household registration system is called another revolution to "liberate" farmers after the household contract responsibility system.

7.2.3 Strengthening the Protection of the Legitimate Rights and Interests of Farmers and Migrant Workers

1. Farmers' land and property rights and interests

The right to land contract management is one of the most important rights for farmers. China has removed control over land contracting and rural housing mortgage financing, which allows farmers to obtain property income. Only by ensuring that farmers' right to subsistence and development through property rights can we truly realize urban-rural integration. To solve the problem of farmers' land rights and interests, the *Decision of the CPC Central Committee on Several Major Issues Concerning Comprehensively Deepening the Reform* proposes that "we will endow farmers with more property rights;" and "We will ensure rural households' usufruct of their homestead, and improve the rural homestead system through reform. We will select several pilot areas to steadily and prudently push forward the mortgage, guarantee and transfer of farmers' residential property rights, and expand the channels for farmers to increase their property income."

2. Rights and interests of migrant workers

Since the State Council promulgated *Several Opinions of the State Council on Solving the Problems of Migrant Workers* in 2008, relevant ministries and commissions and many provinces have introduced specific measures to implement the Opinions, and protecting the personal and property rights of migrant workers in accordance with the law has aroused attention from and been recognized by all sectors of society. With the establishment of relevant systems, the living conditions of migrant workers have been greatly improved. After realizing the set goals, China has shifted its focus of work, and more institutional arrangements and measures to expand the scope of protection to benefit the children of migrant workers' families have come one after another, such as the *Opinions of the State Council on Further Strengthening the Work to Serve Migrant Workers*, the *National New-Type Urbanization Planning (2014–2020)*, and the *Circular of the General Office of the State Council on Transmitting the Opinions of the Ministry of Education and other Ministries and Commissions on Strengthening the Work for Access to Higher Education Examination Entrance for Migrant Workers' Children after Receiving Compulsory Education*. These follow-up measures show that the work of protecting the legitimate rights and interests of migrant workers in accordance with the law is continuous and progressive. It should also be noted that in recent years, many rural migrant workers have settled in urban areas as registered permanent urban residents. In the past, household registration was a criterion to distinguish identities, and the policies emphasized excluding "outlanders" and "migrants" so that the rural "migrant population" was largely excluded from urban social security and various public services. Deepening the reform of the household registration system can fundamentally solve this problem, promote the "institutional entry" of rural migrants, endow migrants legal citizenship, and enhance the provision of social services to migrants to realize equalization of public services for rural migrants and local residents.

7.3 Abolishing the System of Reeducation Through Labor and Improving Community-Based Corrections

In 1957, the *Decision of the State Council on the Issue Concerning Reeducation through Labor* formally established reeducation through the labor system. The subsequent regulations for reeducation through labor mainly include the *Supplementary Regulations of the State Council on Reeducation through Labor* in 1979, the *Measures for Trial Implementation of Reeducation through Labor* issued by the Ministry of Public Security in 1982, and the *Regulations on the Handling of Reeducation through Labor Cases by Public Security Organs* issued by the Ministry of Public Security in 2002. Some departmental regulations and local government regulations also involved this system.

Tracing the roots of the reeducation through the labor system, we found that it was not a unique system of the PRC. It inherited the notion of both education and parenting in the traditional Chinese national governance culture and transplanted the Western concept of punishment into the eastward spread of Western culture in modern times. Its institutional orientation also changed from assistance to punishment and maintenance of social order and security. Especially after the 1980s, when China launched a campaign for severe crackdown on crimes, reeducation through labor as a supplement to criminal sanctions had ever played an active role in maintaining social order. As the negative effects of the severe crackdown emerged, it withdrew from the stage of history. The re-education through labor system was also fading away in China in the 1990s. It was then mainly applicable to those who violated the administration of public security and existed in the gap between administrative violations and criminal violations, and the scope of its application continued to shrink. In the later period, reeducation through the labor system was mainly targeted at idlers, thieves, prostitutes, drug addicts, and public security disruptors. Over time, its functions were gradually replaced with the promulgation of the relevant laws, which provided the legal basis for punishment of the abovementioned violators or restrictions on their acts. For example, the *Regulations on Penalties for Administration of Public Security* was replaced by the *Law on Penalties for Administration of Public Security* promulgated in 2006, which expanded the scope of punishment for violations specified by the abovementioned *Regulations* and specified detailed measures for penalties for administration of public security for wrongful acts that do not constitute crimes. The law is at a higher level in legal hierarchy and has a solid foundation of legitimacy. The *Law on Narcotics Control* promulgated in 2007 stipulates that community-based drug rehabilitation and compulsory isolation for drug rehabilitation should be implemented for drug addicts. This means that this measure was no longer applicable to approximately half of persons receiving reeducation through labor. The amendments to the *Criminal Law* clarify the nature of some just acts and criminalize serious violations such as pickpocketing, burglary, theft with a lethal weapon, and extortion and blackmail that have directly infringed on the legitimate rights and interests of citizens. The *Law on Penalties for Administration of Public Security* and the *Criminal Law* have set clear provisions on the division of responsibilities among different organs. Penalties for the administration of public security or compulsory isolation for drug rehabilitation should be handled by the public security organs in strict accordance with the statutory authority and procedures; suspected crime cases should be handled by the judicial organs strictly in accordance with the procedures prescribed by the *Criminal Procedure Law*. Those who are dissatisfied with the penalties made in accordance with the former may initiate administrative reconsideration or administrative litigation in accordance with the law, and those who are dissatisfied with the judgment or ruling made in accordance with the latter must safeguard their legitimate rights and interests through appeals and protests.

With the improvement of the relevant systems and the popularization of the notion of the rule of law, the legitimacy of reeducation through labor as a means closely related to political control was constantly questioned by various parties, and it was criticized because its improper implementation tended to lead to infringement on citizens' right of personal freedom and right of body. Reeducation through labor should be administrative punishment in nature, but from the perspective of length of time for restriction on personal freedom, the minimum length of time for reeducation through labor was longer than the maximum length of time for criminal punishments such as public surveillance and criminal detention. Therefore, arguably, the sanctions of reeducation through labor were overly severe in this regard because the acts subject to punishments under the system were largely only wrongful acts that did not constitute crimes. In the practice of re-education through labor, cases of illegal use of violence also occurred from time to time, and there was no effective supervision and control over acts such as extorting confessions by torture or illegal use of police equipment. Several typical cases that occurred in 2012 brought the reeducation through the labor system to the forefront of public opinion. Taking various realistic factors into consideration, reeducation through the labor system could no longer meet the requirements of judicial protection of human rights and the requirements of advancing the rule of law in China, and the historical conditions for abolishing reeducation through labor gradually matured.

In early 2013, the top leaders of the Committee of Political and Legal Affairs of the CPC Central Committee announced the decision to actively promote the reform of the reeducation through labor system, saying that after the decision was approved by the NPC Standing Committee, we would "suspend" the reeducation through labor system. Since the beginning of 2013, reeducation through the labor system has been applied under strict control. Reeducation through labor measures was no longer adopted for those who made persistent trivial and irrational complaints or complaints that disrupted the public order. In November 2013, the *Decision of the CPC Central Committee on Several Major Issues Concerning Comprehensively Deepening the Reform* announced that "We will abolish Laojiao, or re-education through labor, improve laws for the punishment and correction of unlawful and criminal acts, and improve the community-based correction system." In December 2013, the 6th Session of the Standing Committee of the 12th National People's Congress adopted the *Decision on Repealing Legislation on Reeducation through Labor*, which means that the reeducation through labor system that had been operated for more than 50 years was officially withdrawn from the historical stage in accordance with the legal procedures. The *White Paper: Progress in China's Human Rights in 2013* objectively summarized and evaluated the abolition process of the reeducation through labor system: With over 50 years of operation in China, the system of reeducation through labor played a positive role in protecting public security, maintaining social order, ensuring social stability, and educating and rescuing lawbreakers in certain historical circumstances. However, over time, its functions were gradually replaced with the implementation of laws such as the *Law on Penalties for Administration of Public Security* and the *Law on Narcotics Control* and with improvements in the *Criminal Law*. Additionally, as the relevant laws became increasingly applicable in cases of reeducation through labor, the correction system played a lesser role over the years. Since March 2013, the system has been basically suspended in China. On December 28, 2013, the Standing Committee of the NPC passed a decision on abolishing legal provisions pertaining to reeducation through labor, putting an end to the system. It was also decided that persons who were receiving reeducation through labor as prescribed by law should be released and exempted from their remaining terms.

The abolition of the reeducation through the labor system is a milestone event in the history of China's legal system and an important manifestation of China's endeavors to safeguard citizens' rights and the rule of law. What steps should be taken after the reform and how to establish and support community-based correction systems became a hot topic of discussion among legal professionals and the focus of the work of related departments. Community-based correction work was launched earlier in China, and the *Circular on the Pilot Work of Community-based Corrections* was issued as early as 2003 by the Supreme People's Court, the Supreme People's Procuratorate, the Ministry of Public Security, and the Ministry of Justice. In 2011, ten ministries and commissions, including the Supreme People's Court and the Supreme People's Procuratorate, jointly issued the *Pilot Work Plan for the Committees on Education and Correction of Illegal Acts*, listing Lanzhou, Jinan, Nanjing, and Zhengzhou as pilot areas for education and correction of illegal acts. In 2012, the Supreme People's Court, the Supreme People's Procuratorate, the Ministry of Public Security, and the Ministry of Justice jointly promulgated the *Implementation Measures for Community-based Corrections*. After reeducation through the labor system was abolished, community-based corrections work was gathering pace. The Supreme People's Court, the Supreme People's Procuratorate, the Ministry of Public Security, and the Ministry of Justice jointly promulgated the *Opinions on Comprehensively Promoting Community-based Correction Work*. In November of the same year, six ministries, including the Ministry of Justice, jointly promulgated the *Opinions on Organizing Social Forces to Participate in Community-based Correction Work*. The *Opinions on Further Strengthening the Management of the Work Connection and Cooperation of Community-based Corrections* promulgated in 2016 gives the direction for strengthening the work connection and coordination of community-based corrections and ensuring the legal application and standardized operation of community-based corrections. To date, many expert drafts of the *Law on Community-based Corrections* have been published, and the promulgation of the official *Law on Community-based Corrections* is just around the corner.

7.4 Judicial Protection of Human Rights and Attention to Special Groups of People

The judiciary is the last line of defense to safeguard social fairness and justice. Judicial protection of human rights is an important part of the human rights cause and can best reflect the level of development of a country's human rights cause. The Communist Party of China and the Chinese government always uphold the principal position of the people, fully protect the rights and interests of the people, fully realize the rights of the people, make laws in a scientific way, enforce them strictly, administer justice impartially, and ensure that everyone abides by the law, thereby promoting the modernization of China's system and capacity for governance. Regarding judicial protection of human rights, the *Decision of the CPC Central Committee on Several Major Issues Concerning Comprehensively Deepening the Reform* proposes to improve the judicial system to protect human rights, stating that

"The state respects and protects human rights. We will further standardize the legal procedures for sealing, sequestering, freezing and confiscating properties involved in a legal case. We will improve the mechanism for preventing and correcting wrong cases and the accountability system, prohibit extorting confession by torture, corporal punishment and maltreatment, and strictly implement rules that illegal evidence is not adopted. We will gradually reduce the number of charges that could lead to the death penalty." This shows that judicial protection of human rights is an important part of advancing the rule of law in China and has new historical significance because it is part of the strategic arrangements for comprehensively deepening the reform.

Improving the judicial protection of human rights by improving the judicial power operating mechanism is the sublimation of the connotation of China's human rights development. Judicial protection of human rights involves the fair trial procedures of courts, full respect of the binding force of judgments, and prompt and effective enforcement of judicial judgments. Impartial trial of criminal cases also entails real mutual restraint between the courts, procuratorates, and public security organs in related case-handling links, respect of rights to silence and defense, dignity of criminal suspects and defendants, and avoidance of extorting confessions by torture.

The personal rights of the accused, detainees and criminals are protected. On December 14, 2012, the *Measures for the Implementation of the Regulations on Detention Houses* came into effect. Pursuant to the Measures, detention houses should install and use surveillance video and other technical preventive equipment to implement real-time and comprehensive security monitoring of detainees. The surveillance video recordings should be retained for a minimum of 15 days. If a detainee dies or suffers bodily harm during detention, he or she may file a claim for state compensation, and the detention house should record and retain relevant surveillance video recordings. In 2014, the Ministry of Public Security promulgated the *Regulations on Audio and Video Recordings of Interrogation of Criminal Suspects by Public Security Organs*, requiring all localities to gradually expand the scope of audio and video recording of interrogation to cover all criminal cases. The Supreme People's Procuratorate revised and improved the *Provisions of the People's Procuratorate on the Implementation of the Synchronized Audio and Video Recording Throughout the Process of Interrogation of Duty Criminal Suspects*, requiring strictly recording audio and video throughout the process of interrogation of criminal suspects in the future, and specifying the principles, methods and procedures of recording, management and use of audio and video recordings, etc. The abovementioned documents establish the principles of full-process audio and video recording, full-angle video recording, separation of recorders and interrogators, consistency between audio and video recording and interrogation transcripts, and suspension of interrogation when the recording system fails, as well as the principle of exclusion of illegal evidence, that is, when an audio or video recording of interrogation is selectively made, edited, or abridged, the relevant evidence shall be excluded. These documents have played an important role in strengthening the protection of judicial human rights.

Judicial organs are authorized to carry out the pilot program of the fast-track sentencing procedure for criminal cases. The NPC Standing Committee promulgated the *Decision Authorizing the Supreme People's Court and the Supreme People's Procuratorate to Launch the Pilot Program of Fast-Track Sentencing Procedure for Criminal Gases in Certain Areas* to carry out the pilot program of fast-track sentencing procedure in Beijing, Tianjin, Shanghai, Chongqing, Shenyang, Dalian, Nanjing, Hangzhou, Fuzhou, Xiamen, Jinan, Qingdao, Zhengzhou, Wuhan, Changsha, Guangzhou, Shenzhen, and Xi'an. The fast-track sentencing procedure concerns cases involving dangerous driving, traffic offenses, theft, fraud, forcible seizures, personal injury, picking quarrels and making trouble, or any other violation where the circumstances are minor and the accused may be sentenced to imprisonment of not more than one year, criminal detention, control, or a fine. If the facts are clear, the evidence is sufficient, the defendant voluntarily confesses the crime, and the parties do not dispute the application of law, the relevant procedure shall be simplified, provided that it is in conformity with the basic principles of the Criminal Procedure Law, and the litigation rights of the parties concerned are fully protected. This move helps increase the trial efficiency of criminal cases, reasonably allocate and save effective judicial resources. The fast-track sentencing procedure for criminal cases promotes the efficient distribution of complex and simple cases and helps resolve the dilemma of heavy caseload and lack of staff. Meanwhile, it is also of positive significance for defendants, especially for criminal suspects who have been detained. The time of the court session is closely related to the time of detention, and the fast-track sentencing procedure allows justice to come faster and minimizes the possibility of overdue detention due to delays in the trial process.

In 2014, the Supreme People's Court, the Supreme People's Procuratorate, the Ministry of Public Security, the Ministry of Justice, and the National Health and Family Planning Commission jointly issued the *Provisions on Temporary Service of Sentences Outside Prisons*, and the Ministry of Justice issued the *Regulations on Strengthening Management of Daily Life and Hygiene Work of Prisons*, along with other regulatory documents to improve the level of law enforcement and effectively safeguard the legitimate rights of detainees.

Improving the judicial assistance system. The Committee of Political and Legal Affairs of the CPC Central Committee, the Ministry of Finance, the Supreme People's Court, the Supreme People's Procuratorate, the Ministry of Public Security, and the Ministry of Justice jointly issued the *Opinions on Establishing and Improving the National Judicial Assistance System (for Trial Implementation)*, and the Supreme People's Procuratorate issued *Several Opinions Regarding the Implementation of the Opinions on Establishing and Improving the National Judicial Assistance System (for Trial Implementation)*, which initially established the framework of China's judicial assistance system. Assistance measures such as deferment or reduction of the payment or exemption of litigation costs are taken to ensure that litigants can participate in litigation normally and safeguard their legitimate rights and interests in accordance with the law. Public security departments and judicial administrative departments at various levels are jointly promoting the construction of legal aid stations in detention houses. Legal aid agencies have dispatched lawyers on duty in detention houses to provide legal advice and other assistance to effectively safeguard the legitimate rights and interests of the accused and detainees.

In short, the Chinese judiciary always takes fairness and justice as its unremitting pursuit and the protection of human rights as its ultimate goal and has made new progress continuously. The *New Progress in the Judicial Protection of Human Rights in China in 2016* has comprehensively summarized the achievements China has made in human rights protection in the field of justice since the 18th CPC National Congress: "The reform of the judiciary has been driven to a deeper level, with improvements in the allocation of judicial powers and responsibilities, judicial accountability and opening-up, and the protection of lawyers' right to practice their profession. Channels of public participation in justice have been expanded, and the judicial protection of human rights has been improved. China has implemented a case-filing register system, revamped and improved its litigation system, and strictly enforced principles of legality, in dubio pro reo, exclusion of unlawful evidence. The state is resolved in preventing and correcting miscarriages of justice, and the procedures for protecting human rights in judicial practice have been raised to higher standards. The judiciary exercises its power independently and impartially in accordance with the law, leading to strengthened public credibility. Further efforts have been made in terms of state compensation and legal aid. Judicial fairness and justice are safeguarded, and citizens' rights are effectively protected. Crime suspects, defendants and criminals are treated in a more civilized manner, punishments are meted out in a more standardized way, and the personal dignity, safety, and legal property of detainees are all well protected, as are their rights of appeal, accusation, and impeachment." The *Report on the Work of the Supreme People's Court* in 2018 stated that Chinese courts have strengthened efforts to protect human rights in judicial practices. The people's courts at various earnestly implemented the amnesty order of President Xi Jinping and the amnesty decision of the Standing Committee of the National People's Congress and released a total of 31,527 convicts in accordance with the law. The people's courts implemented litigation systems for open trial and court debate to effectively protect the litigation rights of the parties and implemented the criminal policy of combining leniency with rigidity. The Supreme People's Court shared no efforts in the review of death sentences to ensure that the death penalty should only be applied to a very small number of criminals who have committed extremely serious crimes. The Supreme People's Court, together with the Ministry of Justice, launched the pilot program of full coverage of defense by lawyers in criminal cases and carried out the work on duty lawyers for legal aid. The people's courts strengthened the trial of juvenile cases, improved mechanisms for social investigations and sealing of misdemeanor records, and actively carried out return visits to give assistance and education. The number of juvenile crime cases has declined for five consecutive years, and the healthy growth of minors has been effectively protected. Opinions on strengthening judicial assistance were issued, 2.67 billion yuan of judicial assistance was distributed to help victims who failed to obtain effective compensation eliminate their difficulties in life, and rights relief was strengthened to convey judicial warmth. The *Work Report of the Supreme People's Procuratorate* stated that the procuratorates at various levels continuously strengthened legal supervision over criminal, civil, and administrative litigation, strengthened judicial protection of human rights, and strove to ensure that the people can see in every judicial case that justice is served and redressed a number of criminal cases involving unjust, false, or wrongful charges.

7.5 Preventing Miscarriages of Justice in Criminal Cases and Improving State Compensation

The *Criminal Procedure Law* revised in 2012 includes the content of "respect and protect human rights" and upholds the spirit of respecting and protecting human rights while revising and improving provisions on investigation measures, review and prosecution, trial procedures, execution procedures, evidence systems, defense systems, and compulsory measures. This is a major advancement in China's human rights cause, and it is of great significance to protect citizens' litigation rights, punish crimes, and protect the people. Preventing miscarriages of justice in criminal cases, promptly redressing the existing cases involving unjust, false, or wrongful charges, and improving the national compensation system are important tasks in judicial protection of human rights.

In 2013, the Committee of Political and Legal Affairs of the CPC Central Committee issued the *Guiding Opinions on Effectively Preventing Miscarriages of Justice in Criminal Cases*, reiterating the principle of no punishment in doubtful cases, the principle of evidentiary adjudication, the strict standard of proof, and protection of defence lawyers' defense rights, etc., and began to establish an accountability system for lifelong quality of case-handling for the people's police, judges, and prosecutors.

In the same year, the Ministry of Public Security issued documents such as the *Circular on Strengthening and Improving Law Enforcement to Prevent Miscarriages of Justice*, requesting public security officers to take correct attitude towards thought of law enforcement further and enforce law for people, reinforce the mechanism and system preventing miscarriages of justice, improve the law enforcement system and case handling criteria to prevent cases of misjudgment and to strengthen comprehensive, complete and real-time scrutiny of law enforcement to prevent miscarriages of justice at source.

In the same year, to ensure the quality of handling cases, the Supreme People's Procuratorate issued *Several Opinions on Effectively Performing Procuratorial Functions to Prevent and Correct Miscarriages of Justice*, emphasizing that procuratorial organs as state organs for legal supervision assume dual responsibilities for investigating crimes and protecting innocent people from being subject to criminal sanctions, and requiring prosecutors to scrutinize all activities concerning evidence, procedures and application of laws so as to ensure that there is no unjustness, connivance, error or omissions. Meanwhile, the Opinions requires the procuratorial personnel to firmly establish the idea of socialist rule by law and reiterate the concept of human rights protection (procuratorial personnel should always adhere to paying equal attention to the punishment of crimes and the protection of human rights and enhance the awareness of human rights). The Opinions requires resolutely correcting the serious problems in the tracking and supervision mechanism for the investigation work after case filing, supervision over interrogation outside detention house, supervision over trial activities, legal supervision over death penalty review cases, supervision over penalty execution and regulatory activities, etc.

In the same year, the Supreme People's Court promulgated the *Opinions on Establishing and Improving the Working Mechanisms for the Prevention of Miscarriages of Justice in Criminal Cases*. Among the principles that the court needs to follow, the principle of human rights protection is on top of the list. The Opinions emphasizes that "People's court shall adhere to the principle of respecting and protecting human rights. People's courts shall respect the status of defendants as subjects of litigation, protect the defendants' right to defense and other litigation rights, and protect the innocents from criminal liabilities." This clarifies the close relationship between the prevention of miscarriages of justice in criminal cases and the protection of human rights. Emphasizing the principle of in dubio pro reo, the Opinions stipulates that the defendant should be declared innocent in cases with insufficient conviction evidence; the rules for exclusion of illegal evidence are adopted, and confessions collected through torture and extortion and other illegal means should be excluded; when a confession is collected through the interrogation outside the case-handling site or through the interrogation during which no audio and video recording is made in accordance with the law, or if the circumstance of illegal obtainment of confession is impossible to rule out, the relevant confession should be excluded.

A relatively large number of defendants were acquitted of charges by courts at various levels, which shows a quick response of the court system to the policy for preventing miscarriages of justice in criminal cases. From 2013 to 2016, the Supreme People's Court supervised and guided courts at various levels to redress 34 major criminal cases involving unjust, false, or wrongful charges through trial supervision procedures.

In March 2011, the *Provisions of the Supreme People's Court on the Trial Procedure for State Compensation Cases of the Compensation Committees of the People's Courts* were promulgated. These provisions are applicable to matters involving the trial procedure for state compensation cases of the compensation committees of the people's courts above the intermediate level and other state agencies or lower-level people's courts as the organs liable for compensation. On August 9, 2013, to unify and regulate the work of handling self-compensation cases by people's courts and to ensure the timely and fair handling of the state compensation claims made by the claimants, the Supreme People's Court promulgated the *Provisions on the Procedures in Handling Self-compensation Cases by People's*

Courts. To date, operational procedures have been established for the two types of state compensation cases tried by people's courts. For example, Zhao Zuohai, who was wrongfully convicted of murder and jailed for 11 years, received 650,000 yuan in government compensation after the case was redressed. Although the right to freedom can hardly be measured by money, the improvement of the state compensation system is to compensate citizens who have suffered damages on the premise that errors in the exercise of public power are recognized at the national level. It is after all a way to prove their innocence and can indeed play a role of providing assistance to solve their living difficulties.

On June 27, 2016, the leading Group for Comprehensively Deepening Reforms of the 18th CPC Central Committee deliberated and adopted the *Opinions on Pushing Forward the Reform of the Criminal Litigation System Centering on Trials* in the 25th meeting. This marked the initiation of the reform of the trial-centered criminal procedure system. The Opinions emphasizes the basic principle of the presumption of innocence and specifies the requirements for organs of public security, the procuracy and the court involving the entire judicial process of investigation, prosecution, trial, and supervision to ensure that the criminal procedure system becomes a legitimate way to achieve the ultimate goal of fairness and justice and ensure that innocent persons are not subject to criminal sanctions punishing criminal acts in accordance with the law to prevent miscarriage of justice.

7.6 Cracking Down on Two Types of Crimes and Protecting Women and Children

7.6.1 Repealing the Crime of Whoring with Underage Girls

On September 5, 1986, the State Council promulgated the *Regulations of the People's Republic of China on Penalties for Administration of Public Security*, which clearly stipulates in Article 30 that whoever has sexual relations with a girl under the age of 14 shall be deemed to have committed rape and shall be punished in accordance with the provisions of Article 139 of the Criminal Law.

In response to the increasingly serious situation of prostitution and whoring in certain places, the NPC Standing Committee adopted the *Decision on Prohibition of Prostitution and Whoring* on September 4, 1991 to specifically crack down on the acts of organizing prostitution, forcing prostitution, inducing, taking in and introducing prostitution and whoring with underage girls. It specifies that whoever has sexual relations with a girl under the age of 14 shall be deemed to have committed rape and shall be punished in accordance with the provisions of the Criminal Law.

The crime of whoring with underage girls first appeared as an independent crime in the criminal law revised in 1997. This crime was listed separately because in the actual law enforcement process, some localities handled the behavior of whoring with underage only as common whoring behavior and imposed administrative penalties instead of investigating the perpetrator for criminal responsibilities. The *Decision on Prohibition of Prostitution and Whoring* in 1991 could hardly effectively protect the legitimate rights of underage girls. To severely punish the act of whoring with underage girls and effectively protect underage girls, the *Criminal Law* revised in 1997 separated the act of whoring with underage girls from the crime of rape and reclassified it as an independent crime. Article 360 stipulates that "Whoever whores with a girl under the age of 14 shall be sentenced to fixed-term imprisonment of not less than five years and shall also be fined." Article 263 stipulates that "Whoever rapes a woman by violence, coercion or any other means shall be sentenced to fixed-term imprisonment of not less than three years but not more than 10 years. Whoever has sexual intercourse with a girl under the age of 14 shall be deemed to have committed rape and shall be given a heavier punishment." However, the original intention of the above provisions had not been realized. In judicial practice, the crime of whoring with underage girls was generally given a lighter penalty because as a crime of disrupting the order of social administration, it did not belong to the aggravating circumstances in the crime of rape, and the maximum penalty was only 15 years of imprisonment. In some cases, punishment did not fit the crime, which was likely to give rise to judicial corruption.

On August 29, 2015, the *Amendment* (IX) *to the Criminal Law of the People's Republic of China* adopted at the 16th meeting of the Standing Committee of the 12th National People's Congress repealed the crime of whoring with underage girls and reclassifying it as rape. Article 236 states that having sexual intercourse with underage girls should be deemed to have committed rape and given harsher punishment. The crime of whoring with underage girls was repealed mainly due to the following considerations.

Article 34 of the *Convention on the Rights of the Child* stipulates that States Parties undertake to protect the child from all forms of sexual exploitation and sexual abuse and prevent "the exploitative use of children in prostitution or other unlawful sexual practices." The *Optional Protocol to the Convention on the Rights of the Child on the Sale of Children, Child Prostitution and Child Pornography* states that "child prostitution" is the practice where a child sells his or her body for sexual activities in return for remuneration or any other form of consideration. This definition shows that the so-called "child prostitution" is actually the exploitative use of children and a crime that infringes on children's rights. As a state party to the *Convention on the Rights of the Child*, China should be bound by the Convention. The establishment of the crime of whoring with underage girls objectively led to the phenomenon of "stigmatization" of underage girls. As victims, underage girls were presupposed as "prostitution." In such cases, the offender failed to receive due punishment, and the victims also suffered discrimination from public opinion, making them unable to get out of the shadow of being harmed and even worsening the situation of the victims, which was not conducive to the rescue and long-term development of children.

The process from establishment to repealing of the crime of whoring with underage girls essentially revolved around the basic human rights principle of maximizing the interests of children. The purpose of establishment and abolition is to protect underage girls from harm. Arguably, the two completely different choices were intended for the same destination. The reason for the constant change in the name of crime in criminal law lies in the practical effects of legal provisions. When the crime of whoring with underage girls could hardly achieve its original intention to protect the rights of underage girls, although scholars who advocate retention of the crime have put forward a sufficient legal basis, although the abolition of the crime might cause a chain reaction of difficulties in the application of other provisions, and this may be questioned to undermine the stability of the law, Chinese legislators still repeal the crime of whoring with underage girls based on the principle of putting the child first and non-discrimination resolutely. This result can be deemed the victory of human rights principles.

7.6.2 Cracking Down Human Trafficking

Human trafficking dates back to ancient times in the world. Crimes such as trafficking in women and children, slaves, and laborers have all left a shameful imprint in human history. To date, the crime of human trafficking is still rampant and presents new characteristics, such as better organization forms and proliferation of cross-border human trafficking. The crime of human trafficking has a bad impact and greater harm. It not only infringes on the victims' personal right and right of freedom but also does great harm to the victims' family members, impairing their physical and mental health or even making them desperate. Even worse, human trafficking is closely related to intentional homicide, intentional injury, rape, organizing prostitution, forced labor, forced begging and other secondary crimes. If not effectively controlled, it will be extremely harmful to society. Therefore, fighting against the crime of human trafficking is a consensus of the international community and an indispensable and an important part of human rights protection.

The victims of human trafficking crime in China are mainly women and children. Therefore, this crime in China's *Criminal Law* is called "the crime of trafficking women and children." For a long time, the government and relevant departments have been committed to severely cracking down on the crime of trafficking women and children. In recent years, the guiding idea of the Chinese government for this task has shifted from "combating trafficking" to "anti-trafficking." The action measure has also shifted from relying mainly on the crackdowns of judicial organs to the participation of all social forces to prevent and combat trafficking in women and children. In 2007, the State Council issued *China's National Plan of Action on Trafficking in Women and Children (2008–2012)*. As China's first plan of action on combating trafficking in women and children, it marks the start of a comprehensive governance mode in which the whole society participates in prevention, combating, and rescue. In March 2013, the Chinese government promulgated the second action plan, *China's Action Plan Against Human Abduction and Trafficking (2013–20)*. According to the plan, a long-term anti-trafficking mechanism integrating precautionary measures, methods for countering such crimes, rescue work and rehabilitation efforts is also expected to be created. The mechanism will be conducive to curbing the rise of human trafficking cases and ensuring that victims of trafficking are rehabilitated and relocated in a timely manner. A nationwide network involving the whole society to prevent and combat the crime of trafficking in women and children has been formed and has shown great power.

To crack down on trafficking in accordance with the law, a system should be established first. In 2010, the Supreme People's Court, the Supreme People's Procuratorate, the Ministry of Public Security, and the Ministry of Justice jointly issued the *Opinions on Legally Punishing the Crimes of Abducting and trafficking in Women and Children*, which clarifies the standards for the application of relevant laws and puts forward operational opinions on issues such as jurisdiction over cases, case filing, and collection of evidence. The Ministry of Public Security has also established a hard and fast rule, stating that whoever reports the missing of a child under the age of 14 or a girl between the age of 14 and 18, this shall be unconditionally filed as a criminal case, and the rapid investigation mechanism shall be activated immediately after the case is reported; in addition to the criminal investigation departments, the police substations can also handle cases of trafficking in women and children. *China's Action Plan Against Human Abduction and Trafficking (2013–20)* proposes to "comprehensively rectify the key areas and the 'buyer's market" for trafficking in human beings, and reduce the occurrence of human trafficking. The *Amendment (IX) to the Criminal Law*, which came into effect on November 1, 2015, made an amendment to the crime of trafficking in women and children. The original Criminal Law stipulates that "Whoever buys an abducted woman or child but does not obstruct the woman from returning to her original place of residence as she wishes or does not maltreat the child nor obstruct his or her rescue may be exempted from being investigated for criminal responsibility," which was amended to "Whoever buys an abducted woman or child but does not maltreat the child nor obstruct his or her rescue may be given lighter punishment; or does not obstruct the woman from returning to her original place of residence as she wishes, may be given a lighter or mitigated punishment." This means harsher punishment on trafficking in women and children. Later, the Supreme People's Court issued the *Interpretation of the Supreme People's Court on Several Issues Concerning the Application of Law in the Trial of Criminal Cases of Trafficking in Women and Children*. The interpretation clarifies the meaning of legal terms such as "stealing or robbing infants or babies" and "obstructing rescue", distinguishes trafficking in women from matchmaking crime and noncrime, and reflects the spirit of giving harsher punishment on crimes of trafficking in women and children in accordance with the law. On the one hand, China is advancing the rule of law and combating such crimes. On the other hand, China is also actively participating in international cooperation and has actively signed the relevant international treaties. The *Protocol to Prevent, Suppress and Punish Trafficking in Persons, especially Women and Children, supplementing the United Nations Convention against Transnational Organized Crime* (the Palermo Protocol) came into effect for China on March 10, 2010.

The application of advanced science and technology has effectively strengthened the effectiveness of anti-trafficking work. In April 2009, the Ministry of Public Security formally established the "anti-trafficking DNA database." The Ministry of Public Security requests that for birth parents of the abducted children, birth parents of the missing children who themselves request to collect blood, abducted children who have been rescued, children of unknown origin suspected of being the victims of abduction, and vagrants and begging children of unknown origin, their blood samples must be collected for DNA testing, and their DNA information must be recorded in the national DNA database. The blood collection work must follow the principle of proximity, and the public security organs must arrange blood collection in the place where the child was missing, where the child lives, and where the child was found. The public security organs should not collect any charge for any reason in case reporting, finding, investigating, collecting blood, testing, and comparing. The DNA database for antitrafficking helped thousands of abducted children find their birth parents. On this basis, in 2017, some CPPCC members proposed to further create a nationwide DNA database including newborns and children to further make use of science and technology to improve the quality and effectiveness of antitrafficking work.

Apart from public security organs, courts, procuratorates and other functional departments, China's anti-trafficking work has formed a pattern in which the whole society participates and makes joint efforts to combat the crime of human trafficking. Mainstream media have produced and broadcast large-scale charitable people-searching programs based on their resource advantages. Meanwhile, several film and television works focusing on human trafficking crimes have debuted, arousing a strong social response. New media are playing a huge role in antitrafficking, and new media with a wide range of spreads and fast spreading speeds, such as Weibo and WeChat, etc. provide brand-new and efficient platforms for anti-trafficking work. The role of nongovernmental forces in antitrafficking should not be underestimated. The Baobeihuijia charitable website established by the Baobeihuijia Volunteer Association has successfully helped nearly 3,000 people find their loved ones until mid-March 2019, and more than 43,000 Jiaxunbaobai and more than 39,000 Baobeixunjia registered users to find information on their loved ones through this platform. On May 15, 2016, the platform for emergency release of missing child information jointly established by the Ministry of Public Security and the Internet company was officially launched. After receiving the relevant information, the police will release it to the public as soon as possible through the official Weibo of new media such as the emergency release platform for missing children information of the Ministry of Public Security, online maps, and mobile payment. Meanwhile, missing children information will automatically be pushed to relevant people around the place where the child was missing through corresponding channels so that more people can obtain accurate information from official channels in a timely manner, assist the public security organs to quickly detect the child abduction cases, find missing children as soon as possible, and form a good anti-trafficking situation of mass prevention and treatment.

China is facing an arduous task in legal system building for anti-trafficking, there are still problems behind the achievements, and the legal system for anti-trafficking still needs to be further improved.

As the victims of human trafficking in China are mainly women and children, the abduction and trafficking of men over the age of 14 are excluded from the crime of trafficking in persons of the prevailing criminal law. However, according to the *Palermo Protocol*, "trafficking in persons" refers to the recruitment, transportation, transfer, harboring or receipt of persons, by means of the threat or use of force or other forms of coercion, of abduction, of fraud, of deception, of the abuse of power or of a position of vulnerability or of the giving or receiving of payments or benefits to achieve the consent of a person having control over another person, for the purpose of exploitation. Exploitation shall include, at a minimum, the exploitation of the prostitution of others or other forms of sexual exploitation, forced labour or services, slavery or practices similar to slavery, servitude or the removal of organs. In reality, "trafficking" and "exploitation" targeting men over the age of 14 do exist. For example, there was a real case in which the perpetrator deceived, kidnapped, transported, and abducted men over the age of 14 to work in a black brick kiln in Shanxi. There were also criminals who trafficked women, children and men over the age of 14 in southwestern China to neighboring countries for labor exploitation. The above behaviors were punished according to criminal law as behaviors of illegal detention, forced labor, and intentional injury. However, it was more appropriate to classify such behaviors into the crime of "trafficking in persons" because the definition of victim should be broader, and the facts should be ascertained by recognition of potential "labor exploitation" rather than simply emphasizing the "sales relationship" to better meet the current or regional anti-trafficking needs. The deficiencies of the current criminal law thus have aroused widespread attention from scholars and practitioners, and practitioners are taking relevant improvement actions. UN-ACT is a UNDP project ensuring a coordinated approach to more strategically and effectively combat trafficking in persons in the Greater Mekong Subregion (GMS) and beyond. The project has reached its final stage. The core task of the second phase of the project is to solve the trafficking problem under the framework of labor export. The project incorporates factors such as men, population mobility safety, and labor exploitation into the issue of trafficking. This is different from Chinese law, and it can also be seen as a local practice of China's anti-trafficking legal reform.

In addition to the change in the names of the above two crimes, the personal rights of women and children are fully protected. Since 2014, the state has stepped up efforts to improve the response mechanism of minors' social protection to prevent, monitor, report and investigate cases of violence to children and provide necessary assistance. A social protection network for minors covering both urban and rural areas is being formed. The guardianship system "based on family guardianship, guaranteed by social supervision and supplemented by state guardianship" is also being implemented in various places, and the work pattern for social protection of minors integrating "families, the society, and the government" will soon be in place. At the end of 2014, the Supreme People's Court, the Supreme

People's Procuratorate, the Ministry of Public Security, and the Ministry of Civil Affairs jointly issued *Several Opinions on Handling Guardians' Infringements on Minors' Rights and Interests in Accordance with the Law* to severely crack down on the phenomenon of guardians' infringements on the rights and interests of minors. The Opinions has detailed the requirements for the trial of cases of transfer of guardianship of minors, established a mechanism for reporting and handling cases of guardianship infringements, and clarified the responsibilities of departments of civil affairs and judicial organs. The Ministry of Civil Affairs issued the *Opinions on Regulating the Adoption of Children with Extremely Indigent Biological Parents and of Abandoned Orphans*, the *Measures for the Management of Families with Children Entrusted to Their Care*, the *Opinions on Establishing a Guiding Mechanism for Charitable Deeds Concerning Children* and other regulatory documents to explore the provision of classified security for children living in difficult circumstances and continuously strengthen subsistence security of children living in difficult circumstances.

Chapter 8
The Rule of Law in Building an Honest and Clean Government: Catching Bother "Flies" and "Tigers"

He Tian and Bin Xu

8.1 The Rule of Law in Building An Honest and Clean Government in China

Improving the legal system and strengthening supervision are the directions of the rule of law in building an honest and clean government in China. China's rule of law system for building an honest and clean government has formed several components of legislation, justice, law enforcement, and law-abiding and discipline-abiding. In terms of legislation, a sound criminal legal system has been in place in recent years. Judicial organs have played an important role in the rule of law in building an honest and clean government, and the procuratorates and the courts have become the guarantee of the rule of law in this regard. The law enforcement organs have changed from the previous disciplinary supervision committees to the present supervisory committees integrating part of the judicial and law enforcement functions. The law-abiding and discipline-abiding system is mainly implemented through regulatory documents on party member discipline, official discipline, and work style.

Since the 18th CPC National Congress, the Party Central Committee with Xi Jinping at the core has made a strategic decision to exercise "strict Party self-governance in all respects." Exercising strict Party self-governance in all respects has been a major strategic deployment made by the Party Central Committee since the 18th CPC National Congress. It is an important part of the strategic blueprint of "Four Comprehensives" and the basic guarantee to completing the building of a moderately prosperous society in all respects and deepening reform and opening up and advancing law-based governance in an all-around way. Strong Party leadership is central to this task; being thorough is fundamental; strictness is key; and discipline is crucial. "In all respects" means management and

H. Tian (✉) · B. Xu
Institute of Law, CASS, Bejing, China

H. Tian and Y. Lv (eds.), *The Chinese Path of Rule of Law Construction*, China Insights, https://doi.org/10.1007/978-981-16-4130-5_8

discipline should be imposed on the whole Party, on its 80 million members and on its four million organizations; this should encompass all aspects of Party development, all sectors and all departments, and the focus should be on the "critical minority." "Strict" means genuine, bold and sustained management and discipline. "Self-governance of the Party" means that the entire Party, from the Central Committee to Party committees at the provincial, municipal and county levels, from central Party organizations and groups in national government agencies to branches at grassroots levels, must assume their primary responsibilities; Party secretaries must treat Party development as their duty; Party discipline commissions at all levels must be responsible for supervision, be sure to impose discipline, and hold people accountable.

Anticorruption is an important part of exercising strict governance over the Party. From the perspective of the historical process of world modernization, the proliferation of corruption was a phenomenon that appeared in the transition from a traditional society to a modern society. Most countries, including the United States, have experienced such a process. Since the reform and opening up, China has also experienced such transitional corruption. After five years of continuous efforts, we have achieved important phased results in ensuring full and strict governance over the Party, and the anti-corruption campaign has built into a crushing tide, is being consolidated, and continues to develop. The Communist Party of China is striving to create effective mechanisms so officials dare not be corrupt, are unable to be corrupt and have no desire to commit corruption so as to ensure there are no restricted zones or "common practice." The unprecedented anti-corruption efforts since the reform and opening up heralded that the CPC has entered a "new normal" in its anti-corruption endeavors. In 2017, the 19th CPC National Congress summarized past anti-corruption achievements, stating that "No place has been out of bounds, no ground left unturned, and no tolerance shown in the fight against corruption. We have taken firm action to 'take out tigers,' 'swat flies,' and 'hunt down foxes.' The goal of creating a deterrent against corruption has been initially attained; the cage of institutions that prevents corruption has been strengthened; and moral defenses against corruption are in the making. The anti-corruption campaign has built into a crushing tide, is being consolidated, and continues to develop."

Anti-corruption is the spirit of the central government and has been transformed into a concrete discipline and long-term mechanism. Recently, the central government has proposed from a strategic perspective to deepen the reform of the national supervision system, expand the scope of supervision, integrate supervision forces, and build a centralized, unified, authoritative and efficient national supervision system. Since the 18th CPC National Congress, China has made important progress in advancing the rule of law in building an honest and clean government. While improving the intra-Party supervision system, it has continuously strengthened external supervision, formed a joint force of internal and external supervision, and basically achieved the initial anti-corruption goal.

8.2 New Political Environment

On the eve of the 18th CPC National Congress, the CPC Central Committee investigated and handled the problem involving Bo Xilai's serious disciplinary violation, and the world was anticipating the anti-corruption measures proposed by the Communist Party of China at the 18th CPC National Congress. "Things must corrupted before got grubby." The possible consequences of government corruption are extremely severe. Long-term accumulated contradictions will lead to strong dissatisfaction and resentment of the people, social instability, the collapse of the regime, and instability of the state power.

Improving the Party's conduct has become the first starting point in fighting against corruption. General Secretary Xi Jinping solemnly pointed out during the 1st Group Study Session of the Political Bureau of the 18th CPC Central Committee: "In real life, some Party members and officials have problems of one kind or another, but it is after all a quandary of faith and spirit." The report to the 18th CPC National Congress requires "Putting people first, exercising governance for the people and always maintaining close ties with them" and emphasizes that "We should make determined efforts to improve the style of writing and the conduct of meetings, and reject undesirable practices such as mediocrity, laziness, laxity and extravagance, the practice of just going through formalities, and bureaucratism. We should use the Party's fine conduct to enhance Party cohesiveness, win popular support and improve the conduct of the government and the general public." On December 4, 2012, the meeting of the Politburo of the CPC Central Committee deliberated and adopted the eight-point frugality code on improving Party and government conduct and keeping close contact with the people.

The eight points in the *Eight-Point Frugality Code on Improving Work Style and Keeping Close Contact with the People* specifically refer to the following: (1) Leaders must keep in close contact with the grassroots. They must understand the real situation facing society through in-depth inspections at grassroots. Greater attention should be focused on places where social problems are more acute, and inspection tours must be carried out more thoroughly. Inspection tours as a mere formality should be strictly prohibited. Leaders should work and listen to the public and officials at the grassroots level, and people's practical problems must be addressed. There should be no welcome banner, no red carpet, no floral arrangement or grand receptions for officials' visits. (2) Meetings and major events should be strictly regulated, and efficiency should be improved. Political Bureau members are not allowed to attend ribbon-cutting or cornerstone-laying ceremonies or celebrations and seminars unless they obtain approval from the CPC Central Committee. Official meetings should get shortened and be specific to the point, with no empty and rigmarole talks. (3) The issuing of official documents should be reduced. (4) Officials' visits abroad should only be arranged when needed in terms of foreign affairs with fewer accompanying members, and on most of the occasions, there is no need for a reception by overseas Chinese people, institutions and students at the airport. (5) There should be fewer traffic controls when leaders travel by cars to avoid unnecessary inconvenience to the public. There should be fewer traffic controls arranged for the leaders' security of their trips to avoid unnecessary inconvenience to the public. (6) The media must not report on stories about official events unless there is real news value. The regulations also ban worthless news reports on senior officials' work and activities and said such reports should depend on work needs, news value and social effects. (7) Leaders should not publish any works by themselves or issue any congratulatory letters unless an arrangement with central leadership has been made. Official documents without substantial content and realistic importance should be withheld. Publications regarding senior officials' work and activities are also restricted. (8) Leaders must practise thrift and strictly follow relevant regulations on accommodation and cars.

Since the release of the Eight-Point Frugality Code known as the "Rigid Eight Rules," the Party's work style has been comprehensively improved. By the end of 2018, a total of 271,407 violations against the Eight-Point Frugality Code were investigated and handled.

Curbing profligacy is also an important part of the endeavors to improve Party and government officials' work style and maintain close ties with the people. To this end, the CPC Central Committee and the State Council promulgated the *Circular on Prohibiting the Use of Logos Such as Special Supply and Exclusive Supply by Central and State Organs*, the *Regulations on Practicing Thrift and Opposing Waste in Party and Government Organs*, the *Administrative Measures for Conference Fees for Official Business of Central and State Organs*, the *Regulations on the Administration of Domestic Official Reception by Party and Government Organs*, the *Circular on Prohibiting the Use of Public Funds for Purchasing, Printing and Sending New Year Cards and Other Items*, the *Circular on Putting A Stop to the Construction of New Government Buildings and Checking up Office Buildings by Party and Government Organs* and other regulations, requiring departments at various state and fuonaries to practice thrift and waste levels. Among them, the *Opinions of the General Office of the State Council on Enforcing the Three-point Decision on Curbing Government Spending and Further Strengthening Supervision and Inspection* and the *Regulations on Practicing Thrift and Opposing Waste in Party and Government Organs* are the regulations on opposing waste and practicing thrift in Party and government organs, requiring following the principle of budget before expenditure and strengthening budget management. The *regulations* stipulate that party and government organs should establish and improve an information disclosure system for opposing waste and practicing thrift and disclose their budget and final accounts information and information on government procurement, domestic official reception, conferences, trainings, office buildings, and audit results of official expenditures and consumption by public funds in an appropriate manner in accordance with the principles of timeliness, convenience, and diversity.[1] The *Regulations on Practicing Thrift and*

[1]Zhou Xiaowen, "Criminal Regulation over Vicious Profligacy by Public Funds," master's degree thesis, Southwest University of Political Science and Law, 2014.

Opposing Waste in Party and Government Organs further clarifies the criteria and supervision measures for official reception. The *Opinions of the General Office of the State Council on Enforcing the Three-point Decision on Curbing Government Spending and Further Strengthening Supervision and Inspection* clearly requires that we should enforce strict control over the total number of people on the government payroll, put a resolute stop to the construction of new government buildings, strengthen relevant supervision measures, and establish a chief administrator responsibility system.

While the initial results have been achieved in improving the work style and punishing corruption, General Secretary Xi Jinping proposed the strategic blueprint of "The Four-pronged Comprehensives Strategy" during an inspection tour in Jiangsu Province. "Four Comprehensives" refers to a complete four-pronged strategy that aims to comprehensively accomplish a moderately prosperous society, deepen reform, advance rule of law, and strengthen strict Party governance. The proposal of the strategic blueprint of "Four Comprehensives" fully demonstrates the overall framework of the governance of the country by the new central leadership group, making the key links, key areas and main directions of the work of Party and the country clearer at present and in the future. With more rigorous internal logic, it provides a strong guarantee for pushing the reform and opening up and socialist modernization to a new stage.

Under the guidance of the "Four Comprehensives" strategy, starting in April 2015, the Communist Party of China launched the "Three Stricts and Three Honests" educational campaign for leading officials with the title at the county level and above. "Three Stricts and Three Honests" was mentioned by General Secretary Xi Jinping in his speech when participating in a panel discussion among the Anhui delegation during the 2nd Session of the 12fth National People's Congress of the People's Republic of China. "Three Stricts and Three Honests" means the requirement that Party members "be strict in moral conduct, in exercising power, and in self discipline, and be honest in decision-making, in doing pioneering work, and in personal behavior." The General Office of the Central Committee of the Communist Party of China issued the *Program for Implementation of the Educational Campaign of Three Stricts and Three Honests for Leading Officials at the County Level and Above*. The educational campaign integrates regular education into intensive activities to study and practice the Party's mass line, strengthens the atmosphere of strict governance over the Party, and sets a benchmark for leading officials. The central authorities severely investigated and dealt with cases involving serious disciplinary violations by officials. The resolute investigation and punishment of corrupt officials demonstrates the clear attitude and firm determination of the Party Central Committee to hold the Party Constitution in great esteem, strictly enforce Party discipline, promote comprehensive and strict governance over the Party, and resolutely punish corruption.

To govern a country and a society, the key is to establish rules and observe rules. The Party Constitution is the general constitution that all Party members must follow, and it is also the general rule. "Two Studies, One Action" means Party members must gain a good understanding of the Party Constitution, Party regulations, General

Secretary Xi Jinping's major policy addresses and meet Party standards. In February 2016, the General Office of the CPC Central Committee issued the *Educational Program for All party members to Study the Party Constitution, Party Regulations, and a Series of Speeches to Meet Party Standards*. In 2017, the General Office of the CPC Central Committee further issued the *Opinions on Promoting Normalization and Institutionalization of "Two Studies, One Action,"* which states that to promote the normalization and institutionalization of "Two Studies, One Action," we must adhere to full coverage and normalization, emphasize innovation, pursue substantial results, combine studies with action, integrate studies into daily life through basic systems such as theoretical learning center groups of Party committees (Party members leadership groups), and prevent formalism.

Since the 18th CPC National Congress, the Party Central Committee has explored the practice of strict Party self-governance in all respects and has gradually formed and improved theories in this regard. The improvement of the theories must be based not only on a deep understanding of the attributes of the Communist Party of China but also on a comprehensive prediction of the real situation in Party building in the new era. Exercising strict Party self-governance in all respects is a top priority for Party building. Since the 18th CPC National Congress was convened, and Party building shows new characteristics: driving the rule of law in building an honest and clean government with exercising strict Party self-governance in all respects as a "handgrip" and maintaining the Party's advanced nature and purity as the "main line." Reviewing the history of ideological development in recent years, before the 18th CPC National Congress, the Party had repeatedly emphasized preserving the Party's purity. After the 18th CPC National Congress, preserving the Party's purity was gradually raised to be one of the Party's "main lines" in the new era. In 2014, the idea of "exercising strict Party self-governance in all respects" was clearly proposed at a review meeting on the campaign to heighten awareness of and implement the mass line. In the process of exploration and practice, the logic of thinking-practice-ideology has made this Party building idea clearer, which is highly integrated with comprehensively deepening reforms, comprehensively advancing the rule of law, and building a moderately prosperous society in all respects. Exercising strict Party self-governance in all respects is related to the effectiveness of Party building, and it has become one of the major strategic deployments of the Party Central leadership group with Xi Jinping at its core, and a new political environment has been created.

8.3 Establishing the Rule of Law System for Building an Honesty and Clean Government

General Secretary Xi Jinping emphasized: "We must apply the rule of law in both thinking and action in fighting corruption, strengthen state legislation for fighting corruption, establish the system of intra-Party regulations for fighting corruption and ensure the legal system operate effectively." The construction of a rule of law system for building a clean government first requires applying the rule of law in both thinking and planning to guide and steer the work of improving Party conduct and upholding integrity and conscientiously resolve major contradictions and problems incompatible with the requirements of the rule of law based on the major strategy of vigorously advancing the rule of law and the practice of discipline inspection and supervision work.

8.3.1 Improving the System of Intra-Party Regulations

Inner-party regulations refer to all the rules and regulations formulated by central Party organizations, the CPC Central Commission for Discipline Inspection, all departments and commissions under central leadership, and the party committees of all provinces, autonomous regions, and municipalities directly under the Central Government to regulate the work, activities, and behaviour of Party members. The Party Constitution is the most fundamental intra-Party regulation and the basis for formulating other intra-Party regulations. In 1990, the CPC Central Committee promulgated the *Interim Regulations of the Communist Party of China on the Procedures for Formulation of Inner-Party Regulations*, in which the term intra-Party regulation was officially used. The Party Constitution revised in 1992 at the 14th CPC National Congress clearly stated that the main task of the Party's discipline inspection committees at various levels was to "uphold the Party Constitution and other regulations of the Party." Since then, the "intra-Prty regulations" have been officially written into the Party Constitution. In May 2012, the CPC Central Committee promulgated the *Regulations on the Formulation of Intraparty Regulations of the Communist Party of China*, marking that the regulations within the Party were formulated in a more standard and scientific manner.

The Communist Party of China has been in power for more than 60 years and has issued many "red-head documents" and regulations, but it has never carried out centralized clean-up work. There are also problems of incompatibility, incoordination, and inconsistency in the system of the Party's regulations. The *Decision of the CPC Central Committee on Several Major Issues Concerning Comprehensively Advancing the Rule of Law* adopted by the 4th Plenary Session of the 11th CPC Central Committee emphasized strengthening the construction of the system of the Party's regulations to form a complete set of regulations within the party. To this end, it is imperative to summarize the experience of the Communist Party of China in the history of construction of the system of the Party's regulations through check-up work and explore the internal laws of the Party's institutional building to provide scientific guidance for deepening the reform of the system for Party building.

In August 2013, the *Decision of the CPC Central Committee on Repealing and Declaring the Invalidation of a Number of Intraparty Regulations and Regulatory Documents* was promulgated. Pursuant to the document, more than 50 departments, including the General Office of the CPC Central Committee, conducted a comprehensive screening of more than 23,000 central documents issued between the founding of the PRC and June 2012. After checking up, of the 1,178 central intra-Party regulations and regulatory documents, 322 were repealed, and 369 were declared invalid, accounting for 58.7%. Only 487 remained valid, among which 42 needed to be revised in due course. Through the check-up work, the relevant departments obtained a clear picture of all the central intra-Party regulations and solved the problems of incompatibility and inconsistency in the system of intra-Party regulations. This has effectively maintained the coordination and unity of the system of intra-Party regulations to promote its compliance and enforcement.

8.3.2 Strengthening the Management and Supervision of Public Power

The Central Party Committee's management and expectations of the "critical minority" have become increasingly rigorous since the 18th CPC National Congress. "Leading an ox by its nose" is an important method in Xi Jinping's governance theory. He pointed out that if work is to be effective in all areas, the focus must be placed on the "key minority of officials in important positions." In his view, this "critical minority" has both a duty to lead and a duty to serve as exemplars. Only if leading officials lead well and act as role models can the "critical minority" pull the "great majority" along with it, thereby causing the latter to follow the former. The higher the ranks of leading officials, the more important their positions, the greater their powers, and the more strictly they should be supervised —this fully illustrates the spirit of focusing on the "critical minority."

Power must be exercised under accountability, the exercise of power must be supervised, and those derelict in their duties will be held accountable. The Communique of the 6th Plenary Session of the Commission for Discipline Inspection of 18th CPC Central Committee stated that there was an urgent need to formulate practical and feasible regulations on Party accountability to enforce strict Party self-governance through an accountability system. At this meeting, General Secretary Xi Jinping clearly requested that the accountability system should be integrated, and the accountability mechanism should be improved to ensure that those who fail to perform their duties will be strictly held accountable. The formulation of regulations on accountability within the Party is a realistic need to refine, systematize and legalize accountability within the Party[2] and an urgent requirement to strengthen strict Party self-governance in all respects.

---

[2]See "Regulations on Accountability of the Communist Party of China Issued by the CPC Central Committee," http://news.xinhuanet.com/politics/2016-07/17//_1,119,232,150.htm, latest access time: July 18, 2017.

The current accountability system within the Party is fragmented, and relevant accountability provisions are scattered in the *Regulations On Disciplinary Actions of the Communist Party of China*, the *Administrative Supervision Law*, the *Civil Servant Law*, and the *Interim Provisions on the Implementation of the Accountability System for the Leading Officials of the Party and Government.* Meanwhile, there are many principled provisions for which there is a large room for flexible interpretation in operation. This shows that the accountability mechanism within the Party still needs to be improved. Since the 18th CPC National Congress, documents on strengthening the Party's integrity and self-discipline have gradually formed a strict integrity system. The CPC Central Committee has successively issued the most stringent Party regulations, such as the *Regulations On Disciplinary Actions of the Communist Party of China*, the *Guidelines of the Communist Party of China Integrity and Self-Discipline*, the *Code of Conduct for Intraparty Political Life Under New Circumstances*, and the *Regulations on Accountability of the Communist Party of China*.

Regarding means of punishment, pursuant to the *Regulations on Accountability of the Communist Party of China*, leading officials will face punishment according to the severity of their wrongdoings, such as being named and shamed within certain ranks; receiving oral or written warnings; being suspended from their posts, transferred, or forced to resign, demotion, or dismissal; and being subject to punishment for violating Party discipline.[3] The *Regulations* also responded to the policy of "comprehensively and strictly govern the party" put forward since the 18th National Congress of the Communist Party of China. Leading Party officials and organizations should be held accountable for poor leadership of the Party; insufficient promotion of political, theoretical, organizational and disciplinary work within the Party; insufficient combating of corruption; and improper conduct in the most pressing issues that concern the people, including education, medical services and ecological protection.

Regarding the appointment of officials, in January 2014, the CPC Central Committee issued the newly revised *Regulations on the Work of Selecting and Appointing Leading Party and Government Officials by the Party's Central Committee*, requiring the criteria for evaluating the quality of officials in the basic conditions, principles, and requirements for officials selection and appointment. The revised *Regulations on the Work of Selecting and Appointing Leading Party and Government Officials by the Party's Central Committee* embodies the new spirit and requirements of the Party Central Committee for official cultivation. It is of great significance for lower-level institutions to better implement the spirit of the central government, establish a sound scientific official selection and appointment mechanism, and deal with prominent issues in official selection.

How can we select good officials and appoint them? Fundamentally, this must be guaranteed by a scientific and effective institutional mechanism. The selection and

---

[3]Refer to "Strengthening the Building of the Whole Party through Accountability and Interpreting Loyalty by Accountability—Thoroughly Implementing the Regulations on Accountability of the Communist Party of China," *Sichuan Party Building*, Issue 8, 2016.

appointment of officials involves complex and sensitive areas and must be controlled by a sound system. The newly revised *Regulations on the Work of Selecting and Appointing Leading Party and Government Officials by the Party's Central Committee*, as the general regulations on selection and appointment of officials in the new era, must regulate the selection and appointment of officials with its extremely coercive and binding force. While clarifying the specific applicable circumstances, the *Regulations* further stipulate that the basic conditions and qualifications as prescribed by laws should not be broken, and a series of restrictions should be established. For example, the number of consecutive tenures of service should not be exceeded; officials should not be promoted to higher grades two levels at a time; if the probationary period has not expired or a one-year probationary period has not been served, officials should not be promoted exceptionally; and stricter restrictions should be imposed on the two aspects of process disclosure and examination and approval. Meanwhile, the *R*egulations have made strict and detailed regulations on the "reappointment" and "naked officials" issues that have been widely considered in society in recent years. The revised Regulations list six specific circumstances where officials should not be included in the list of candidates to be observed for promotion, including "naked officials" officials whose spouses have emigrated or those who do not have spouses but whose children have all left the country.

8.4 Strengthening the Practice of Party Discipline and Maintaining the Normalization of Anticorruption

On the basis of reorganizing the conduct of the Party and government, the CPC Central Committee further strengthened the practice of Party discipline. General Secretary Xi Jinping stated in his important expositions on state governance that it is necessary to insist on fighting "tigers" and "flies" together. The spirit of the speech has run through the entire process of anti-corruption work since the 18th National Congress of the Communist Party of China and the construction of the Party's work style and clean government. Discipline inspection and supervision organs in various places unswervingly do a good job in discipline supervision and accountability.

8.4.1 Full Coverage of the Disciplinary Inspection (Anti-Corruption Inspection) by the CPC Central Committee

Disciplinary inspection is an important way for the CPC Central Committee to strengthen Party discipline and supervision. Disciplinary inspection is an important system stipulated by the Party constitution, an important measure to strengthen Party building, an important means of strictly governing the party and maintaining party discipline, and an important form of strengthening internal party supervision. Presently, the CPC Central Committee and provinces, autonomous regions, and municipalities directly under the Central Government implement an inspection system and establish special inspection agencies to inspect and supervise the leading groups of lower-level Party organizations and their members.

Since the 18th CPC National Congress, the inspection leadership group of the CPC Central Committee has organized 12 rounds of inspection tours, including inspection of Party organizations in 277 local governments, departments and entities, "return inspections" of 16 provinces, autonomous regions and municipalities directly under the central government, and "flexible inspections" into four institutions under the central authorities. As of the end of April 2017, the inspection leadership group had successfully completed disciplinary inspections into Party organizations in 8,362 localities, departments, and enterprises and institutions, realizing that no place has been out of bounds, no ground left unturned, and no tolerance shown in the fight against corruption. Disciplinary inspections of the central authorities involve four stages. The first stage is the 4th round of inspection in 2014, covering 31 provinces, autonomous regions and municipalities and the Xinjiang Production and Construction Corps; the second stage is the 8th round of inspection in 2015, covering the key state-owned enterprises and financial institutions under the central government; the third stage is the 11th round of inspections in 2016, covering central departments and public institutions; the fourth stage is the inspections into centrally administered colleges and universities during the 12th round of inspection in 2017. The inspection leadership group of the CPC Central Committee has been taking the 19th round of inspection since 2018.

The inspection work yielded fruitful results owing to the greater flexibility of inspection work after innovative methods were adopted and a wider scope was covered. There are diverse forms of inspection, including routine inspection, special inspection, flexible inspection and reexamination. Among them, only the 12 rounds of inspection launched by the 18th CPC Central Committee included special inspections at 29 centrally administered universities, reexaminations in 4 provinces and autonomous regions, and flexible inspections at 4 units.

In addition, "three nonfixed items" are bright spots; that is, the leader of the team of disciplinary inspectors is not fixed, the inspection subjects are not fixed, and the relationship between the inspectors and the inspection subjects is not fixed. Previously, the leader of the Central Leading Group for Inspection Work generally served for a term of 5 years. There are also local inspection teams, financial inspection teams, and corporate inspection teams within the Central Leading Group for Inspection Work. Wang Ying, deputy bureau-level inspector of the Central Leading Group for Inspection Work, introduced that after the 18th CPC National Congress, the leader of the Central Leading Group for Inspection Work was authorized and appointed for each inspection tour; there are no longer such divisions as local, enterprise and financial teams within the Central Leading Group for Inspection Work; the specific tasks of the team of inspectors were temporarily determined based on the tasks of each round of inspection.

With the continuous deepening of inspection work, disciplinary inspection was also gradually institutionalized. In August 2015, the revised *Regulations of the Communist Party of China on Inspection Work* were officially promulgated. The *Regulations* emphasize full coverage of inspections and coordinating all the inspection work of the nation, such as moves in a chess game. The inspection scope of the central inspection team covers the "Four Major Institutions" at provincial and sub-provincial levels, i.e. the Party committee, the government, the people's congress and the Chinese People's Political Consultative Conference (CPPCC). Special inspection provisions were added to the *Regulations*. After 21 months, the *Regulations* were revised again. The *Decision on Amending Regulations of the Communist Party of China on Inspection Work* was deliberated and adopted, summarizing and absorbing the innovative achievements of inspection work.

8.4.2 Preventing and Punishing Corruption

A sound legal system is a prerequisite and basis to ensure that there must be laws to go by, the laws must be observed and strictly enforced, and lawbreakers must be prosecuted. To establish an anti-corruption-related legal system within the Party, we should improve existing laws and regulations and tighten the institutional cage; more importantly, we should strengthen legislation in important areas. In practice, similar violations or cases, expulsion from the Party and giving warnings are implemented within the scope permitted by the principles and regulations, and there is a large room for discretion.[4]

Therefore, the Party and the state should seriously explore how to bridge the gap between Party disciplines and state laws, further strengthen the formulation of anti-corruption-related laws and regulations, and eliminate the space for public power rent-seeking. As far as the CPC Central Committee is concerned, it should keep abreast of the new situation and meet the anti-corruption requirements, pay attention to the new characteristics and trends of negative corruption, step up efforts in top-level planning, and strengthen the construction of systems that link up with the work and operation procedures. At the local level, in some places, some systems have been tested first, and good experience should be reflected in the operation and implementation level for accumulation and sublimation.[5]

Exercising strict governance over the Party and governing the country by law are complementary to each other. Only by exercising strict governance over the Party

---

[4]Fu Jing, "Promoting Party Style and Clean Government Building and Anti-corruption Work Based on the Rule of Law Thinking," *China Discipline Inspection and Supervision News*, October 21, 2014, 6th edition.

[5]Zhou Xiaowen, "The Criminal Regulation of Vicious Profligacy of Public Funds," master's degree thesis, Southwest University of Political Science and Law, 2014.

can the Party's strong leadership be guaranteed. Only under the leadership of the Communist Party of China can the country be governed in an orderly manner. Strict governance over the Party is a dual requirement for party organizations and party members and cadres in terms of party disciplines and laws. Governing the country by law is the governance of public power and private rights according to the law on the whole. Exercising strict governance over the Party and governing the country by law will be consolidated, fixed, and promoted in an institutionalized form in the comprehensive deepening of reforms.

8.4.3 Strong Anti-Corruption Momentum

Since the 18th CPC National Congress, the whole party has been taking a "zero-tolerance" attitude toward fighting corruption. A large number of corrupt officials have been investigated and punished, there is no upper limit on the ranking of corrupt officials who are subject to punishment, and anti-corruption operations with an extremely high density involve a wide range of areas. These are new circumstances that have not appeared in previous anti-corruption strategies. More than 150 senior officials were dismissed one after another, and more than 20 primary-level officials were punished. Within two years, the number of persons who were given Party disciplinary sanctions and the number of high-ranking officials who were investigated have repeatedly set new highs. Punishment efforts spread to all regions, and the high-ranking officials in 31 provinces, autonomous regions and municipalities were investigated and punished.

8.5 Punishing Corruption and Strengthening International Cooperation in Fighting Against Corruption

"China insists that we must show zero tolerance for corruption and strengthening international cooperation in fighting against corruption." In 2015, at the second phase of the 10th G20 Summit, President Xi Jinping proposed that China would support the G20 to strengthen international pragmatic cooperation in overseas fugitive repatriation and asset recovery. December 9th is the International Anticorruption Day determined by the United Nations. On this day, the United Nations will advocate the concept of "everyone has duty to assist in eliminating corruption." In recent years, China has strengthened efforts in the field of international anticorruption cooperation and achieved remarkable results.

8.5.1 Cross-Border Fugitive Repatriation and Asset Recovery

In November 2014, under the auspices of China, the APEC Informal Leaders' Summit emphasized the efforts in anticorruption cooperation and adopted the *Beijing Declaration on Anticorruption*. The Declaration stated that an APEC Network of Anti-Corruption Authorities and Law Enforcement Agencies (ACT-NET) would be established to carry out comprehensive cooperation in fugitive repatriation and asset recovery in the Asia–Pacific region, and countries in the region would join forces to combat cross-border corruption. To date, the ACT-NET in the Asia–Pacific region has been initially established, and the "dream of escape" of corrupt officials will be shattered. Soon thereafter, the G20 Summit endorsed the *G20 Anti-Corruption Action Plan 2015–2016* to improve the anti-corruption cooperation network, strengthen mutual legal assistance, recover corrupt assets, and refuse to provide a safe haven for corrupt officials.[6] As of the end of 2018, the public security organs had launched the "Fox Hunt", and a total of 4,600 fugitives had been arrested from more than 120 countries and regions.

Meanwhile, China has further strengthened international political mutual trust in anticorruption cooperation. On May 8, 2015, China and Russia jointly signed and issued the *Joint Statement of the People's Republic of China and the Russian Federation on Deepening the Comprehensive Strategic Partnership of Coordination and Advocating Win-win Cooperation,* which for the first time included strengthening anti-corruption cooperation in the joint statement between two countries, highlighting the importance of international anti-corruption cooperation. The year 2015 marks the 10th anniversary of the establishment of the Anti-Corruption Working Group of the U.S.-China Joint Liaison Group on Law Enforcement Cooperation. China and the United States have reached a consensus on strengthening cooperation and jointly combating transnational crimes: "Anti-corruption has become increasingly important in both China and the United States. The anti-corruption work becomes a bright spot of bilateral relationship."

In 2015, China achieved great results in the field of extradition cooperation. China has acceded to more than 20 international criminal multilateral conventions that contain provisions on legal assistance in extradition. China has also actively participated in international judicial practice involving human rights issues related to extradition, and its extradition requests have been supported by international judicial institutions. In June 2015, the Inter-American Court of Human Rights made a judgment on the case involving Huang Haiyong's appealing against Peru's extradition and ruled that the person sought Huang Haiyong lost the case and the requested state Peru won the case, thus supporting the Peruvian government's extradition decision and China's extradition request. When China is participating more extensively in extradition matters and assuming international human rights

---

[6]"China's Rule of Law in 2014 and Development Trends in 2015," http://www.cssn.c</fx/fx_yzyw/201,504/t20150402_1,573,559.html, latest access time: July 18, 2017.

obligations, it will inevitably be involved in international judicial practices. The continuous progress and development of China's rule of law and human rights protection will surely lay an important foundation for the conclusion of extradition treaties and related practices.

8.5.2 Strengthening International Cooperation, the Anti-Corruption Action Being Effective

Since 2016, public security organs across the country have conscientiously implemented the CPC Central Committee's decision and deployment on overseas fugitive repatriation and asset recovery and launched the "Skynet" and "Fox Hunt" campaigns, which have achieved significant results. As of October 2016, public security organs across the country have successfully captured 409 fugitives of various types from 61 countries and regions. In September 2016, at the G20 Hangzhou Summit, China gave full play to its role as the chairman of the G20 Anti-Corruption Working Group and promoted the adoption of the *G20 High Level Principles on Cooperation on Persons Sought for Corruption and Asset Recovery*, and the *G20 Anti-Corruption Action Plan 2017–2018*, and established a Research Center on International Cooperation Regarding Persons Sought for Corruption and Asset Recovery in G20 Member States. The *G20 High Level Principles on Cooperation on Persons Sought for Corruption and Asset Recovery* ground-breakingly proposed that we would implement our stance of zero tolerance against corruption, zero loopholes in our institutions and zero barriers in our actions.

8.6 Innovating the Reform of the Integrity and Self Discipline System and Initiating the Reform of the Supervisory System

After implementing the strict intra-Party discipline, to integrate anti-corruption resources, the reform of the supervisory system was launched. The communique of the 6th Plenary Session of the 18th CPC Central Committee stated that "Party committees at all levels shall support and ensure that the people's congresses, governments, supervisory organs, and judicial organs at the same level supervise state organs and public officials in accordance with the law." This was the first time that supervisory organs were put side by side with the people's congresses and the governments. In December 2016, the NPC Standing Committee adopted the *Decision on Carrying the Pilot Program for the Reform of the National Supervision System in Beijing, Shanxi Province, and Zhejiang Province*, officially implementing the reform plan in the three regions. Meanwhile, a series of systems related to supervisory commissions are also being further improved in advancing the rule of law.

8.6.1 Top-Level Design: Establishing Supervisory Commissions

The 6th Plenary Session of the 18th CPC Central Committee deliberated on and adopted the *Regulations on Inner-Party Supervision of the Communist Party of China*, which stipulates that Party committees at all levels shall support and ensure that the people's congresses, governments, supervisory organs, and judicial organs at the corresponding level supervise state organs and public officials in accordance with the law. For the first time, the term "supervisory organ" appeared alongside the people's congress, government, and judicial organ. In November 2016, the General Office of the CPC Central Committee issued the *Pilot Plan for the Reform of the National Supervision System in Beijing, Shanxi Province, and Zhejiang Province* and disclosed for the first time to the outside world the basic goals and ideas of this round of supervisory reform. On December 25, the 25th Session of the Standing Committee of the 12th National People's Congress adopted the decision on the pilot reform of the national supervisory system by a majority of votes. On January 8, 2017, the 7th Plenary Session of the 18th Central Commission for Discipline Inspection concluded and put forward the "timetable" for the reform of the supervisory system in 2017: the pilot areas will first complete the transfer of relevant departments of the procuratorial organs to ensure that the establishment of supervisory commissions at the provincial level was completed by the end of March 2017 and the establishment of supervisory commissions at the city and county levels by the end of June. On March 17, 2018, the 1st Session of the 13th National People's Congress deliberated on and adopted the State Council's institutional reform plan to be incorporated into the Ministry of Supervision into the newly established National Supervision Commission. On March 20, 2018, the *Supervision Law of the People's Republic of China* was adopted by voting at the 1st Session of the 13th National People's Congress. On March 23, 2018, the National Supervision Commission of the People's Republic of China was inaugurated in Beijing. Pursuant to the law, the National Supervision Commission of the People's Republic of China is the highest supervisory organ.

The newly established supervisory commissions have integrated three powers and twelve actions. The three powers include supervision, investigation and punishment. That is, the supervisory organs should oversee and inspect public employees' performance of their duties in accordance with the law, just use of authority, clean governance, and upholding ethics; investigate duty-related violations or crimes such as graft, misuse of authority, neglect of duty, rent-seeking behavior, tunneling, playing favoritism and committing irregularities, and wasting public funds, and make decisions on punishments; transfer suspected criminal cases to the procuratorates in accordance with the law. While exercising the above powers, supervisory commissions may take twelve actions: interview, interrogation, questioning, inquiry, freezing, collecting and obtaining, sealing, seizure, search, inspection and examination, identification, and detention.

8.6.2 Pilot Reform

Since the pilot program was launched, the reform of the national supervisory system has drawn wide attention all the time. The important progress in the reform of the supervisory system is to absorb a wealth of practical experience from the pilot reform, summarize and refine it in a timely manner and upgrade it to the fundamental system of the country, and incorporate it into the scope of the Constitution. Judging from the past institutionalization process, the *Regulations on Inner-Party Supervision of the Communist Party of China* formally put forward the legal term "supervisory organ." The *Pilot Plan for the Reform of the National Supervision System in Beijing, Shanxi Province, and Zhejiang Province* issued in late 2016 has drawn up a road map and timetable for pilot reform over the past year. The plan proposed completing the establishment of provincial supervision commissions at the end of March 2017 and completing the establishment of supervision commissions at the city and county levels at the end of June.

In this pilot program, the most prominent institutional innovation lies in supervisory commissions at the national, provincial, prefecture and county levels being established and working together with the Party's disciplinary inspection commissions as one office while keeping their own identity. According to the system, the supervisory organs perform disciplinary inspection and supervision functions under the leadership of the Party committees. The relevant leadership mechanisms have been explored and practiced in the pilot process, and a complete set of working mechanisms and operating modes have been initially formed. On the basis of the overall pilot framework, some pilot regions have also adopted different institutional measures according to actual local conditions. For example, in some pilot regions, the supervisory organs were renamed to be stationed discipline inspection and supervision groups to horizontally extend the supervisory functions. Some pilot regions attach importance to township disciplinary inspection officials and regard them as the tentacles of the "neural network" of the national supervision system at the primary level and encourage them to play a role in assisting the supervision work of township party committees through the empowerment mechanism. Generally, from the pilot reform to the operation of the national system, a good institutional innovation mechanism has been formed from the local to the central level. The pilot reform provides experience for the continuously institutionalized development of the supervisory system.[7] The 8th Plenary Session of the 1st Session of the 13th National People's Congress voted to pass the *Supervision Law of the People's Republic of China*.

In October 2017, the General Office of the CPC Central Committee issued the *Pilot Program for Promoting the Reform of the National Supervision System throughout the Country*. In November, the 30th Session of the Standing Committee

[7]"Beijing, Zhejiang, and Shanxi's Supporting Work Gradually Started After Becoming the Pilot Regions for the Reform of the Supervisory System," http://cpc.people.com.cn/n1/2017/0213/c164113-29,075,950. html, latest access time: July 18, 2017.

of the 12th National People's Congress adopted the *Decision on Launching the Pilot Work of Reform of the National Supervision System throughout the Country*. On November 7, the much-watched *Supervision Law (Draft)* began to solicit public opinion. The draft was formulated on the basis of the *Administrative Supervision Law* forming the fundamental law on the national supervision system. The draft specifies the organizational mode, powers and responsibilities of supervisory commissions at various levels. The National Supervisory Commission is created by the National People's Congress and is responsible for supervision work throughout the country. Supervisors are supervision personnel who exercise supervisory powers in accordance with the law. The state implements a hierarchical system for supervisors and has formulated measures for the hierarchical establishment, evaluation and promotion of supervisors. On this basis, the draft stipulates that the supervisory organs will exercise supervision over those exercising public power.

8.7 Exercising Strict Governance Over the Party

The 19th CPC National Congress in 2017 proposed that China will further secure a sweeping victory in the fight against corruption in the new era and improve the Party and state supervision system. On March 11, 2018, the 1st Session of the 13th National People's Congress adopted an amendment to the Constitution. Article 125 stipulates that the National Supervision Commission of the People's Republic of China is the highest supervisory organ. In addition, the 1st Session of the 13th National People's Congress deliberated and adopted the institutional reform plan of the State Council, which merged the Ministry of Supervision and the Bureau of Corruption Prevention of the People's Republic of China into the newly formed National Supervision Commission.

Clean governance, which is closely integrated with the country's modern governance, shows a trend of modernization. The level of clean governance is an important manifestation of the ruling party's ability to govern. After ruling for nearly 70 years, the Communist Party of China has accumulated a wealth of experience in its ruling practice, but many practical problems have also arisen. Along with the torrent of reform and opening up, some Party members failed to adhere to communist beliefs and forgot their original aspirations to govern the people. They have developed a serious tendency to corruption, causing negative social impacts and intensifying class conflicts at a certain level. This is a political issue that the Communist Party of China must face in the new era.

Since the 18th CPC National Congress, the Party Central Committee with Xi Jinping at its core has made a firm resolution to thoroughly tackle corruption within the Party and has achieved remarkable results. The endeavors of the new central collective leadership in domestic institutional building and international cooperation reflect its political determination to seek new development and uphold the Party's fine style. There is still a long journey ahead fraught with many challenges.

Appendices

Table A.1 Legislation of the National People's Congress and its standing committee during 2012–2018

Year	No	Time of promulgation	Title of law
2012	1	February 29, 2012	The Clean Production Promotion Law of the People's Republic of China (revised)
	2	March 14, 2012	The Criminal Procedure Law (revised)
	3	April 27, 2012	The Military Insurance Law (enacted)
	4	June 30, 2012	The Exit and Entry Administration Law (enacted)
	5	June 30, 2012	Measures for Election of Deputies From the Chinese People's Liberation Army to the National People's Congress and Local People's Congresses at or Above the County Level (revised)
	6	August 31, 2012	The Civil Procedure Law (revised)
	7	August 31, 2012	The Law on Popularization of Agricultural Technology (revised)
	8	October 26, 2012	The Mental Health Law (enacted)
	9	October 26, 2012	The Prison Law (revised)
	10	October 26, 2012	The Law on Lawyers (revised)
	11	October 26, 2012	The Law on the Protection of Minors (Revised)
	12	October 26, 2012	The Law on the Prevention of Juvenile Delinquency (revised)
	13	October 26, 2012	The Law on Penalties for Administration of Public Security (revised)
	14	October 26, 2012	The Law on State Compensation (revised)
	15	October 26, 2012	The People's Police Law (revised)
	16	October 26, 2012	The Postal Law (revised)
	17	December 28, 2012	The Labor Contract Law (revised)
	18	2December 28, 2012	The Agricultural Law (revised)

(continued)

H. Tian and Y. Lv (eds.), *The Chinese Path of Rule of Law Construction*,
China Insights, https://doi.org/10.1007/978-981-16-4130-5

Table A.1 (continued)

Year	No	Time of promulgation	Title of law
	19	December 28, 2012	The Law on the Protection of Rights and Interests of the Elderly (revised)
	20	December 28, 2012	The Law on Securities Investment Fund (revised)
2013	1	April 25, 2013	The Tourism Law (enacted)
	2	June 29, 2013	The Special Equipment Safety Law (enacted)
	3	June 29, 2013	The Seed Law (revised)
	4	June 29, 2013	The Infectious Disease Prevention and Control Law (revised)
	5	June 29, 2013	The Non-governmental Education Promotion Law (revised)
	6	June 29, 2013	The Securities Law (revised)
	7	June 29, 2013	The Animal Epidemic Prevention Law (revised)
	8	June 29, 2013	The Coal Law (revised)
	9	June 29, 2013	The Law on the Prevention and Control of Environmental Pollution by Solid Waste (revised)
	10	June 29, 2013	The Law on the Administration of Tax Collection (revised)
	11	June 29, 2013	The Import and Export Commodity Inspection Law (revised)
	12	June 29, 2013	The Customs Law (revised)
	13	June 29, 2013	The Grassland Law (revised)
	14	June 29, 2013	The Law on the Protection of Cultural Relics (revised)
	15	August 30, 2013	The Trademark Law (revised)
	16	October 25, 2013	The Consumer Rights Protection Law (revised)
	17	December 28, 2013	Resolution of the Standing Committee of the National People's Congress on Approving the Decision of the State Council on the Issue of Reeducation through Labor (repealed)
	18	December 28, 2013	Resolution of the NPC Standing Committee on Approving the State Council's Supplementary Provisions on Reeducation through Labor (repealed)
	19	December 28, 2013	The Marine Environmental Protection Law (revised)
	20	December 28, 2013	The Drug Administration Law (revised)
	21	December 28, 2013	The Measurement Law (revised)
	22	December 28, 2013	The Fisheries Law (revised)
	23	December 28, 2013	The Customs Law (revised)
	24	December 28, 2013	The Tobacco Monopoly Law (revised)
	25	December 28, 2013	The Company Law (revised)
2014	1	April 24, 2014	The Environmental Protection Law (revised)
	2	April 24, 2014	The Interpretation of the NPC Standing Committee on Article 341 and Article 312 the Criminal Law
	3	April 24, 2014	The Interpretation of the NPC Standing Committee on Article 158 and Article 159 of the Criminal Law of the PRC

(continued)

Table A.1 (continued)

Year	No	Time of promulgation	Title of law
	4	April 24, 2014	The Interpretation of the NPC Standing Committee on Article 30 of the Criminal Law of the PRC
	5	April 24, 2014	The Interpretation of the NPC Standing Committee on Article 266 of the Criminal Law of the PRC
	6	April 24, 2014	The Interpretation of the NPC Standing Committee on Article 271, Paragraph 2 of the Criminal Procedure Law of the PRC
	7	April 24, 2014	The Interpretation of the NPC Standing Committee on Article 254 Paragraph 5 and Article 257 Paragraph 2 of the Criminal Procedure Law of the PRC
	8	June 27, 2014	The Military Facilities Protection Law (revised)
	9	August 31, 2014	The Safety Production Law (revised)
	10	August 31, 2014	The Budget Law (revised)
	11	August 31, 2014	The Meteorological Law (revised)
	12	August 31, 2014	The Government Procurement Law (revised)
	13	August 31, 2014	The CPA Law (revised)
	14	August 31, 2014	The Securities Law (revised)
	15	August 31, 2014	The Insurance Law (revised)
	16	November 1, 2014	The National Security Law (repealed)
	17	November 1, 2014	The Counterespionage Law (enacted)
	18	November 1, 2014	The Administrative Procedure Law (revised)
	19	November 1, 2014	The Interpretation of the NPC Standing Committee Article 99 Paragraph 1 of the General Principles of the Civil Law of the PRC and Article 22 of the Marriage Law of the PRC
	20	December 28, 2014	The Waterway Law (enacted)
2015	1	February 27, 2015	The Decision of the NPC Standing Committee on Authorizing the State Council to Temporarily Adjust and Implement the Relevant Laws and Regulations in 33 Pilot Counties (Cities, Districts) including Daxing District, Beijing
	2	March 15, 2015	The Legislation Law (revised)
	3	April 24, 2015	The Advertising Law (revised)
	4	April 24, 2015	The Food Safety Law (revised)
	5	April 24, 2015	The Tax Collection Administration Law (revised)
	6	April 24, 2015	The Law on the Prevention and Control of Environmental Pollution by Solid Waste (revised)
	7	April 24, 2015	The Gun Control Law (revised)
	*	April 24, 2015	The Securities Investment Fund Law (revised)
	9	April 24, 2015	The Urban and Rural Planning Law (revised)
	10	April 24, 2015	The Measurement Law (revised)
	11	April 24, 2015	The Compulsory Education Law (revised)
	12	April 24, 2015	The Postal Law (revised)

(continued)

Table A.1 (continued)

Year	No	Time of promulgation	Title of law
	13	April 24, 2015	The Railway Law (revised)
	14	April 24, 2015	The Notarization Law (revised)
	15	April 24, 2015	The Tobacco Monopoly Law (revised)
	16	April 24, 2015	The Drug Administration Law (revised)
	17	April 24, 2015	The Cultural Relics Protection Law (revised)
	1*	April 24, 2015	The Port Law (revised)
	19	April 24, 2015	The Flood Control Law (revised)
	20	April 24, 2015	The Insurance Law (revised)
	21	April 24, 2015	The Civil Aviation Law (revised)
	22	April 24, 2015	The Livestock Law (revised)
	23	April 24, 2015	The Electricity Law (revised)
	24	April 24, 2015	The Auction Law (revised)
	25	April 24, 2015	The Law on the Protection of the Rights and Interests of the Elderly (revised)
	26	April 24, 2015	The Animal Epidemic Prevention Law (revised)
	27	April 24, 2015	The Electronic Signature Law (revised)
	28	April 24, 2015	The Employment Promotion Law (revised)
	29	April 24, 2015	The Decision of the NPC Standing Committee of the National People's Congress on Authorizing Pilot Reform of the People's Juror System in Certain Regions
	30	July 1, 2015	The National Security Law (enacted)
	31	August 29, 2015	The Law on Promoting the Transformation of Scientific and Technological Achievements (revised)
	32	August 29, 2015	The Amendment (IX) to the Criminal Law
	33	August 29, 2015	The Election Law (revised)
	34	August 29, 2015	The Local Organic Law (revised)
	35	August 29, 2015	The Law of People's Deputies (revised)
	36	August 29, 2015	The Air Pollution Prevention and Control Law (revised)
	37	August 29, 2015	The Commercial Bank Law (revised)
	38	August 29, 2015	The Decision of the NPC Standing Committee on Approving the Treaty on Criminal Judicial Assistance between the People's Republic of China and the United Kingdom of Great Britain and Northern Ireland
	39	November 4, 2015	The Seed Law (revised)
	40	December 27, 2015	The Anti-Domestic Violence Law (enacted)
	41	December 27, 2015	The Anti-Terrorism Law (enacted)
	42	December 27, 2015	The Population and Family Planning Law (revised)
	43	December 27, 2015	The National Medal and National Honorary Title Law (enacted)
	44	December 27, 2015	The Education Law (revised)

(continued)

Table A.1 (continued)

Year	No	Time of promulgation	Title of law
2016	1	February 26, 2016	The Law on the Exploration and Development of Resources in the Deep Seabed Area (enacted)
	2	March 16, 2016	The Charity Law (enacted)
	3	April 28, 2016	The Law on the Administration of Domestic Activities of Foreign NGOs (enacted)
	4	July 2, 2016	The Asset Appraisal Law (enacted)
	5	July 2, 2016	The Energy Conservation Law (revised)
	6	July 2, 2016	The Wild Animal Protection Law (revised)
	7	July 2, 2016	The Water Law (revised)
	8	July 2, 2016	The Flood Control Law (revised)
	9	July 2, 2016	The Occupational Disease Prevention Law (revised)
	10	July 2, 2016	The Waterway Law (revised)
	11	July 2, 2016	The Environmental Impact Assessment Law (revised)
	12	September 3, 2016	The National Defense Traffic Law (enacted)
	13	September 3, 2016	The Law on Foreign-capital Enterprises (revised)
	14	September 3, 2016	The Law on Sino-foreign Equity Joint Ventures (revised)
	15	September 3, 2016	The Law on Sino-Foreign Cooperative Enterprises (revised)
	16	September 3, 2016	The Investment Protection Law of Taiwan Compatriots (revised)
	17	September 3, 2016	The Decision of the NPC Standing Committee on Authorizing the Supreme People's Court and the Supreme People's Procuratorate to Carry out the Pilot Work of the Leniency System for Confessing Guilt and Punishment in Criminal Cases in Certain Areas
	18	November 7, 2016	The Cyber Security Law (enacted)
	19	November 7, 2016	The Film Industry Promotion Law (enacted)
	20	November 7, 2016	The Private Education Promotion Law (revised)
	21	November 7, 2016	The Marine Environmental Protection Law (revised)
	22	November 7, 2016	The Foreign Trade Law (revised)
	23	November 7, 2016	The Maritime Traffic Safety Law (revised)
	24	November 7, 2016	The Customs Law (revised)
	25	November 7, 2016	The Archives Law (revised)
	26	November 7, 2016	The Law on Sino-Foreign Cooperative Enterprises (revised)
	27	November 7, 2016	The Sports Law (revised)
	28	November 7, 2016	The Civil Aviation Law (revised)
	29	November 7, 2016	The Law on the Prevention and Control of Environmental Pollution by Solid Waste (revised)

(continued)

Table A.1 (continued)

Year	No	Time of promulgation	Title of law
	30	November 7, 2016	The Coal Law (revised)
	31	November 7, 2016	The Highway Law (revised)
	32	November 7, 2016	The Meteorological Law (revised)
	33	November 7, 2016	The Tourism Law (revised)
	34	November 7, 2016	The Interpretation of the NPC Standing Committee on Article 104 of the Basic Law of the Hong Kong Special Administrative Region of the PRC (legislative interpretation)
	35	December 25, 2016	The Traditional Chinese Medicine Law (enacted)
	36	December 25, 2016	The Public Cultural Service Guarantee Law (enacted)
	37	December 25, 2016	The Environmental Protection Tax Law (enacted)
	38	December 25, 2016	The Decision of the NPC Standing Committee on the Launch of the Pilot Work of Reform of the National Supervision System in Beijing, Shanxi Province and Zhejiang Province
	39	December 25, 2016	The Decision of the NPC Standing Committee on Authorizing the State Council to Temporarily Adjust the Application of the Relevant Provisions of the Civil Service Law of the PRC in Some Regions and Some Central Organs in Beijing
	40	December 25, 2016	The Decision of the NPC Standing Committee on Authorized the State Council to Temporarily Adjust the Application of the Relevant Provisions of Social Insurance Law in 12 Pilot Cities including Handan, Hebei Province
	41	December 25, 2016	The Decision of the NPC Standing Committee on Temporarily Adjusting the Application of Relevant Laws and Regulations during the Reform of the Officer System
2017	1	February 24, 2017	The Red Cross Law of the PRC (revised)
	2	February 24, 2017	The Enterprise Income Tax Law of the PRC (revised)
	3	March 15, 2017	The General Provisions of the Civil Law of the PRC (enacted)
	4	April 27, 2017	The Law of the PRC on Surveying and Mapping (revised)
	5	April 27, 2017	The Decision of the NPC Standing Committee on Extending the Period of the People's Juror System Reform Pilot Program
	6	June 27, 2017	The National Intelligence Law of the PRC (enacted)
	7	June 27, 2017	The Civil Procedure Law of the PRC (revised)
	8	June 27, 2017	The Water Pollution Prevention and Control Law of the PRC (revised)
	9	June 27, 2017	The Administrative Procedure Law of the People's Republic of China (revised)
	10	September 1, 2017	The Nuclear Safety Law of the PRC (enacted)

(continued)

Table A.1 (continued)

Year	No	Time of promulgation	Title of law
	11	September 1, 2017	The National Anthem Law of the PRC (enacted)
	12	September 1, 2017	The Law of the PRC on the Promotion of Small and Medium-sized Enterprises (revised)
	13	September 1, 2017	The Judge Law of the PRC (revised)
	14	September 1, 2017	The Law of the PRC on Prosecutors (revised)
	15	September 1, 2017	The Civil Servants Law of the PRC (revised)
	16	September 1, 2017	The Lawyers Law of the PRC (revised)
	17	September 1, 2017	The Notarization Law of the PRC (revised)
	18	September 1, 2017	The Arbitration Law of the PRC (revised)
	19	September 1, 2017	The Administrative Reconsideration Law of the PRC (revised)
	20	September 1, 2017	The Administrative Punishment Law of the PRC (revised)
	21	November 4, 2017	The Public Library Law of the PRC (enacted)
	22	November 4, 2017	The Standardization Law of the PRC (revised)
	23	November 4, 2017	The Anti-Unfair Competition Law of the PRC (revised)
	24	November 4, 2017	The Amendment (X) to the Criminal Law of the PRC (revised)
	25	November 4, 2017	The Accounting Law of the PRC (revised)
	26	November 4, 2017	The Marine Environmental Protection Law of the PRC (revised)
	27	November 4, 2017	The Law of the PRC on the Protection of Cultural Relics (revised)
	28	November 4, 2017	The Customs Law of the PRC (revised)
	29	November 4, 2017	The Law of the PRC on Chinese-Foreign Cooperative Enterprises (revised)
	30	November 4, 2017	The Maternal and Infant Health Care Law of the PRC (revised)
	31	November 4, 2017	The Civil Aviation Law of the PRC (revised)
	32	November 4, 2017	The Highway Law of the PRC (revised)
	33	November 4, 2017	The Port Law of the PRC (revised)
	34	November 4, 2017	The Law of the PRC on the Prevention and Control of Occupational Diseases (revised)
	35	November 4, 2017	The Law of the PRC on the Administration of Domestic Activities of Foreign NGOs (revised)
	36	November 4, 2017	The Decision of the NPC Standing Committee on Adding the National Laws Listed in Annex III of the Basic Law of the Hong Kong Special Administrative Region of the PRC
	37	November 4, 2017	The Decision of the NPC Standing Committee on Adding the National Laws Listed in Annex III of the Basic Law of the Macao Special Administrative Region of the PRC

(continued)

Table A.1 (continued)

Year	No	Time of promulgation	Title of law
	38	November 4, 2017	The Decision of the NPC Standing Committee on Temporarily Adjusting the Application of Relevant Laws and Regulations during the Reform of the Chinese People's Armed Police Force
	39	November 4, 2017	The Decision of the NPC Standing Committee of the National People's Congress on Extending the Authorization of the State Council to Temporarily Adjust the Time Limit for Implementing Relevant Laws and Regulations in the Administrative Areas of 33 Pilot counties (cities, districts) including Daxing District, Beijing City
	40	November 4, 2017	The Decision of the NPC Standing Committee on the Pilot Work of Supervision System Reform
2018	1	February 24, 2018	The Decision of the NPC Standing Committee of the National People's Congress on Extending the Authorization of the State Council to adjust the application of the relevant provisions of the Securities Law of the PRC in the implementation of the reform of the registration system for stock issuance
	2	Mzrch 11, 2018	Amendment to the Constitution of the PRC(enacted)
	3	Mzrch 20, 2018	The Supervision Law of the PRC (enacted)
	4	April 27, 2018	The People's Juror Law of the PRC (enacted)
	5	April 27, 2018	Protection of Heroes and Martyrs Law of the PRC (enacted)
	6	April 27, 2018	Frontier Health and Quarantine Law of the PRC (revised)
	7	April 27, 2018	Import and Export Commodity Inspection Law of the PRC (revised)
	8	April 27, 2018	National Defense Education Law of the PRC (revised)
	9	April 27, 2018	Mental Health Law of the PRC (revised)
	10	April 27, 2018	Counterterrorism Law of the PRC (revised)
	11	April 27, 2018	National Intelligence Law of the PRC (revised)
	12	April 27, 2018	The Decision of the NPC Standing Committee on the establishment of Shanghai financial court
	13	April 27, 2018	The Decision of the NPC Standing Committee on the institutional reform of the State Council involving the adjustment of the responsibilities of administrative organs stipulated by law
	14	June 22, 2018	The Decision of the NPC Standing Committee on the responsibilities of the Constitution and Law Committee of the National People's Congress
	15	June 22, 2018	The Decision of the NPC Standing Committee on the exercise of maritime rights protection and law enforcement functions and powers by China maritime police

(continued)

Table A.1 (continued)

Year	No	Time of promulgation	Title of law
	16	August 31, 2018	Individual Income Tax Law of of the PRC (revised)
	17	October 26, 2018	International Criminal Judicial Assistance Law of the PRC (enacted)
	18	October 26, 2018	Fire Fighting and Rescue Regulationsof the PRC (enacted)
	19	October 26, 2018	Criminal Procedure Law of the PRC (revised)
	20	October 26, 2018	Organic Law of the People's Courts of the PRC (revised)
	21	October 26, 2018	Organic Law of the People's Procuratorate of the PRC (revised)
	22	October 26, 2018	Company Lawof the PRC (revised)
	23	October 26, 2018	Wildlife Protection Law of the PRC (revised)
	24	October 26, 2018	Metrology Law of the PRC (revised)
	25	October 26, 2018	Air Pollution Prevention and Control Law of the PRC (revised)
	26	October 26, 2018	The Protection of Persons with Disabilities Law of the PRC (revised)
	27	October 26, 2018	The Protection of Women's Rights and Interests law of the PRC (revised)
	28	October 26, 2018	Advertisement Law of the PRC (revised)
	29	October 26, 2018	Energy Conservation Law of the PRC (revised)
	30	October 26, 2018	Sand Prevention and Control Law of the PRC (revised)
	31	October 26, 2018	The Promotion of Agricultural Mechanization Law of the PRC (revised)
	32	October 26, 2018	Agricultural Product Quality and Safety Law of the PRC (revised)
	33	October 26, 2018	The Circular Economy Promotion Law of the PRC (revised)
	34	October 26, 2018	Tourism Law of the PRC (revised)
	35	October 26, 2018	Environmental Protection Tax Law of the PRC (revised)
	36	October 26, 2018	Public Library Law of the PRC (revised)
	37	October 26, 2018	Ship Tonnage Tax Law of the PRC (revised)
	38	December 29, 2018	Rural Land Contract Law of the PRC (revised)
	39	December 29, 2018	Civil Service Law of the PRC (enacted)
	40	December 29, 2018	Organic Law of the Villagers Committee of the PRC (revised)
	41	December 29, 2018	the Organization of Urban Neighborhood Committees Law of the PRC (revised)
	42	December 29, 2018	Farmland Occupation Tax Law of the PRC (enacted)
	43	December 29, 2018	Vehicle Purchase Tax Law of the PRC (enacted)
	44	December 29, 2018	Product Quality Law of the PRC (revised)

(continued)

Table A.1 (continued)

Year	No	Time of promulgation	Title of law
	45	December 29, 2018	Compulsory Education Law of the PRC (revised)
	46	December 29, 2018	Import and Export Commodity Inspection Law of the PRC (revised)
	47	December 29, 2018	Budget Law of the PRC (revised)
	48	December 29, 2018	Food Safety Law of the PRC (revised)
	49	December 29, 2018	Electricity Law of the PRC (revised)
	50	December 29, 2018	Higher Education Law of the PRC (revised)
	51	December 29, 2018	Port Law of the PRC (revised)
	52	December 29, 2018	Corporate Income Tax Law of the PRC (revised)
	53	December 29, 2018	Labor Law of the PRC (revised)
	54	December 29, 2018	The Protection of the Rights and Interests of the Elderly law of the PRC (revised)
	55	December 29, 2018	Environmental Noise Pollution Prevention and Control Law of the PRC (revised)
	56	December 29, 2018	Environmental Impact Assessment Law of the PRC (revised)
	57	December 29, 2018	Private Education Promotion Law of the PRC (revised)
	58	December 29, 2018	Civil Aviation Law of the PRC (revised)
	59	December 29, 2018	Occupational Disease Prevention and Control Law of the PRC (revised)
	60	December 29, 2018	Social Insurance Law of the PRC (revised)
	61	December 29, 2018	The Decision of the NPC Standing Committee of the National People's Congress on Extending the Authorization of the State Council to Temporarily Adjust the Time Limit for Implementing Relevant Laws and Regulations in the Administrative Areas of 33 Pilot counties (cities, districts) including Daxing District, Beijing City

Table A.2 The State Council's administrative regulations during 2012–2018

Year	No	Time of promulgation	Title of administrative regulation
2012	1	February 23, 2012	The Detention Center Regulations (enacted)
	2	March 1, 2012	The Regulations on the Administration of Marine Observation and Forecasting (enacted)
	3	March 30, 2012	The Regulations on Compulsory Insurance Motor Vehicle Traffic Accident Liability (revised)
	4	April 5, 2012	The Regulations on School Bus Safety Management (enacted)
	5	April 28, 2012	The Special Provisions on Labor Protection of Female Employees (enacted)
	6	June 4, 2012	The Regulations on the Administration of Foreign Labor Service Cooperation (enacted)
	7	June 28, 2012	The Regulations on the Construction of Barrier-free Environment (enacted)
	8	August 29, 2012	The Regulations on Environmental Protection of Meteorological Facilities and Meteorological Observations (enacted)
	9	September 9, 2012	The Meteorological Supervision Regulations (enacted)
	10	October 13, 2012	The Domestic Waterway Transportation Management Regulations (enacted)
	11	October 22, 2012	The Regulations on the Recall of Defective Automobile Products (enacted)
	12	October 24, 2012	The Administrative Regulations on Futures Trading (revised)
	13	November 9, 2012	The Decision of the State Council on Amending and Repealing Certain Administrative Regulations (5 administrative regulations were revised; 5 administrative regulations were repealed)
	14	November 9, 2012	The Regulations on the Administration of Enterprise Name Registration (revised)
	15	November 9, 2012	The Funeral Administration Regulations (revised)
	16	November 9, 2012	The Detailed Rules for the Implementation of the Tax Collection and Administration Law (revised)
	17	November 9, 2012	The Road Traffic and Transport Regulations (revised)
	18	November 9, 2012	The Regulations on Emergency Rescue, Investigation and Handling of Railway Traffic Accidents (revised)
	19	November 12, 2012	The Agricultural Insurance Regulations (enacted)

(continued)

Table A.2 (continued)

Year	No	Time of promulgation	Title of administrative regulation
2013	1	January 21, 2013	The Regulations on the Administration of Credit Reporting Industry (enacted)
	2	January 30, 2013	The Regulations on the Protection of the Right to Network Dissemination of Information (revised)
	3	January 30, 2013	The Implementation Regulations of the Copyright Law (revised)
	4	January 30, 2013	The Computer Software Protection Regulations (revised)
	5	January 31, 2013	The Regulations on the Protection of New Varieties of Plants (revised)
	6	May 30, 2013	The Regulations on the Administration of Foreign-funded Insurance Companies (revised)
	7	July 12, 2013	The Regulations on the Administration of the Entry and Exit of Foreigners (enacted)
	8	July 18, 2013	The Measures for the Administration of Coal Production Licenses (repealed)
	9	July 18, 2013	The Decision of the State Council on Repealing and Amending Some Administrative Regulations (25 regulations were revised)
	10	August 17, 2013	The Railway Safety Administration Regulations (enacted)
	11	September 1, 2013	The Detailed Rules for the Implementation of the Law on the Entry and Exit of Foreigners (repealed)
	12	September 9, 2013	The Regulations on the Protection of the Security of the Three Gorges Project on the Yangtze River (enacted)
	13	October 2, 2013	The Regulations on Urban Drainage and Sewage Treatment (enacted)
	14	November 9, 2013	The Measures for reporting balance of payments statistics (revised)
	15	November 11, 2013	The Regulations on the Prevention and Control of Pollution from Large-scale Livestock and Poultry Farming (enacted)
	16	December 7, 2013	The Decision of the State Council on Amending Some Administrative Regulations (16 regulations were revised)
	17	December 11, 2013	The Measures of Having A Holiday for National Annual Leaves and Memorial Days (revised)
	18	December 28, 2013	The Decision of the State Council on the Issue of Reeducation through Labor (repealed)
	19	December 28, 2013	The Supplementary Provisions of the State Council on Reeducation through Labor (repealed)

(continued)

Table A.2 (continued)

Year	No	Time of promulgation	Title of administrative regulation
2014	1	January 17, 2014	The Implementation Regulations for the Law on Keeping Confidentiality of State Secrets (enacted)
	2	February 16, 2014	The Regulations on Water Supply Management of the South-to-North Water Diversion Project (enacted)
	3	February 19, 2014	The Decision of the State Council on Repealing and Revising Certain Administrative Regulations (8 regulations were revised)
	4	February 19, 2014	Provisions for the Contribution of Capital by Parties to Joint Ventures Using Chinese and Foreign Investment (repealed)
	5	February 19, 2014	Supplement to Provisions for the Contribution of Capital by Parties to Joint Ventures Using Chinese and Foreign Investment (repealed)
	6	February 21, 2014	Interim Measures for Social Assistance (enacted)
	7	March 1, 2014	The Implementation Regulations for the Law on Keeping Confidentiality of State Secrets (repealed)
	8	March 7, 2014	The Regulations on the Supervision and Administration of Medical Devices (revised)
	9	April 25, 2014	The Regulations on Personnel Management Regulations of Public Institutions (enacted)
	10	April 29, 2014	The Implementation Regulations for the Trademark Law (revised)
	11	July 29, 2014	The Decision of the State Council on Revising Certain Administrative Regulations (21 regulations were revised)
	12	August 7, 2014	Interim Regulations on Enterprise Information Disclosure (enacted)
	13	November 24, 2014	Interim Regulations on Real Estate Registration (Enacted)
	14	November 27, 2014	Regulations on the Administration of Foreign Banks (revised)
2015	1	January 30, 2015	The Implementation Regulations for the Government Procurement Law (enacted)
	2	February 9, 2015	The Museum Regulations (enacted)
	3	February 17, 2015	The Deposit Insurance Regulations (enacted)
	4	June 12, 2015	The Regulations on the Administration of Construction Engineering Survey and Design (revised)

(continued)

Table A.2 (continued)

Year	No	Time of promulgation	Title of administrative regulation
	5	June 14, 2015	The Administrative Measures for Chinese Citizens Travelling to and from Taiwan Region (revised)
	6	October 21, 2015	The Interim Regulations on Residence Permits (enacted)
	7	November 11, 2015	The Map Management Regulations (enacted)
2016	1	February 6, 2016	The Decision of the State Council on Amending Some Administrative Regulations (66 administrative regulations were revised)
	2	March 10, 2016	The National Social Security Fund Regulations (enacted)
	3	April 23, 2016	The Regulations on Administration of Vaccine Circulation and Vaccination (revised)
	4	May 17, 2016	The Farmland Water Conservancy Regulations (enacted)
	5	June 19, 2016	The Customs Inspection Regulations (revised)
	6	November 11, 2016	The Regulations on Radio Administration (revised)
	7	November 30, 2016	The Administrative Regulations on the Approval and Filing of Enterprise Investment Projects (enacted)
2017	1	February 1, 2017	The Regulations on Education for the Disabled (revised)
	2	February 7, 2017	The Regulations on Disability Prevention and Rehabilitation of the Disabled (enacted)
	3	March 1, 2017	The Decision of the State Council on Revision and Repealing of Certain Administrative Regulations (some provisions of 36 administrative regulations were revised; 3 administrative regulations were repealed)
	4	March 16, 2017	The Regulations on Administration of Pesticide (revised)
	5	April 14, 2017	The Regulations on Land Acquisition Compensation and Resettlement for Construction of Large and Medium-sized Water Conservancy and Hydropower Projects (Revised)
	6	May 4, 2017	The Regulations on the Supervision and Administration of Medical Devices (revised)
	7	May 28, 2017	The Implementation Regulations for the Statistics Law of the PRC (enacted)
	8	July 16, 2017	The Regulations on Environmental Protection Administration of Construction Projects (revised)

(continued)

Table A.2 (continued)

Year	No	Time of promulgation	Title of administrative regulation
	9	August 2, 2017	The Regulations on the Supervision and Administration of Financing Guarantee Companies (enacted)
	10	August 6, 2017	The Measures for Investigation and Punishment of Unpermitted and Unlicensed Business Operations (enacted)
	11	August 22, 2017	The Volunteer Service Regulations (enacted)
	12	August 26, 2017	The Regulations on Religious Affairs (revised)
	13	September 27, 2017	The Regulations on Civilian Personnel of the Chinese People's Liberation Army (revised)
	14	October 1, 2017	Measures for Investigation, Punishment and Banning of Unlicensed Business Operations (repealed)
	15	October 5, 2017	The Regulations on the Administration of Buildings, Halls, and Institutions of Organizations (enacted)
	16	October 7, 2017	The Decision of the State Council on Revising Some Administrative Regulations (some provisions of 15 administrative regulations were revised)
	17	December 1, 2017	Interim Regulations on the Construction and Administration of Buildings and Halls (repealed)
2018	1	March 2, 2018	Interim Regulations on Express Delivery (enacted)
	2	March 19, 2018	Interim Regulations on Private Enterprises of the PRC (repealed)
	3	March 19, 2018	Detailed Rules for the Implementation of the Water Pollution Prevention Law of the PRC (repealed)
	4	March 19, 2018	Regulations on the Administration of Quality Prospecting Qualifications (repealed)
	5	March 19, 2018	Regulations on the Management of Breeding Livestock and Poultry (repealed)
	6	March 19, 2018	Trial Measures for Reeducation through Labor (repealed)
	7	March 19, 2018	Decision of the State Council on Amending and Repealing Certain Administrative Regulations (Some provisions of 18 administrative regulations were revised; 5 administrative regulations were repealed)
	8	June 28, 2018	Olympic Symbol Protection Regulations (revised)
	9	June 29, 2018	Interim Regulations on the Human Resources Market (enacted)

(continued)

Table A.2 (continued)

Year	No	Time of promulgation	Title of administrative regulation
	10	July 31, 2018	Regulations on the Prevention and Treatment of Medical Disputes (enacted)
	11	August 11, 2018	National Economic Census Regulations (revised)
	12	September 18, 2018	Decision of the State Council on Amending Some Administrative Regulations(Some clauses of 10 administrative regulations were revised)
	13	October 10, 2018	Administrative Division Management Regulations (enacted)
	14	November 11, 2018	Methods for the Design and Wearing of Fire Fighting and Rescue Signs of the PRC (enacted)
	15	November 11, 2018	Regulations on Patent Agency (revised)
	16	December 18, 2018	Regulations for the Implementation of the Individual Income Tax Law of the PRC (revised)

Table A.3 Solicitation of Public Opinions for Draft Laws during 2012–2016

No	Title of law draft	Time for opinions soliciting	Number of participants	Pieces of opinions
1	The Asset Appraisal Law (Draft)	2012—02—29 to 2012—03—31	6372	156,122
2	The Amendment to the Law on Popularization of Agricultural Technology (Draft)	2012—04—27 to 2012—05—31	1180	3244
3	The Securities Investment Law (Revised Draft)	2012—07—06 to 2012—08—05	1132	88,226
4	The Amendment to the Labor Contract Law (Draft)	2012—07—06 to 2012—08—05	131,912	557,243
5	The Law on the Protection of the Rights and Interests of the Elderly (Revised Draft)	2012—07—06 to 2012—08—05	1418	56,861
6	The Amendment to the Budget Law (Draft for Second Deliberation)	2012—07—06 to 2012—08—05	19,115	330,960
7	The Amendment to the Environmental Protection Law (Draft)	2012—08—31 to 2012—09—30	9582	11,748
8	The Tourism Law (Draft)	2012—08—31 to 2012—09—30	544	2270
9	The Special Equipment Safety Law (Draft)	2012—08—31 to 2012—09—30	124	527
10	The Amendment to the Trademark Law (Draft)	2012—12—28 to 2013—01—31	145	544
11	The Amendment to the Consumer Protection Law (Draft)	2013—04—28 to 2013—05—31	1408	3240
12	The Amendment to the Environmental Protection Law (Draft for Second Deliberation)	2013—07—19 to 2013—08—18	822	2434
13	The Amendment to the Consumer Protection Law (Draft for Second Deliberation)	2013—09—06 to 2013—10—05	640	1344
14	The Asset Appraisal Law (Draft for Second Deliberation)	2013—09—06 to 2013—10—05	1360	32,642
15	The Amendment to the Law on the Protection of Military Facilities (Draft)	2013—12—31 to 2014—01—30	15	25
16	The Amendment to the Administrative Procedure Law (Draft)	2013—12—31 to 2014—01—30	1483	5436
17	The Amendment to the Work Safety Law (Draft)	2014—03—02 to 2014—04—01	3181	7142
18	The Waterway Law (Draft)	2014—04—25 to 2014—05—24	445	1487

(continued)

Table A.3 (continued)

No	Title of law draft	Time for opinions soliciting	Number of participants	Pieces of opinions
19	The Food Safety Law (Revised Draft)	2014—07—01 to 2014—07—31	2468	8877
20	The Counter Espionage Law (Draft)	2014—0*—31 to 2014—09—15	81	211
21	The Administrative Procedure Law Amendment (Draft for Second Deliberation)	2014—0*—31 to 2014—09—20	1586	2300
22	The Advertising Law (Revised Draft)	2014—0*—31 to 2014—09—30	1403	23*0
23	The Amendment to the Legislation Law (Draft)	2014—0*—31 to 2014—09—30	230	609
24	The Anti-Terrorism Law (Draft)	2014—11—04 to 2014—12—03	1023	3295
25	The Amendment (IX) to the Criminal Law (Draft)	2014—11—04 to 2014—12—03	15,096	51,362
26	The Advertising Law (revised draft for second deliberation)	2014—12—30 to 2015—01—19	1726	2238
27	The Food Safety Law (revised draft for second deliberation)	2014—12—30 to 2015—01—19	878	2943
28	The Amendment to the Legislation Law (Draft for Second Deliberation)	2014—12—30 to 2015—01—19	109	218
29	The Air Pollution Prevention and Control Law (Revised Draft)	2014—12—30 to 2015—01—29	971	5047
30	The Amendment to the Law on Promoting the Transformation of Scientific and Technical Achievements (Draft)	2015—03—02 to 2015—04—01	97	260
31	The National Security Law (Draft for Second Deliberation)	2015—05—06 to 2015—06—05	288	1020
32	The Law on Administration of Foreign NGO (Draft for Second Deliberation)	2015—05—05 to 2015—06—04	255	1*03
33	The Seed Law (Revised Draft)	2015—05—05 to 2015—06—04	1559	8022
34	The Cyber Security Law (Draft)	2015—07—06 to 2015—08—05	1564	4240
35	The Air Pollution Prevention and Control Law (revised raft for second deliberation)	2015—07—06 to 2015—08—05	566	1762
36	The Amendment (IX) to the Criminal Law (Draft)	2015—07—06 to 2015—08—05	76,239	110,737
37	The Asset Appraisal Law (draft for third deliberation)	2015—09—08 to 2015—10—07	753	3820

(continued)

Table A.3 (continued)

No	Title of law draft	Time for opinions soliciting	Number of participants	Pieces of opinions
38	A Package of Amendments to Education Laws (Draft)	2015—09—08 to 2015—10—07	120	280
39	The National Medal and National Honorary Title Law (Draft)	2015—09—08 to 2015—10—07	52	140
40	The Anti-Domestic Violence Law (Draft)	2015—09—08 to 2015—10—07	8792	42,203
41	The Charity Law (Draft)	2015—10—31 to 2015—11—30	452	1843
42	The Law on Resource Exploration and Development in Deep Seabed Areas (Draft)	2015—11—06 to 2015—12—05	30	83
43	The Film Industry Promotion Law (Draft)	2015—11—06 to 2015—12—05	131	309
44	The Traditional Chinese Medicine Law (Draft)	2015—12—30 to 2016—01—29	13,290	32,487
45	The Amendment to Wild Animal Protection Law (Revised Draft)	2015—12—30 to 2016—01—29	1640	6205
46	The Charity Law (revised draft for second deliberation)	2016—01—11 to 2016—01—31	169	661
47	The Amendment to the Private Education Promotion Law (Draft for Second Deliberation)	2016—01—07 to 2016—02—06	321	1448
48	The Wild Animal Protection Law (revised draft for second deliberation)	2016—04—27 to 2016—05—20	241	878
49	The National Defense Traffic Law (Draft)	2016—05—04 to 2016—06—03	28	57
50	The Public Cultural Service Guarantee Law (Draft)	2016—05—04 to 2016—06—03	50	152
51	The Cyber Security Law (Draft for Second Deliberation)	2016—07—05 to 2016—08—04	231	969
52	The General Provisions of Civil Law (Draft)	2016—07—05 to 2016—08—04	13,802	65,093
53	The Red Cross Law (Revised Draft)	2016—07—05 to 2016—08—04	102	473
54	The Environmental Protection Tax Law (Draft)	2016—09—06 to 2016—10—07	118	300
55	The Amendment to the Marine Environmental Protection Law (Draft)	2016—09—06 to 2016—10—07	33	49
56	The Film Industry Promotion Law (Draft for Second Deliberation)	2016—09—06 to 2016—10—07	49	266

(continued)

Table A.3 (continued)

No	Title of law draft	Time for opinions soliciting	Number of participants	Pieces of opinions
57	The Traditional Chinese Medicine Law (Draft for Second Deliberation)	2016—09—06 to 2016—10—07	1298	2951
58	The Public Cultural Service Guarantee Law (Draft for Second Deliberation)	2016—11—14 to 2016—12—13	27	102
59	The Surveying and Mapping Law (Revised Draft)	2016—11—14 to 2016—12—13	37	146
60	The Nuclear Safety Law (Draft)	2016—11—14 to 2016—12—13	485	2762
61	The Red Cross Law (Revised Draft for Second Deliberation)	2016—11—14 to 2016—12—13	31	155
62	The Small and Medium-sized Enterprise Promotion Law (Revised Draft)	2016—11—15 to 2016—12—14	51	241
63	The General Provisions of Civil Law (Draft for Second Deliberation)	2016—11—18 to 2016—12—17	960	3038
64	The General Provisions of Civil Law (Draft for Third Deliberation)	2016—12—27 to 2017—01—26	660	2096
65	The Amendment to the Water Pollution Prevention Law (Draft)	2016—12—27 to 2017—01—26	75	237
66	The E-Commerce Law (Draft)	2016—12—27 to 2017—01—26	194	922
67	Anti-Unfair Competition Law (Revised Draft)	2017—02—26 to 2017—03—05	465	1521
68	Standardization Method (Revised Draft)	2017—05—16 to 2017—06—14	252	1101
69	Nuclear Safety Law (Draft for Second Deliberation)	2017—05—16 to 2017—06—14	127	409
70	National Intelligence Law (Draft)	2017—05—16 to 2017—06—14	251	773
71	Public Library Law (Draft)	2017—06—28 to 2017—07—27	101	458
72	Farmers' Professional Cooperative Law (Revised Draft)	2017—06—28 to 2017—07—27	127	422
73	Soil Pollution Prevention and Control Law (Draft)	2017—06—28 to 2017—07—27	140	724
74	National Anthem law (Draft)	2017—06—28 to 2017—07—27	361	731
75	SME Promotion Law (Revised Draft for Second Deliberation)	2017—06—28 to 2017—07—27	38	157

(continued)

Table A.3 (continued)

No	Title of law draft	Time for opinions soliciting	Number of participants	Pieces of opinions
76	Anti-Unfair Competition Law (Revised Draft for Second Deliberation)	2017—09—05 to 2017—09—24	98	354
77	Standardization Method (Revised Draft for Second Deliberation)	2017—09—05 to 2017—09—24	129	446
78	Tobacco Tax Law (Draft)	2017—09—06 to 2017—10—05	18	56
79	Organic Law of the People's Procuratorate (Revised Draft)	2017—09—04 to 2017—10—03	410	1226
80	Organic Law of the People's Court (Revised Draft)	2017—09—04 to 2017—10—03	180	578
81	Electronic Commerce Law (Draft for Second Deliberation)	2017—11—07 to 2017—11—26	291	692
82	Supervision Law (Draft)	2017—11—07 to 2017—12—06	3771	13,268
83	Rural Land Contract Law (Revised Draft)	2017—11—07 to 2017—12—06	313	859
84	Ship Tonnage Tax Law (Draft)	2017—11—07 to 2017—12—06	19	69
85	Prosecutor law (Revised Draft)	2017—12—29 to 2018—01—27	7992	10,438
86	Judge law (Revised Draft)	2017—12—29 to 2018—01—27	11,356	13,650
87	People's Juror Law (Draft)	2017—12—29 to 2018—01—27	202	641
88	International Criminal Judicial Assistance Law (Draft)	2017—12—29 to 2018—01—27	36	305
89	Basic Medical Hygiene and Health Promotion Law (Draft)	2017—12—29 to 2018—01—27	31,665	57,075
90	Heroes and Martyrs Protection Law (Draft)	2017—12—29 to 2018—01—27	420	1108
91	Soil Pollution Prevention and Control Law (Draft for Second Deliberation)	2017—12—29 to 2018—01—27	102	494
92	Criminal Procedure Law (Revised Draft)	2018—5—09 to 2018—06—07	1190	2620
93	Personal Income Tax Law Amendment (Draft)	2018—6—29 to 2018—07—28	67,291	131,207
94	Organic Law of the People's Procuratorate (Revised Draft for Second Deliberation)	2018—6—29 to 2018—07—28	296	1140
95	Organic Law of the People's Court (Revised Draft for Second Deliberation)	2018—6—29 to 2018—07—28	330	1028

(continued)

Table A.3 (continued)

No	Title of law draft	Time for opinions soliciting	Number of participants	Pieces of opinions
96	Electronic Commerce Law (Draft for Third Deliberation)	2018—6—29 to 2018—07—28	317	1473
97	Criminal Procedure Law (Revised Draft for Second Deliberation)	2018—9—05 to 2018—10—04	424	996
98	Regulations on Fire Rescue Ranks of Comprehensive Fire Rescue Team (Draft)	2018—9—05 to 2018—10—04	5683	13,938
99	Cultivated Land Occupation Tax Law (Draft)	2018—9—05 to 2018—10—04	96	179
100	Vehicle Purchase Tax Law (Draft)	2018—9—05 to 2018—10—04	120	178
101	Divisions of the Civil Code (Draft)	2018—9—05 to 2018—10—04	111,208	440,491
102	Drug Administration Law (Revised Draft)	2018—11—01 to 2018—12—01	601	1844
103	Civil Service Law (Revised Draft)	2018—11—01 to 2018—12—01	29,374	56,778
104	Basic Medical and Health Promotion Law (Draft for Second Deliberation)	2018—11—01 to 2018—12—01	3244	6023
105	Rural Land Contract Law (Revised Draft for Second Deliberation)	2018—11—01 to 2018—12—01	362	934

Postscript

This book is one of the Understanding China Series published by China Social Sciences Press. We hope to demonstrate the development of China's rule of law with a brief description in recent years so that Chinese and foreign readers can have a direct understanding of China's achievements, shortcomings and future prospects in the process of ruling the country by law and building a socialist country ruled by law.

It contains nine parts of introduction, involving legislation, a government under the rule of law, judicial system, the rule of law in civil, commercial and economic affairs, the rule of law in social affairs, human rights protection, the rule of law in building an honest and clean government. It is a further summary and enrichment based on the empirical observation of the development of the rule of law in China in recent years by scholars from the Institute of law, Institute of international law and other related units by Chinese Academy of Social Sciences. The book is completed by many scholars, and the specific division of labor is as follows.

Introduction: Tian Chuncai, Tian He;
Chapter one: Liu Yanpeng;
Chapter two: Wang Xiaomei;
Chapter three: Hu Changming;
Chapter four: Xie Hongfei and Xia Xiaoxiong;
Chapter five: Yao Jia;
Chapter six: Li Yanjie;
Chapter seven: Zhao Jianwen, Sun Qian, Liu Renwen, Liu Huawen, Wang Yiming, etc.
Chapter eight: Tian He, Xu Bin, etc.

Zhao Jianying, Secretary of the Party Committee and President of China Social Sciences Press, and Wang Yin, Assistant to the Editor-in-Chief, attach great importance to the compilation and publication of this book, and we would like to express my sincere gratitude.

December 2018 Editors

H. Tian and Y. Lv (eds.), *The Chinese Path of Rule of Law Construction*,
China Insights, https://doi.org/10.1007/978-981-16-4130-5

References

1 Monographs

Chen, L., & Liu, L. (Eds.). (2017). *Proceedings of the seminar on solving the contradictions in heavy caseload and shortage of staff under the background of judicial reform*. Law Press China.

Chen, S. (Ed.). (2017). *Commentary on the General Provisions of Civil Law*. Law Press China.

Chen, W. (2004). *Judge's profession and judicial reform*. China Renmin University Press.

Chen, W. (Ed.). (2008). *Criminal pretrial procedure and human rights protection*. China Legal Publishing House.

Chen, Z. (Ed.). (2017). *International cooperation in the field of human rights and a Chinese Perspective*. China University of Political Science and Law Press.

China Human Rights Research Association. (2012). *Cultural traditions, values and human rights*. China Intercontinental Press.

Feng, L. (2008). *Research on the legalization of the relationship between central and local legislation*. Peking University Press.

Feng, Y. (2016). *China under the rule of law: Comparison between China and the west and road models*. Beijing Normal University Press.

Gao, Q., et al. (2009a). *Basic judicature*. Law Press China.

Gao, Q., et al. (2009b). *Rural judicature*. Law Press China.

Ge, Z. (2015). *Welfare and services for the disabled in China*. Shandong People's Publishing House.

Gu, P. (1991). *Social conflicts and litigation mechanism*. Sichuan People's Publishing House.

Guo, W., et al. (2005). A summary of research on China's Finance and Taxation Law in 2004. In Liu, J. (Ed.), *Finance and Taxation Law* (Vol. 7). Law Press China.

He, W. (1998). *The concept and system of judicature*. China University of Political Science and Law Press.

Hou, M. (2007). *Study on the supreme people's court of China: Proceeding from judicial influence*. Law Press China.

Hu, X. (Ed.). (2009). *Towards harmony: 60 years of China's social security development*. China Labor and Social Security Publishing House.

Hu, Y. (2016). *Judicial reform*. Social Sciences Academic Press (China).

Huai, X. (2006). *The courts and judges*. Law Press China.

Jiang, G. (2018). *China supervision law studies*. China University of Political Science and Law Press.

Jiang, H. (2018). *Knowledge and action of judicial reform*. Law Press China.

Li, B. (2010). *On human rights*. Social Sciences Academic Press (China).

Li, J. (2004). Summary of research on China's Finance and Taxation Laws in 2002. In Liu, J. (Ed.), *Finance and Taxation Law Review* (Vol. 4). Law Press China.

H. Tian and Y. Lv (eds.), *The Chinese Path of Rule of Law Construction*, China Insights, https://doi.org/10.1007/978-981-16-4130-5

Li, L. (2003). *Legislation towards constitutionalism*. Law Press China.
Li, L. (Ed.). (2009). *Public participation in the legislation process*. China Social Sciences Press.
Li, L. (2016). *China's road to the rule of law*. China Social Sciences Press.
Li, L. (Ed.). (2017). *Twenty years of China's Rule of Law (1997–2017)*. Social Sciences Academic Press (China).
Li, Y. (2013). *The rule of law issues in China's social insurance*. China Social Sciences Press.
Liang, H. (2013). *For the Civil Law of China*. China Social Sciences Press.
Lin, Y., & Liu, X. (Eds.). (2018). *The social relief system in contemporary China: Assistance to people most in need and poverty alleviation*. The People's Press.
Liu, S. (2011). *Research on the legislative cost-benefit analysis system*. China University of Political Science and Law Press.
Liu, S. (2012). *Judicial reform: Minor problems and general direction*. Law Press China.
Liu, Y. (2017). *Research on legislation of larger cities*. China Social Sciences Press.
Lv, Y., & Tian, H. (2017). *Government transparency in China (2009–2016)*. Social Sciences Academic Press (China).
Mo, J. (2005). *International covenants on human rights and China*. World Knowledge Publishing House.
Qiang, S. (2007). *Legislator's jurisprudence*. SDX Joint Publishing Company.
Qin, Q., Ye, H., et al. (2018). *Research on the reform of national supervision system*. Law Press China.
Shen, G. (2018). *Exploration of the road to the rule of law in China*. Shanghai People's Publishing House.
Su, L. (2016). *The rule of law and its native resources* (3rd edn.). Peking University Press.
Sun, D. (2003). *Research on Taiwan's authoritarian regime and its transformation*. China Social Sciences Press (China).
Sun, X. (2018). *Right system and scientific norms: Notes on civil code legislation*. Social Sciences Academic Press (China).
Social Insurance Administration of the Ministry of Human Resources and Social Security. (2017). *China social insurance development annual report 2016*. China Labor and Social Security Publishing House.
Tan, S. (Ed.). (2007). *International covenants on human rights and China's legal system construction*. Wuhan University Press.
Tan, S. et al. (2009). *Research on China's judge system*. Law Press China.
Tang, L. (2017). *A commentary on judicial reform* (23rd edn.). Xiamen University Press.
Tian, H., Lv, Y., et al. (2017a). *China's local rule of law practice (2005–2016)*. Social Sciences Academic Press (China).
Tian, H., Lv, Y., et al. (2017b). *Survey on the national conditions for the rule of law in China (2006–2016)*. Social Sciences Academic Press (China).
Tian, H., & Lv, Y. (Eds.). (2017a). *The development of the rule of law in China: Achievements and prospects (2002–2016)*. Social Sciences Academic Press (China).
Tian, H., & Lv, Y. (Eds.). (2017b). *The rule of law in civil and commercial economy in China (2002–2016)*. Social Sciences Academic Press (China).
Tian, H., & Lv, Y. (Eds). (2017c). *The rule of law in social affair in judicial system in China (2002–2016)*. Social Sciences Academic Press (China).
Tian, H., & Lv, Y. (Eds.). (2017d). *The criminal rule of law in China (2002–2016)*. Social Sciences Academic Press (China).
Tian, H., & Lv, Y. (Eds.). (2017e). *The rule of law of the government in China (2002–2016)*. Social Sciences Academic Press (China).
Tian, H., & Lv, Y. (Eds.). (2018a). *The scale of the rule of law*. Social Sciences Academic Press (China).
Tian, H., & Lv, Y. (Eds.). (2018b). *China's legislation and the system of people's congress (2002–2016)*. Social Sciences Academic Press (China).

Tian, H., & Lv, Y. (Eds.). (2018c). *The rule of law in human rights in China (2002–2016)*. Social Sciences Academic Press (China).
Tian, H., & Lv, Y. (Eds.). (2018d). *The rule of law in social affair in China (2002–2016)*. Social Sciences Academic Press (China).
Wang, B. (2015). *The dynamics and statics of commercial law and economic law*. Law Press China.
Wang, L. (2015). *The rule of law: Good law and good governance*. Peking University Press.
Wang, Q., & Liu, J. (Eds.). (2003). *Judicial protection of human rights in China*. Xiamen University Press.
Wang, X. (2010). *Wang Xiaoye's comments on the anti-monopoly law*. Social Sciences Academic Press (China).
Wang, X., Li, Y., Zhang, W., et al. (2017). *Judicial Transparency in China (2011–2016)*. Social Sciences Academic Press (China).
Wu, P. (2015). *Research on children's welfare and rights in China*. China University of Political Science and Law Press.
Wu, Y. (2008). *The judge's role and judicial behavior*. Encyclopedia of China Publishing House.
Xian, K. (2015). *On the human rights of special groups—Research on the legal rights and interests of special groups*. Guangming Daily Press.
Xiao, Y. (1998). *The contemporary judicial system*. China University of Political Science and Law Press.
Xu, H., et al. (2017). *Research on the rule of law in social governance*. Law Press China.
Yu, R. (Ed.). (2013). *The local legislation quality evaluation index system*. Law Press China.
Yue, L. (Ed.). (2017). *Criminal justice and human rights in China*. Law Press China.
Zhai, J. (2013). The status quo and future of China's fiscal and taxation law. In Liu, J. (Ed.), *Fiscal and Taxation Law Review* (Vol. 3). Law Press China.
Zhang, J. (2017). *Research on modern supervision system and legal system in China*. China Legal Publishing House.
Zhang, S. (2018). *A new perspective of the theory on the economic laws in contemporary China*. China Renmin University Press.
Zhang, W. (2016). *Public law and modernization of national governance*. Law Press China.
Zhang, W. (2017). *Private law and economic construction under the rule of law*. Law Press China.
Zhang, W. (2018). *Social law and the construction of a society ruled by law*. Law Press China.
Zhang, X. (1998). *Women and human rights*. Xinhua Press.
Zheng, G. (Ed.). (2018). *China social security development report 2017*. China Labor and Social Security Press.
Zheng, G. (Ed.). (2012). *Interpretation and application guidelines of the social insurance law of the People's Republic of China—Attaching the interpretation of the military personnel insurance law*. China Labor and Social Security Press.
Zhou, D. (2000). *Foreign court organizations and judge systems*. The People's Court Press.
Zhu, L. (Ed.). (2011). *Research on democratization and scientization of local legislation: A case study of Beijing*. Renmin University of China Press.
Zhuo, Z. (2011). *Research on laws and politics*. Law Press China.
Zuo, W., et al. (2000). *Changes and reforms—Study on the modernization of the court system*. Law Press China.
Zuo, W., et al. (2004). *Study on the supreme court*. Law Press China.

2 Papers

[England] Derek Bell. (2013). Justice, democracy and environment: A concept of liberal environmental citizenship (X. Yang, Trans.) *Journal of Nanjing University of Technology* (Social Science Edition), (1).

Chen, B. (2018). The contemporary transformation of social law and the construction of social law in China. *Economic Law Review*, (1).

Chen, D. (1998). The democratic legitimacy of legislation and legislation paramountcy—Criticism of legislation in China. *Peking University Law Journal*, (6).

Chen, G., & Lan, Z. (2018). Major achievements in the reform of the supervision system and expectations for improvement. *Administrative Law Review*, (4).

Chen, L. (2017). Real right law is coming in the world's attention. *National People's Congress of China*, (4).

Chen, S. (2014). The functional positioning of government and market in the mechanism of commercial law. *China Legal Science*, (5).

Chen, W. (2007). On the nationalization of judicial power—From the perspective of the localization of governance of judicial power. *Hebei Law Science*, (9).

Chen, W. (2018). Theoretical investigation and practical issues of duty-related crime supervision. *Journal of Renmin University of China*, (4).

Ding, Y. (2002). Summary of the 2002 annual meeting of the finance and taxation law research association of the chinese law society. *China Legal Science*, (6).

Feng, Y. (2005). Research on the knowledge base of law and economics paradigms. *Journal of Renmin University of China*, (4).

Feng, Y., & Wang, B. (2014). Analysis on the scientific standards of scientific legislation. *Journal of Renmin University of China*, (1).

Huang, Q. (2007). Reflections on modern judicial concepts—A review of Mr. Deng Zhenglai's 'Where is Chinese Law Should Go,. *Fujian Law Science*, (4).

Huang, X. (2010). The development process and trends of self-regulatory organizations in China's securities industry. *China Finance*, (11).

Huang, Y., & Jiang, X. (2014). The definition of 'relevant markets' in the internet industry. *Open Journal of Legal Science*, (6).

Huang, Z. (2014). The second order structure of consumers' collective damage compensation litigation. *Global Law Review*, (5).

Jiang, D. (2015). Getting business licenses before getting administrative permits' and regulatory innovation—Reshaping the 'Creditable Country' with a coordinated regulatory model. *Study on China Administration for Industry & Commerce*, (11).

Jiang, M. (2018). On the legislative purpose and basic principles of the supervision law. *Administrative Law Review*, (4).

Jiang, P., & Wu, J. (2010). The market economy and the rule of law economy—A dialogue between economists and jurists. *Journal of China University of Political Science and Law*, (6).

Jiang, Y. (2012). Judicial dilemma and outlet of definition of relevant market in the internet industry. *Jurists Review*, (6).

Li, H. (2006). The evolution of the concept of commercial trial in China. *Nanjing University Law Review*, Spring.

Li, L. (1998). Theory and practice of the division of legislative powers. *Chinese Journal of Law*, (5).

Li, S. (2017). The general provisions of civil law is the basic law for establishing and improving the basic civil system. *The People's Congress of China*, (4).

Li, Z. (2014). A brief discussion on the practice and application of the concept of commercial trial. *People's Justice*, (15).

Liang, H. (1999). Uniform contract law: Successes and shortcomings. *China Legal Science*, (3).

Lin, J., & Chen, W. (2013). On the value function of social assistance law and its institutional construction. *Jiangxi Social Sciences*, (2).

Liu, K., & Zhang, Q. (2014). Legislative changes of China's corporate capital system and solutions to the problems. *Journal of Henan University of Finance, Economics and Law*, (5).

Liu, L. (2015). The basic concepts, basic features and implementation suggestions of the new budget law. *Law Science Magazine*, (4).

Liu, S. (2006). Re-discussion on the 'Judicial Reform' of the People's Courts. *Open Journal of Legal Science*, (1).

Miao, L. (1996). On the determination of 'Non-Conflict' standards in local legislative work. *Jurists Review*, (5).

Peng, G. (2018). The status quo, problems and prospects of social law construction. *China Institutional Reform and Management*, (11).

Sun, B. (2006). A discussion on the scientific standards of legislative quality. *Journal of Inner Mongolia University for Nationalities*, (2).

Sun, B. (2008). On local exclusive legislative power. *Contemporary Law Review*, (2).

The Commercial Law Research Center of Central China Normal University. (2009). Analysis about China's thirty year commercial law & commercial jurisprudence. *Law Science Magazine*, (2).

Tong, Z. (2006). How the *Real Right Law* (draft) makes use of the constitutional gate—Comments on the controversies over unconstitutional and constitutional interpretations arising from an open letter. *Open Journal of Legal Science*, (3).

Wang, B. (2010). Concept and thinking of commercial trial. *Shandong Justice*, (2).

Wang, L. (2012). On the judgment standards for invalid contracts. *Journal of Law Application*, (7).

Wang, Q. (2008). Assessment of the rationality of legislation. *Journal of Shanghai Administration Institute*, (4).

Wang, X. (2005). The principle of non-conflict must be correctly understood in local legislation. *The People's Congress of China*, (5).

Wang, X. (2018). The attributes of state supervision power. *Qiusuo*, (7).

Wang, Z. (2007). Explanation on the *Real Right Law of the People's Republic of China (Draft)*—At the 5th session of the 10th National People's Congress on March 8, 2007. *The Communique of the NPC Standing Committee of the People's Republic of China*, (3).

Wei, Z. (2016). What general provisions of civil law do we need—Compare with German Civil Law. *Northern Legal Science*, (3).

Xiao, Y. (2000). Efforts to promote reform to ensure judicial impartiality to enter the new century with a new stance—Speech at the national conference of presidents of high courts. *The Communique of the NPC Standing Committee of the People's Republic of China*, (1).

Yan, K., & Yu, S. (2011). On China's structural tax cuts under the global financial crisis. *Taxation Research*, (1).

Yang, S. (2014). Theoretical explanation of the implementation of the social insurance law and supporting legal guarantees. *Journal of China University of Labor Relations*, (2).

Yu, D. (1988). The need to be legalized: Party-government relations in the primary stage of socialism. *Contemporary Law Review*, (2).

Yu, G. (2008). 30 Years of the rule of law in fiscal and taxation systems in China. *China Taxation*, (12).

Zhang, S. (2014). Reform decisions and consensus of economic law. *Law Review*, (2).

Zhang, S. (2015). Tax system changes and the modernization of rule of law in taxation system. *Social Sciences in China*, (2).

Zhao, X. (2012). Thirty years of chinese commercial law. *China Law*, (3).

Zheng, G. (2013). The status quo and development orientation of social welfare in China. *Journal of Renmin University of China*, (2).

Zhong, C. (2012). Definition of relevant market in the anti-monopoly law enforcement in the internet industry. *Legal Science* (Journal of Northwest University of Political Science and Law), (4).

Zhou, L. (2018). Research on the construction and path of China's supervision system. *Journal of China National School of Administration*, (4).

Zhu, J. (2011). The socialist legal system with Chinese characteristics: Structure, characteristics and trends. *Social Sciences in China*, (3).

Zhu, L. (2001). Research on the issues of the model of legislative system. *Journal of Renmin University of China*, (4).

Zhu, X. (2018). Consolidation and development of the procuratorial system after the reform of the national supervisory system. *Chinese Journal of Law*, (4).
Zuo, W., & Zhu, T. (2002). Who is the subject and how to achieve justice—The argument for the concept of subjectivity of judicature. *Open Journal of Legal Science*, (7).

3 Newspapers

He, X., He, F., & Ma, Y. (2015, January 29). Interpretation and application of provisions of the supreme people's court on several issues concerning the trial of cases by the circuit courts. *People's Court Daily*, (5th edn).
The Research Group of the First Civil Division of the Higher People's Court of Jiangsu Province. (2012, March 13). Guiding consumers to protect their rights and strengthening judicial protection. *Jiangsu Legal News*, (A07 edn).
Wang, M. (2015, September 26). Overcoming the difficulties in the implementation of the judicial accountability system. *People's Court Daily*, (2nd edn).
Wang, Z., & Dai, J. (2015, August 19). Procuratorates legally protecting lawyers' practicing rights. *Procuratorial Daily*, (1st edn).
Yang, L. (2017, March 20). General provisions of civil law: A bright embodiment of contemporary rule of law. *Beijing Daily*, (13th edn).
Zhao, X. (2011, August 20). Backfeeding model and marriage law. *Legal Daily*, (7th edn).

Index

H. Tian and Y. Lv (eds.), *The Chinese Path of Rule of Law Construction*,
China Insights, https://doi.org/10.1007/978-981-16-4130-5

The manufacturer's authorised representative in the EU is Springer Nature Customer Service Centre GmbH, Europaplatz 3, 69115 Heidelberg, Germany. If you have any concerns regarding our products, please contact ProductSafety@springernature.com

Printed and bound by CPI Group (UK) Ltd, Croydon, CR0 4YY
30/09/2026
02225294-0008